My Journey into Tea

A Candid Memoir of the Realities of Small Business Ownership

ELAINE TERMAN

atmosphere press

For my dear husband, Phil. I could not have taken this journey without you by my side. Your loving support and hard work enabled me to become more than I ever thought possible. I am left with eternal love and gratitude.

I had no inkling that tea would become my life and my passion. Or that I'd end up owning my own business, my tea shop, and that shopkeeper would be the title I'd hold the longest of my entire working life.

Growing up, I'd only had an occasional cup of plain old tea bag tea, usually Red Rose, with my Hungarian grandmother after we came in from gardening. I thoroughly enjoyed that quiet time with her. There was something about the reverent way she stirred her tea and gently squeezed the tea bag, but the tea itself wasn't much to get excited about.

Then, in my twenties, something happened that woke me to the true pleasure of tea. It is best described in a page from my *Tea Taster's Journal: A Primer for Those New to the Journey into Tea*:

"James Norwood Pratt, author of the *New Tea Lover's Treasury*, is widely credited with sparking a tea renaissance in the United States. In his premier edition of *The Tea Dictionary*, he defines tea as, 'A miracle of vegetation that became a treasure of the world as medicine, beverage, currency and communion—the wellspring of empires, industries and art.'

"Tea truly is 'a treasure of the world.' Once bitten by the tea 'bug,' your life is never the same. It becomes enriched with ritual, relaxation, better health, and an incredible variety of flavors, textures and characters. Special times are to be had over this wondrous cup.

"My own journey into tea began many years ago in my early adulthood. Finally independent of parents and college, I was on my own journey into life when I bought a small sampler pack of loose-leaf black teas with exotic names like Assam, Ceylon, Darjeeling, Keemun and Yunnan. Before that, only an occasional common tea bag tea had crossed my lips, and with the taste of these new treasures, I was smitten. Each one had its own distinct character, and I would wander back and forth through them, trying to decide which one I liked better. It became a private ritual I would hold whenever I needed peace and tranquility.

"As life takes its twists and turns, I decided I didn't have time to mess with loose tea, tea balls and such, and turned to the convenience of common tea bags again. I gradually lost interest altogether and only rarely had a cup of tea. Then, one miraculous day, while planning to open up my own shop and small tea room, I received my first batch of new tea samples in the mail. That old familiar feeling swept over me, and again I was in love. By now, it has grown into full blown passion. It has enriched my life's journey beyond description. With over ten thousand or so varieties of tea in the world, it looks like it's going to be interesting travels indeed.

"I wish you rich and interesting travels as you embark upon your own Journey into Tea.

~Elaine, TheTeaLady"

I didn't start out with that title, but somewhere along the way, I became TheTeaLady. Only a year into the tea business and feet barely on the ground, everyone kept telling me, "You have to have a website." It was becoming common knowledge: you can't compete in today's world without a website. Sheesh! I didn't want to become some megacorporation. I just wanted to create a relaxing little tea shop with just a few tables and chairs for sharing life over a cup of tea. But, life was changing rapidly, and small and simple just didn't seem to fit anymore. The internet was exploding, and you were nobody if you didn't have an internet presence. Go big or go home, I guess. Seems I had no choice.

So, I dove into this just like I'd done with everything else since the shop's inception. I'd start with nothing but an idea and intense desire and somehow figure it out from there, and I was confident that I'd figure out this website thing as well. Baptism by fire. Suitable for a fire sign Leo, even if this initial year left me feeling a bit singed around the edges.

As always, money was tight. My starting capital was dwindling, and I was guarding every dime left. I was glad to find out that there were templates where you could build your own website. And there were now shopping carts for easy selling of products online. Perfect. That would save a bundle in time and dollars. After figuring out the basics of servers, hosting, SSL security, etc., I bought a website building program, picked a template, and dove in.

First things first. The name. I tried variations of dot-com names with the word tea in them, and either they were too cumbersome, I just didn't like them, or the good ones were already taken: tealady.com, teatime.com, tealeaf.com, tea-with-anything.com that I liked just wasn't available. After trying dozens of variations, I finally hit upon "thetealady.com." Bingo! It was available. And I really liked it.

I hesitated. Could I really claim the title of "thetealady"? I mean, tealady.com was just claiming to be *A* tea lady, but *THE* tea lady? That seemed somehow too grand a title for someone still on the beginning end of the tea learning curve and only a year into the business. It took some serious self-talk to get past my insecurities and fear. *What am I afraid of?* I asked myself. *Why couldn't I be "thetealady"? I'd thought of it first. Didn't I have the right to claim it as my dot-com name, then?*

After about a day or so of inner debate and shoring up my nerves, I checked it again. It was still available, and I took that as a sign that this was meant to be my new internet moniker. With fingers twitching in excited anticipation, I clicked. I'd secured the name of my new website, and that's how I became TheTeaLady.

And that leads me to this story. It is not a sweet tea tale, laced with all things pretty and light. I've never been one to sugarcoat life. I try to stay solidly rooted in reality but allow myself the occasional fantasy. Sometimes, if you're lucky, or just paying attention, life works out, and your unique fairy tale unfolds. But that doesn't mean there aren't loads of hardships along the way. Reread some of those fairy tales. There's always a villain, and the road is riddled with unexpected twists, turns and insurmountable challenges like turning straw into gold. That's what makes for an interesting tale. And like it or not, those twists and turns and bumps in the road are what make our lives interesting as well.

This story is about the American dream or at least my stab at it. Every bit of it is true except names of the guilty have been changed. It's about that dream where you start your own business, become your own boss, finally have control over your life. Where you do what you love, and the money follows you. That's exactly what I wanted and had hoped for. I was in my late forties with enough life under my belt to take a stab at it. I thought, *If not now, When? If I don't do it now, I'll never do it. It's time*, I told myself.

It turned out to be the best thing that ever happened to me. I have grown in ways too numerous to count, learned far more than I'd ever expected, and met so many wonderful people with whom I'd otherwise never have crossed paths. I can now look back upon my life with a real sense of satisfaction. I really did it! And I am richer for it.

I am also poorer, financially, for it. Or, at least I didn't make a lot of money. Of course, that's one of the lessons: *riches are not always in the form of money*. Through all the trials and traumas of small business ownership, I have endured more hardship than I thought I ever could, and more pain than I thought I could bear. Another lesson—you're stronger than you think.

And I have come face to face with true evil. Evil in the

form of cheaters and con artists, government corruption, unscrupulous contractors, landlords, banks, and others. That gave me the best lesson of all: *you can stand up to evil and, win or lose, remain standing with your integrity intact in the end.* And sometimes, you actually do win. That's the sweetest reward of all.

Chapter 1

My Journey: the Allure of Tea

Nature is the manifestation of God for me. Trees are creatures just begging to be hugged. Surround me with nature—land, lush flora, and any variety of animals— and I'm in heaven. I find a peacefulness I cannot attain anywhere else.

A farm in the heartland was the perfect nurturing setting for me to begin my life's journey. There was deep respect for the fields that grew food for the world. The animals were as much my friends as my classmates. My fauna companions were everywhere and diverse in character.

So, nature—the land, the crops, and our animals—became my foundation. My lovely friends. Watching things grow, come to harvest, and wither back to the earth teaches us the cycles of life. It is why, always, I find my renewal in nature. There is a wisdom and serenity there that is so profound to me, so alive and so healing.

I went off to college to major in biology with a chemistry minor, so that I could somehow bring nature into my career life. I was in education for my first degree, and I thought I'd end up being a biology teacher. But, when I graduated, local school districts were so strapped, there was a freeze on hiring.

With no jobs locally, I looked farther away. What I repeatedly found was that all biology or chemistry teachers in all the school districts I'd encountered were also football, basketball, track, or wrestling coaches. To this day, I don't even know how football works, but I was about to lie my way into a job by saying I'd coach whatever team they needed. Obviously, that would never have worked, and I had to accept the fact that I'd probably never find a job teaching what I loved and had trained for.

So, after a year of substitute teaching, which held many trials, tribulations, and even horrors (unruly kids regaling me with stories of what they did to the last sub!), I decided to find another way to manifest my love of the life sciences.

With another year of college and a year of internship, I had my second degree, in medical technology. There I could be immersed in science, working in a hospital lab on human specimens. It felt right. I helped heal people who were sick, and that was rewarding.

I'd started out in chemistry, but soon moved to microbiology, which held more interest for me. We plated specimens on to agar-filled petri dishes. When bacteria appeared on the plate within the next two days, we used our own analysis and judgment to decide if anything pathogenic was there and needed to be worked up. Besides what it looked like on the plate, we used other things like smell to decide if a bug might be pathogenic. Some smelled buttery, one particular bacteria even smelled like grapes. We'd perform various tests, which led to the identification of pathogenic organisms and do sensitivity testing to see which antibiotic each bug would be susceptible or resistant to. That way, the doctor knew exactly which drug would be best to treat the infection.

While I loved my little bacteria, after years of the same old same old, it became too routine. An E. coli was an E. coli, a Pseudomonas was just another Pseudomonas. I got so good at it I could identify many bugs by sight and smell, but, of course, still ran the proper tests to be sure. Then eventually, the identification had become more automated by running the specimen through a machine for confirmation, much like in chemistry. In the boredom of that seldom changing routine, I decided that I needed a change.

I thought perhaps I was ready for a management position, and branching out to a large commercial lab would be different from a hospital setting. I landed a job as lab manager with a small satellite of International Clinical Labs, which was a refreshing change from the hospital setting. I was challenged again, and it was exciting and fun—for a while. After a few years, ICL got bought out by SmithKline Labs, which, after a merger with Beecham turned into SmithKline Beecham Clinical Labs, who then absorbed a local private lab, Westgate Labs. None of that corporate gobbling up was very fun to go through, but it had to be tolerated whether you liked it or not.

After nearly ten years in the private lab business, I experienced that nastiest of the nineties corporate antics—downsizing. That entailed, on one fine Friday afternoon, all of a sudden, without warning, being given the boot. The harsh cruelty of that experience made me pretty certain that I'd never work for corporate America again.

Two more years of wandering around trying to figure out what to do next, eventually led me to the decision to take a stab at "the American dream." So many people harbor the fantasy of owning their own business. Why couldn't I be among those who actually did it?

To fill the time, I was working a part-time job at Read For Literacy until I could answer the questions I had about where to go next. Their offices were located in our beautiful, Art Deco main library in downtown Toledo. It was like being immersed in art just to work there. And being surrounded by all those books! Pure heaven.

I tired of the limits of this job after only about a year, and wondered what I should do. I wanted to quit but hadn't a clue what I would do next. And, I was getting the itch to venture into my own business.

For some odd reason, I've often found answers to my most perplexing problems by randomly flipping through books. So I went downstairs to the stacks and started flipping through.

I landed on *Conversations with God* by Neale Donald Walsh, and this passage popped out at me: "If you cannot find a group whose consciousness matches your own, be the source of one."

So, that was it. The last little push I needed. I decided I would open my own business. I was in my late forties, and I figured if I was ever going to do such an adventurous thing, now was the time. I had enough life experience under my belt to feel ready for both the risk and the challenge.

It really didn't take long for me to get to tea as the core of my business. I started out with a broad focus, including all herbs, and that felt right. They were natural, of the earth. They fit perfectly with my close-to-nature upbringing. Along the way, tea came forward, and it all made sense. Tea is technically an herb, which by broad definition is any useful plant. But I had come to know tea intimately and considered it the greatest, most useful of all plants.

I don't just consider it so, it simply *is* the most useful plant. Besides an almost unlimited variety of teas to drink, it has massively documented health benefits. That made it fit perfectly with my medical background. It can also be used to flavor soups, breads, cookies, and more, ground up and put in smoothies, cakes, or cereals. Extracts of tea are used in body care lotions and serums, oil from tea seed is the healthiest oil for cooking, tea bags reduce bags under eyes, soothe sunburned skin, and spent tea leaves are great for composting. There is a vast and beautiful garden of utilitarian variety that comes from tea.

So, quite early on in the groundwork of this evolving business idea, tea took front and center. I started to learn everything about it I could. Every book, article, source, piqued my interest, and I'd absorb facts, figures, and stats like a thirsty sponge. I sourced the best vendors for the best quality tea. I gathered more sources for procuring tea accessories, body care products, and anything that might be related to tea.

The magic really began when I received my first vendor catalog. That's when the delightful garden of tea suddenly bloomed for me. This catalog had hundreds of teas! Besides the classic black teas, there were pages and pages of flavored black teas and dozens of green teas, a reasonable selection of oolongs and even what was quite rare at that time, two or three white teas. There were formed teas in cakes (Pu-erh) and bird's-nest shapes, and powdered tea, as in matcha. There were tons of flavors available, and some interesting-sounding blends. Besides the tea there were pages and pages of common and exotic tea preparation paraphernalia. Classic teapots, of course, and many newer gadgets I'd never even seen before.

I must have devoured that catalog for a week or more and finally decided to place an order for tea samples, which were free with wholesale orders. I'd seen a couple of tea wares I wanted to try and ordered, among them, my first French press. That, as it turned out, became a cornerstone of my whole tea operation. I picked out as many teas to try as I could without abusing the free sample status.

I was excited beyond words the day my tea treasures arrived. It was absolute joy, like Christmas morning. I was like the proverbial kid in a candy store. Or like a woman getting a package that was marked fromTiffany & Co. I opened the box with robust enthusiasm and excited anticipation for the treasures inside. I quickly found the French press and read the instructions on how to work the thing, as I'd never used one before. I didn't know which tea to sample first, but opened each sample bag several times to sniff and sniff again. It was so difficult. They were all heavenly!

If memory serves me, the aroma of the raspberry was so heady, it won the honor of first brew. Well, infusion, to be more accurate. I had so much to learn about this wonderful new world of tea, including proper terminology, and I couldn't dig into it fast enough.

Waiting for the kettle to boil was one of those sweet moments of heightened anticipation. I put two scoops of the raspberry flavored leaf in the two-cup press using my new "proper cup of tea" measuring spoon. I poured the water over the tea and set the lid, plunger up, on top of the press. With a recommended infusion time of three to five minutes, I set my timer for three minutes, knowing that I like my tea weaker than some do. More delicious anticipation.

Beep, beep, beep. Beep, beep, beep. Time's up! I carefully pushed the plunger down and pumped up and down another couple of times to mix. The leaves danced! Finishing in the down position, the color was consistently darker now. The whole process was delightful to watch. And then it came time. The first pour.

Once customers experienced tea preparation in the French press, they often let go of the romantic idea of the traditional English teapot.

I tasted the first sample, not quite expecting the delightful pleasure I was about to experience. The flavor absolutely burst in my mouth! It was smooth, light, and definitely juicy. This taste of fresh raspberries was like nothing I'd had before in a beverage. That was the moment I learned the difference between real natural flavoring and what we are so often affronted with—overpowering artificial flavors. What a difference it was!

That is why I always loved what others considered the tedious task of bagging tea for the shelves. I could do it for hours, enjoying the intoxicating aromas of each tea. Especially the strawberry teas. The pure essential oils used for flavoring were exceptionally potent in the strawberry teas, and the whole bagging area would smell like a strawberry field.

That was also the moment I learned the difference between quality loose-leaf tea and floor-sweepings tea bag tea. That lowest grade of leaf used in most tea bags, fannings and dust, is literally swept up off the floor at some estates, after the larger, quality leaves are sorted out and sold. That exquisite taste of quality, once experienced, never leaves you.

I've had more than a few customers over the years come back into the shop, tongue-in-cheek scolding me for spoiling them to the taste of good tea. We'd laugh, and then they'd happily browse the shelves, looking for the next gem to add to their personal tea repertoire.

I tasted a few more, and thoroughly enjoyed the next few glorious days it took to get through the several dozen or so samples. I took copious notes of my impressions, picked out more from the catalog that I knew would be winners, and recorded which ones I simply had to have in my tea collection. I had to make myself stop at seventy or so, fearing I would run out of shelf space and overwhelm the customers with too many teas from which to choose.

And I was in love. With all of it. The tea. The aromas. The different sizes, shapes, and colors of the leaves. The French press and the way you got to watch the leaves open. The cute little measuring spoon and all the fun tea paraphernalia. The premium quality, variety, and flavor that comes from fine loose-leaf tea. And I would make it my mission to make others fall in love with it too.

That's also when I decided the tea room would not be Victorian, which always seemed a little stuffy and limited to me. The world of tea was so much bigger than that, which led me to a more contemporary character for the shop, encompassing all that tea has to offer. We would use the contemporary French press for all our tea preparation.

It had several advantages over the traditional teapot. Among them, the leaves stayed in the press, so no dripping baskets or bags. They were not much more difficult to wash or maintain than regular tea pots. I loved their clean lines and trendy look and feel. Mostly, I never tired of watching that moment when the hot water hits the leaves and they dance with joy, fulfilling their life's purpose to bestow their delicious flavors and healthy benefits upon us lucky humans. The French press, with its glass walls, provided an insider view of the process, which would enable me to share that delight with every single customer.

Climbing that steep learning curve was something I was eager to begin. I actually started the planning and achieved a basic overview of the shop before I quit my job. Once I had that, I was ready to throw myself into full-time effort into manifesting this dream of mine. I learned as much as I could as fast as I could so that I could make wise choices about which teas and wares to carry. There was so much to learn, as I was sometimes reminded.

Very early on, one of the retired gentlemen from S.C.O.R.E. (Service Corps of Retired Executives) who helped me with my business plan came into the shop just after I'd opened. He was obviously a seasoned tea drinker and quite pleased to see that I had gotten the shop open. He'd brought me a sample of one of his favorite teas and handed it to me with a challenge. "Do you know what kind of tea this is?" I think he wanted to see if I really knew my stuff.

I remember the small tin with beautiful, long, twisted, dark tea leaves. I'd never seen tea leaves so large before. It was so dark, I thought it must be a black tea and said so. He just smiled, and said, "Keep working, you've got a ways to go." Ouch. That smarted a bit. But, I took his advice and realized I had to keep studying tea. If I was going to be "the tea lady," I'd better know what I was talking about.

I read everything I could get my hands on. I had set up a very functional office space in the shop and whenever I was not ordering, doing books, or some other everyday operational task, I was searching the internet for information on tea. I perused other tea sites: vendors, tea estates, other tea shops and tea rooms. I read many books on tea. I filled in the blanks on the many types and varieties of tea. I realized the tea that my S.C.O.R.E. adviser had brought in was a very high-quality oolong. I made my mind up that I'd not be stumped again.

Oolong was a class I had heard of, of course, but didn't know much about other than that's what you get in most Chinese restaurants. And after a time, I learned what an interesting class of tea it is! Flavors and characteristics vary widely within the class. They can be fruity, floral, nutty, or grainy. You can even get all of those flavor notes out of the same scoop of tea leaf, infused three or four times in a row.

Most oolongs start out with either a grainy or nutty note, to my taste buds. In the lightly oxidized oolongs, with a more green-tea character, it tends to be slight and soft, grainy like oats or rice, and you will often find lovely floral notes. In some oolongs, even vegetable notes come out like corn or squash! And in the more heavily oxidized oolongs, I always get robust nutty, woodsy, or grainy taste notes reminiscent of chestnuts, wheat, rye, or barley, and even mushrooms and hay.

Infuse the same leaf again, and the oolong magic begins to happen. The top notes begin to fade a bit, bringing forth new ones like fruit. I will never forget an oolong we enjoyed for one year. It started out with an interesting nutty note that was reminiscent of chestnuts. In the second infusion, the nuttiness began to subside, and a vague fruity note came to the forefront. Then, in the third cup, with the nutty notes totally gone, an overwhelming splash of apricot asserted its presence. Heavenly!

All of this from a humble cup of tea. Well, three cups actually, but you know what I mean. And I've never experienced anything like it again. The same tea just came out differently the next season. Not lesser, just not ever the same again. But some years, when everything is just right, you get to experience a new and wonderful delight. Mother Nature's magic. Just like in fine wines or any commodity dependent on the terroir. All conditions of climate are simply not the same from year to year. It can be disappointing to come to the end of a particularly good tea, but next year's harvest always holds the potential for a new jewel.

That was the one thing I never tired of: tasting new teas. It must be similar for wine connoisseurs. Always in pursuit of that next intriguing flavor note. It was the same for me with tea. And, as with wine, each year's tea harvest brought those slight variations, even from exactly the same Darjeeling tea bush, from the exactly the same Darjeeling tea estate. That's part of the beauty of tea. Endless variety and intrigue.

There were so many flavored teas to choose from that my head would swim as I tried to decide which ones I thought would have wide popular appeal. Raspberry, for sure. And Strawberry, Peach, Orange Spice, Lemon, Chocolate Mint, French Vanilla, Blueberry, and Black Currant all earned a place on the list.

On a whim, knowing the popularity of fruit flavors, I'd ordered a sample of Wild Blackberry. That was good fortune, since that turned out to be my personal favorite. And my best blend was the blackberry with vanilla, which we called Blackberries and Cream. So delightfully delicious! Something

Peter Rabbit's mum might have served.

There were quite a few flavors available in green teas, too, and even a few in oolongs. Strawberry Green remains my best-selling tea to this date. Peach Apricot Green is a close second and an interesting tea. It starts with a gunpowder base (so named because the leaf is rolled into small pellets reminiscent of gunpowder), which I would never have thought to add flavoring to, but one of my vendors hit a winner when he came up with that one.

Over time, I suppose because I don't like very strong tea, I tended to gravitate toward greens for their light, floral, fruity characters. Monk's Green turned out to be my very favorite. It is a classic Chinese green tea scented with Osmanthus flowers, which smell faintly of peaches. I wasn't a fan of the more well-known Jasmine Green, which to me is akin to drinking perfume. And while I absolutely adore lavender as a fragrance, I cannot stand drinking tea with lavender in it, either.

But the smell of peaches did it for me. I loved the Monk's Green so much I began to drink it frequently, but was careful to switch to different teas occasionally so as not to burn out on this beautiful tea. I'd learned that lesson with an earlier favorite.

My very first favorite flavor was a black tea, Cream Earl Grey. It's a mix of traditional Earl Grey with Vanilla Cream blended in. Earl Grey, by the way, is not a type of tea, as some think, but a flavored English blended black tea. The flavoring in Earl Grey comes from oil of bergamot, a non-edible citrus fruit common throughout the Mediterranean. The fruit itself is too bitter to eat, but the essential oil extracted from the rind is divine and used frequently in perfumes.

My treasured Cream Earl Grey was simply the most heavenly thing I'd ever tasted. Seriously. Exquisite, divine, and almost orgasmic to me. And I drank copious amounts of it. Since I had a hot-water urn on the counter right behind me, it was a daily ritual to fill and refill my press until my leaf was exhausted, and then I'd add fresh leaf to drink some more.

So, for about two years, I drank this, and only this, tea every day. All day long. Two whole years. And then it happened. Burnout. Severe and sudden total burnout. It was as if I'd reached some maximum threshold, some wall that ruined my desire for it, and I sadly, completely lost my taste for it.

The good that came out of that regret was that I was forced to start to enjoy other teas. I was very careful after that, that no matter how much I might like a newly discovered tea treasure, I would never again let myself burn out on it. Oddly, even though it has been many years, I've never gotten my taste back for Cream Earl Grey. I won't be making that mistake with my lovely Monk's Green!

White teas are even lighter than greens, and I discovered that I loved them as much or more. My all-time favorite is one we call Adam's Peak, named after the highest, most-revered mountain in Sri Lanka. There is a larger-than-life footprint in the rock at the top of the mountain. Christians say it is the footprint of Jesus Christ or St. Thomas; Buddhists say it is Buddha's; in Hindu tradition, that of Shiva; Islamics claim it is the foot of Adam. Highly revered by everyone, it seems.

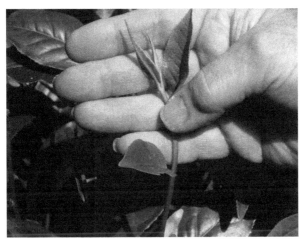

"Two leaves and a bud" make for the most premium of teas. And the unfurled bud, the newest leaf, makes the exquisite Silver Needle tea.

Our lovely Adam's Peak tea is a Ceylon White Tip, meaning that it consists only of the unfurled bud, hand plucked from the very tip of each stem of the tea bush. You may have heard the term used to describe good-quality tea as being "two leaves and a bud." Well, this gem is the bud only. Expensive and highly prized. Bud-only teas come from other places as well. Mostly China, where they are called Silver Needle.

Working with customers throughout the day often took me away from my desk. And as we spent copious amounts of time with customers to educate and turn them on to the wonders of tea, I would often get distracted for a half an hour or more. I'd return to my desk, see my tea press sitting there with the plunger up, tea still steeping, and think, "Oh crap, it's ruined!"

With most teas, they would be ruined. *The* absolutely most important rule in properly preparing a cup of tea is to time it properly. Too much time that the leaf sits in the water brings out too much tannin and other chemical components, yielding unpalatable, bitter notes. It's the biggest mistake people make in preparing tea.

But, since Adam's Peak is such an expensive tea, the first time it happened, I decided I'd plunge the press and drink it anyway. To my amazement, it was not bitter at all! It was a bit stronger in flavor than the regular five-minute infusion, but it was sweet and very palatable.

And there was something else about the character of this particular tea. Sri Lanka gave it its sweetness, the bud gave it its delightful lightness, but there was yet another property of this tea that had me scooping it out quite often. I found out later, when I began to seriously study the health benefits of tea that the bud, that youngest unfurled leaf, holds the greatest quantity of a compound called L-theanine.

L-theanine, it turns out, is the substance in tea that relaxes the brain. That's why, even though tea contains caffeine, you also get a hit of actual chemical relaxation from a cup of tea. And don't we always associate tea with relaxation? Coffee—hype you up. Tea—nice relaxing cup.

Coffee doesn't have L-theanine, just caffeine. So, when you drink ten cups of coffee, you just get more hyped with each cup. Tea, on the other hand, has both caffeine and L-theanine. Caffeine excites the brain; L-theanine relaxes the brain. That's why when you drink ten cups of tea, you don't get the jitters. Just beautifully balanced alertness.

There. That's your chemistry lesson for today.

And that's what made Adam's Peak my personal favorite for quite a while. Especially during the brick-and-mortar years. All white tea, since it is always made from the youngest leaves, is the highest in L-theanine of all the types of tea. I was often stressed with the many challenges of running a small business, so I don't think it's a coincidence that I always gravitated toward white tea on those days. That divine cup of white tea gave me a much-needed hit of calm. Literally. Chemically induced calm.

Customers would often ask me what tea was my favorite. It was difficult to pare it down to just one, but I would always respond that if I got stranded on a deserted island and could only take one tea, it would be a toss-up between Monk's Green and Adam's Peak.

Along my journey to learn everything I could about tea, I discovered another way to get exposure to lots of teas: the World Tea Expo. It is the major tea convention in the US, held in Las Vegas each year, where there are samples of the best teas in the world to sip all day long.

There I met new vendors, discovered the latest tea gadgets, and attended seminars on all aspects of tea. Vendors were eager to show their wares, especially something new and unique. There were often show specials enabling me to try a new product at a discount. I got connected with other tea lovers and tea shop owners. It was sheer ecstasy for anyone in the tea biz.

I met some of the big names in the tea world such as John Harney, who I credit with popularizing fine-quality loose-leaf tea in America, and James Norwood Pratt, author of *The Tea Lover's Treasury* and, before that, *The Wine Bibber's Bible*. I shared a nice luncheon table with Norwood at one of the expos where I enjoyed his colorful stories, especially the one where he shared that he owned a life-size replica of Michelangelo's David!

The expo brought in people from all over the world, which I loved. It made me realize how tea is the most widely consumed beverage in most of the rest of the world. I got to meet people from India, China, Japan, Sri Lanka, and more. I was richer for those meetings, more expanded as a person.

The whole experience fed my soul. And all along the way, I fell more deeply for my beloved tea.

Besides learning about the basic mechanics—the different types of tea, some history, production and harvesting, how to prepare, and how tea leaves are graded for quality—the one attribute I had to thoroughly explore was the vast health benefits of tea. My science background gave me an edge in understanding the more scientific studies that were being done on tea. The more I read, the more benefits I discovered. I was amazed by the constant flow of new research-based information on yet another benefit discovered, or confirmation of suspected benefits from human trials.

When I first started out, tea was exploding in more ways than one. First, the market for fine-quality loose-leaf tea was one of the fastest growing. But parallel to that, the medical science world was busy testing and uncovering the incredible health benefits of tea.

Researchers found out in early in vitro (in the lab) testing that tea does some pretty wonderful things. This interest in tea was exploding throughout the nineties. Then, at the turn of the century/millennium, studies progressed to in vivo (in the body). Double blind human trials. That was when scientists were anxious to confirm that these seeming benefits shown in the lab didn't just work on rats or mice or in petri dishes but carried over into humans. Good news—the human trials started confirming what the in vitro studies indicated—that tea is remarkably healthy for humans.

There were over one thousand studies a year being done on tea at that time, and by now, surely more. What they've shown is jaw dropping when you look at the totality of it. A bit more chemistry here will help in understanding the what and why.

Tea is loaded with antioxidants, those highly beneficial components in foods that undo the oxidative damage caused by, well, life. The nasties we live with such as pollution, pesticides, stress, and poor diet, all cause oxidation of our cells, weakening our organs, and lead to disease and aging. If you look at oxidation in the body as a similar process to oxidation of metal, which results in rust, you can understand that these antioxidants help to undo this oxidative damage that plagues us. Wow, cool.

And while tea contains a rich mixture of polyphenol antioxidants, including catechins and flavonols that are found in many fruits, vegetables, and other healthy foods throughout the human diet, there is one in particular that you won't find in any other food or beverage. EGCG. Epigallocatechin gallate. It's the crème de la crème of antioxidants. There are only three places in all of nature that you will find EGCG. An obscure mushroom that is not consumed, the camellia flowering bush from our gardens, and tea. Real tea only, from the Camellia tea bush, so you won't find EGCG in your cup of herbal tea or Rooibos, the South African Red Bush tea.

It's the one, most powerful antioxidant that helps best to fight not only the formation of cancer cells in the body, but has been shown to reduce tumor size, reprogram cancer cells to die off like normal cells, and even helps inhibit metastasis. Wow, again! Tea isn't just good for you, it's a superfood!

To be brief about it, here's information from one of the handouts I'd give to customers on the **health benefits of regular tea consumption:**

- Guards against free radical damage from radiation that can bring about cancer, diabetes, and it slows the aging process.

- Enhances the function of the immune system.

- Prevents normal cells from turning cancerous.

- Helps chemotherapy to target the cancerous cells.

- Suppresses the formation and growth of tumors.

- Suppresses the metastasis of cancer through the body.

- Helps control cholesterol levels.

- Lowers the risk of stroke by making the platelets less sticky.

- Helps control blood pressure and moderate blood sugar levels.

- Two to three cups daily can reduce the risk of heart attack by 44 percent.

- Helps keep blood sugar at moderate levels.

- Fights foodborne bacteria, such as Salmonella and E. coli.

- Promotes good bacteria in the intestines; encourages bowel regularity.

- Fights viruses, including cold and flu.

- Assists weight loss by blocking the breakdown of starch.

- Provides a mild stimulant effect without causing sleeplessness or

- nervousness; reduces stress.

- Fights bacteria in the mouth that cause cavities and bad breath.

- Improves skin integrity and can actually reduce wrinkles!

- Maintains the body's fluid balance.

- Plus, tea is all natural and contains no additives, artificial flavorings or colors, is calorie free, sodium free, contains fluoride, and has traces of vitamins A, K, C, beta-carotene, folate, and other B vitamins.

All these things, and more, have been confirmed with scientific studies. And even more has come out since I made this list. The most exciting recent group of studies are showing that compounds in tea may help slow or prevent Alzheimer's disease.

Others have discovered how tea helps slow down aging by keeping our telomeres from shrinking. Telomeres are those little thingies (a very scientific term) at the ends of our DNA that shorten with age. Longer telomeres mean you're staying younger, and tea keeps your telomeres from shortening.

Knowing all these incredible but science-backed health facts about tea has me and many other tea devotees choosing it over any other beverage. Every day, and that's the key. When I first dug into the research studies, they were performed on two to three cups of tea per day. They showed scads of positive benefit, if one consumed tea daily.

Then, researchers wondered what would happen with increased consumption. More recent studies have compared two to three cups consumed side by side with a group who drank four to six cups a day. And you know what? They found that more is better. Consuming twice as much tea a day would show twice the benefit. Are you craving a cup of tea yet?

Having sipped many cups of tea over the shop years, I have noticed changes in my body that I don't believe would have happened otherwise. For starters, I've carefully observed the condition of my skin, especially facial wrinkles. Besides drinking tea, I used facial care products that contain green and white tea extract. My theory has always been to fight aging any which way I can, inside and out. (Insert smiley face emoji here.)

So, since my early searches for any and all products containing tea, I have used these on my face. And I've watched closely. When I look at what changes have occurred in this nineteen-year period where the ravages of age began to set in with a vengeance, I observed a slowing down of that process. Less wrinkles than one should have for this ripe age, especially having been an avid sun worshipper in my twenties and thirties.

No skin cancers either, which have become commonplace for many who tanned in the sun. In my day, we used just baby oil. No SPF. The concept of protecting our skin from cancer causing rays hadn't even been conceived of at the time. The whole point was to intensify the sun as much as possible to achieve the darkest tan. And that exposed many to dangerous skin cancers later in life. I've had none.

All of this is anecdotal, but I believe observable data should not be discounted, as the medical field of scientific study might have us believe. Perhaps the most blatant example for me came when I was diagnosed with breast cancer.

I had noticed a small lump probably a good dozen years before I'd been diagnosed. I had it biopsied. Twice. I was told it was nothing. At least nine or ten of those years were daily tea-drinking years. The lump was still there but had never gotten any bigger.

Then one day, after I'd had a routine mammogram, I was told that I should have a newer, more accurate biopsy done, so I did. Weeks later, before I'd gotten the results from my doctor, I got a strange phone call. It was from a nurse at a local hospital's breast cancer support center, asking if there was anything she could do for me.

Whaaaat? Why are you calling me?

Then it dawned on the nurse. I hadn't been told yet, even though it was over a month after my mammogram and biopsy. The doctor had never called, so I assumed everything was OK. But that was when it dawned on me that everything must not be OK.

She suggested I call my doctor's office and would not tell me anything else. But I knew. Everything was definitely not OK. "You have DCIS," he said. I didn't know what that was.

It's ductal carcinoma in situ, in case you don't know either. Cancer within the ducts of the mammary glands. So, he recommended I schedule an appointment with a surgeon, and I began that sidetrack journey. I didn't really want to go on that trip, especially in the middle of running a small business that demanded my constant presence, but I had no choice.

I ended up having two surgeries and took only a week off for each. They felt they "got it all," but I still had to do a seven-and-a-half-week regimen of radiation "just to be sure."

While sitting in the radiation waiting room for a daily regimen over seven and a half weeks, you get to know the others, mostly women, who are going through this tough journey with you. Usually, there was a flow of sympathy and camaraderie between all of us ladies going through this hell together.

One day, one of the ladies who I'd shared daily chit-chat with asked me what I did. That led to discussions of tea, and me sharing my knowledge of the health benefits of regular tea consumption. I made a comment that I really felt tea can help bring about overall better health.

Then a dark voice from across the waiting room rang out, "Well, it didn't help you to not get cancer!" I was so taken aback by this negative attack. All the rest of us seemed to understand how positivity and support was crucial to surviving this ordeal. But this dour woman was clearly still in the anger phase and willing to take it out on anyone vulnerable.

I was shocked at her thrusting her anger at her cancer sisters. It was cruel and wrong. I had to stay silent, as I didn't want to thrust anger back at her. But I wish I could have thought quicker at that moment.

Having thought it through once I'd moved past my shock and anger, there's much I could have said to her. I could have told her that while I did have cancer, I'd had that lump for over a dozen years, discovered before I'd become a regular tea drinker, and that it had gotten no bigger in all that time. I could have added that my cancer was only at stage one. Something had contributed to my low stage outcome after so many years and having studied all the validated research on tea's ability to fight cancer, it may well have been the constant flow of tea in my diet over the previous ten years.

It made me all the more excited to be a tea vendor, with the ability to bring this wonderful treasure to others. I'd use my science background to help others to become aware of the tremendous health benefits that come in every cup of tea. I wanted everyone I could reach to understand that tea was so much more than the Americanized version of taking tea in stuffy Victorian fashion. These were core issues for me. If I was going to pour my heart and soul into my own business, it had to be something for the greater common good. Tea fit that bill perfectly.

So, I looked for every opportunity to share what I'd learned about the amazing, scientifically supported, well-documented, and bountiful health benefits of tea.

Having a background in biology and chemistry, and working as a medical technologist for twenty years, I had a natural interest in the research done on tea. No matter where I looked, the news on tea was always good. I wanted to spread this good news with others beyond just casual mention to shop customers, so I began to prepare more formal lectures on it.

I had no experience in front of an audience of any kind. At first, I'd hold small classes at the shop and always include a heavy dose of info on the latest medical research. I wanted people to know that tea wasn't just another tasty beverage. It was the absolute star among beverages!

That built my confidence in speaking to a group, and from there I expanded to small (and sometimes larger) groups at nursing homes, churches, or any event that would have me. I just loved sharing my knowledge of tea, and found it to be a subject people were very interested in. Health is always a good sell.

I found that I enjoyed it so much and knew my stuff so well that in a short time, I didn't even need notes anymore. Tell me what you want—history, types of tea, how to prepare, or health benefits—and I could talk off the cuff. Usually, it was a combination of all of the above. And always, there were lots of questions on how tea can make you healthier.

Because of my science background, I could go beyond the articles in *Women's Day* and other magazines touting the common knowledge on tea and health. I could digest the medical journal articles that went into the chemistry of how exactly tea is good for us. That enabled me to take my tea knowledge to the next level and become a speaker at my doctor's Integrative Medicine Conference.

It was a real thrill for me to be able to merge my science education with my tea business. I never expected to find that satisfaction, but there it was. Just as creating all the graphics, signage, design, labels, info handouts, etc., for the business was immensely satisfying for my more artistic side.

Because I would be speaking to a largely medical professional audience, I really dug into these lectures in much greater depth than the church lady ones. I did months of research, making sure that every claim I made on the health benefits of tea was backed by double blind research studies and extensive metadata analysis.

I would always get to a point where I just had to stop searching through the research. I'd gathered so many studies, usually stacks three to four inches thick, that all of a sudden, I would become overwhelmed. I put what data I'd gathered into the presentation, and always had more than enough to convince my audience on the science-backed benefits of tea.

Lucky to have a husband specializing in all things audiovisual, Phil made beautiful PowerPoint presentations to enhance my lectures. It helped that he worked at the same hospital where the conference was held, and he ran the audiovisuals for the entire day. It was so great to have these visual aids as part of my presentation, because the information was so technical I needed to have something to follow. No more talking just off the cuff. These lectures would require lots of data and citations from studies, but I could relax a bit, knowing I had someone I trusted to run the presentation.

My first of three lectures at these conferences was titled Green Tea & Cancer. I would search through scores of articles on the subject until I couldn't take in one more bit of data. I knew tea was healthy, but this research wowed even me at the sheer volume of confirmation of the health benefits of tea. It was a joy to present something so well documented to this tough crowd. And, having had cancer kill my father and eventually my husband and having my entire family threatened by it, including myself, I was so heartened to see such hope for treatment in this gift from nature.

The next one was titled Tea & Cardiovascular Health. While green tea is usually touted as the healthiest and almost exclusively the type cited in magazine articles on tea and health, I noticed that many—most in fact—of the studies that verified the benefit of tea to cardiovascular health showed black tea, not green, was the type that reduced the risk of heart attack and every other marker of cardiovascular disease.

It was at least a year or two after I'd noticed this trend that I ran across a metastudy on the research on tea and cardiovascular health, and it pointed out that black tea, not green, oolong, or white tea was the most effective in prevention of heart disease and mortality. My suspicions were confirmed.

Another interesting thing I noticed while researching for this talk was that all around the world, tea and cardiovascular health studies were being done. In the US, China, Japan, India, etc., all these studies were showing astounding results of a direct and significant correlation for the reduced risk of heart disease and mortality. All but England. Every study out of England showed questionable results at best, and in some cases concluded no correlation.

I wondered why that might be. Then, I remembered reading a previous study out of Germany suggesting that milk might bind enough of the antioxidants in tea, rendering them unavailable to do their job, thus seriously reducing the overall health benefits of tea. In most other places around the world, tea is taken straight, with no milk. But in England, milk is a strong standard. So, when the studies in England looked at regular tea drinkers there, they did not find the same correlation the rest of the world did. That fact would seem to indicate that the speculation on milk reducing health benefits in tea is probably true. More research needs to be done to confirm this.

The overall research shows that within thirty minutes of drinking a cup of tea, your blood pressure is measurably lower. Regular (i.e., daily) tea consumption seemed to be the key to lower cholesterol, lessened risk of blood clots, and decreased mortality. Stroke, another aspect of cardiovascular disease, was lessened because tea has been shown to make our platelets less sticky. Sticky platelets cause blood clots. And this was one of those study parameters that showed a direct correlation to reduced risk with increased consumption. One study on strokes showed a 21% risk reduction with a consistent two to three cups of tea a day. The parallel study with participants consuming four to six cups a day yielded a 42% reduction. Double the tea gave double the benefit.

Perhaps the most significant studies were the ones that confirmed that regular tea drinkers are less likely to have heart attacks in the first place. And, if they do have one, they are significantly more likely to survive it. I was eager to share this good news with any audience that would have me.

My third medical tea talk was on the overall health benefits of tea. Talk about being overwhelmed with data and information! But I correlated everything I'd learned over the years and presented to the audience of medical professionals. By the end of my talk, with loads of questions from the group, the excitement was palpable. I was pleased to have gotten another large group of people turned on to tea.

My love affair with tea wasn't just from the perspective of a tea vendor. It has become a very personal, almost sacred thing to me.

Many rituals center around this simple leaf. Some are quite elaborate and sacred, and carry a rigid formality, as in the Japanese Tea Ceremony. Every movement is required to be performed in a particular way, and practitioners study for years before becoming a master of the ceremony.

China has the Gong Fu Tea Ceremony. A little less formal in strict detail but laced with much reverence for the tea and honor and respect for those who partake. Korea has a similar, more relaxed ceremony, where serenity and beauty make up a large part of the ambiance.

The one we are perhaps most familiar with is Afternoon Tea, which follows a ritual started by Anna, the Seventh Duchess of Bedford. This woman, who in retrospect may have been hypoglycemic and couldn't wait until the traditional 8:00 p.m. to eat, would order small sandwiches and desserts to be brought to her room around four o'clock. She soon started to invite friends to join her, and the ritual of Afternoon Tea was born.

It has become quite ritualized in America, at least, where the setting is usually Victorian, with lace and doilies and fine china. Often the tea served seems to be an afterthought, as the scones with clotted cream and jam, tea sandwiches with the crust cut off, and finger desserts take center stage. It is an interesting blend of formality and relaxation as one lingers over several courses and pots and pots of tea.

I'd like to coin the name for an even less formal occasion to be known as the "American Tea Ceremony." I envision the many forms this could take. I know some ladies who make up tea trays for themselves with their favorite tea paraphernalia. For me, the ritual always begins with putting the kettle on, and it even works with an electric kettle. During that time, while waiting for it to whistle or beep, the relaxation would already start to set in. I'd choose which tea called to me for the day, put leaves in the basket, and when the water was ready, fill the pot. After the proper infusion time, I'd pour the tea into my favorite teacup and often grab a book. It all says, "Slow down and relax a bit." That's when true tranquility sets in.

Tea seems such a common thing, just a humble leaf. And yet, tea is quite uncommon. There simply is no other substance with such healing powers, such goodness and nutrition, so much variety, so steeped (pun intended) in history, and so able to impart the rejuvenating serenity we find in tea.

I found my calling in tea, and despite all my education in other arenas, I became destined to spend the largest sector of my career with it. I am quite happy to spend the rest of my days as TheTeaLady.

Chapter 2

Bold (or Bonkers) Beginnings

'd had it. It was one of the dirtiest "downsizings" anyone had ever seen. I knew after that I could never go back to corporate America.

My supervisor had called a few days before and asked me to make sure that my lead courier and right-hand lady would be scheduled in the lab that coming Friday instead of being put out on a route. I knew immediately something was up. I questioned it, and he said that he could not give me any details. I knew then that something *really bad* was up. I had a sinking feeling in the pit of my stomach for the rest of the week.

Friday came and five "suits" showed up from the Detroit lab. They had been there about an hour, calling certain people into meetings where, by the looks on their faces, obviously bad news had been delivered. Each person emerged sullen and serious and was promptly escorted to a private room in the far back corner of the lab. I knew my time was coming.

When it was my turn, I was whisked into the office just as about a dozen others had been before me. I was told that my job was being eliminated. I could sign the papers, not sign the papers, or call an attorney, but any which way, I was being eliminated. Permanently.

I was then herded to that same private far-off room where all of us who were being axed met with an outplacement agency. That was a move that large corporate America has learned to do to reduce the possibility of backlash from their harsh and unprincipled discarding of good employees. Get them to move on as soon as possible, and they won't focus on how badly they've been treated.

I was then escorted under guard to my desk to clean out my belongings. I was watched like a criminal as I gathered my personal belongings. *What the hell is this?* I thought. *I built this lab in this town for you!* This is what corporate America has become. Cruel and heartless. Discarding human beings like crumbs at the end of a meal.

My right-hand courier was made to leave the area so that she and I would have no contact. I was not allowed to say good-bye to any of my coworkers, or even my supervisor from Detroit, who I loved working with and wanted to tell him so. He was a big bear of a guy, kind and capable, and I just wanted to give him a big hug and say good-bye. A couple of months after that day, I made arrangements to meet him for lunch near the Detroit lab, and I did give him that bear hug.

A locksmith was there changing the locks on the building before I'd even gone. I was not allowed to take any of my business cards, which I thought would at least make good bookmarks or scrap paper. What did they think I was going to do with them? I doubt that passing myself off as a laboratory distribution coordinator after termination would get me anywhere. This ruthless disposal of human beings was, from my perspective, a part of their attempt to dehumanize me and take away part of my identity.

And with crushing finality, I was escorted out the building and watched closely until I drove out of the parking lot and away from the building. I knew that day that I could never work for a large corporation again. Never again would I put my psyche at such risk.

I was so traumatized by the suddenness of this loss, and the brutal way in which it was carried out, that I got myself into therapy. The therapist diagnosed me as suffering from PTSD. She said that I hadn't gone through a corporate downsizing, but that they, in their ruthless treatment, had downsized ME as a person. It was strongly recommended, if possible, that I not seek work for a while in order to recover.

So, I took about a year off, the only year since age sixteen that I had not worked. It felt strange, but I wasn't ready to go back to any sort of regular job. I was lost, in a way, where I wasn't quite sure what to do with myself. So, I let go of my fierce work ethic for a while and, on the advice of another good therapist as well, gave myself time to recover.

In that time, I came to the conclusion that I was also finished with my medical career. Med Tech is one of the top ten highest stress jobs out there. It demands 100 percent accuracy, or you could kill someone with an incorrect test result or mishandling of a specimen; or at least cause them to receive incorrect or potentially harmful treatment. Nope, it was time to hang up my lab coat. For good. I would never again give that much of myself to risk being treated so inhumanely.

During that year, I was constantly looking for what I could do next. "Do"—as in work, employment, livelihood. I have always felt that everyone has an obligation to contribute to society. I believe we all come into this world with our own unique sets of talents and abilities. And I think that's the answer to that monumental question, "Why are we here?" I believe it is to discover our own innate talents and share these gifts with others. Simple as that.

I examined potential options, and considered taking my sculpture more seriously, literally making a career out of art. I'd taken classes for many years with a talented local sculptor, JoAnn (Jody) Cousino, and loved working in three dimensions. I could get lost for hours in a lump of clay. Most of her students worked on human figures (usually about a foot tall) and I enjoyed making these maquette-sized people.

I also enjoyed a sort of trompe l'oeil realism, and so I decided to make a life-size bowler hat and formal gloves. For some odd reason, I have a "thing" about bowler hats, and this turned out to be one of my greatest accomplishments. They looked so real, right down to the stitching in the gloves, that I've actually had people try to pick them up to try on, only to realize by the heavy weight that they were sculptures!

Another very realistic piece I did was a larger-than-life teabag. The bag itself is about a foot tall and it even has a string with the paper tab at the end. The painting of the texture on the bag came out so realistic, several people thought it was a real giant tea bag and not a hunk of clay.

People often mistook my foot-tall clay sculpture of a
tea bag for a real giant tea bag.

At one of the classes I took at Bowling Green State University with a wonderful sculptor/instructor, Otto Ockvirk (Do names get any more colorful than that?), it was just me in my mid-thirties, and the rest of the students in their early twenties. They were clearly there just to fulfill a requirement; I was there to learn and practice sculpture techniques. Every day, at the beginning of class around 1:00 p.m., after Otto gave us our assignment for the day, he would leave to let us work on our own. The work time was two hours, as I recall, but everyone except me would be gone by 1:30, usually just as soon as Otto left. I'd often find myself still working well after the two-hour mark.

I remember one particular day vividly when I was carving on a piece of alabaster. Otto had given me some corrective tips on how to hold the mallet so that my wrist would not get so tired. I got into the swing of it (pun intended) after that, and somewhere deep into the afternoon nothing else existed but me and the stone. I finally realized that it was dark out and past six o'clock. I only became aware of the time when I realized I'd exhausted my arms so much I could barely pick up the chisel anymore. The half-hour drive home was a challenge, just to keep my hands on the steering wheel. Fibromyalgia, a chronic exhaustion condition that I've been saddled with, levies harsh payment for overdoing any physical endeavor. It was an oddly surreal experience of having pushed myself so far past my limits.

"Do what you love . . ." they say, don't they? But, as Jody would often remind us, art is a hard way to make a living, and ultimately, I decided that the pressure to sell art would take away the joy for me. It has remained a hobby which I still delight in, and I take great pleasure in using my creativity whenever I can.

So, art was out as my next career move.

What if, I thought, like many people do, *I started my own business? You know . . . reached for the American dream? Be my own boss?* It is an appealing and alluring prospect. You think you will be in control of things. (Add laugh track here.) You think you won't have to answer to incompetent bosses anymore (more laugh track—everybody becomes your boss). You'll get to call all the shots and come and go as you please, instead of punching a time clock. (ROFLOL!)

Still, the prospect was very tempting. And try as I might, I couldn't shake the idea. Every time I thought about going out to find another job with a lab or some other corporate entity, my stomach turned to knots. So, being my own boss began to emerge as the only option.

I started to examine the options and tried to find an idea of what my business would look like. I'd worked in retail out of college and loved it. So, I thought maybe I could set up some sort of retail shop. Now all I had to do is figure out what I could sell. The product had to be right. It had to have meaning for me.

My ideas ran the gamut of things that I thought sounded interesting. *Clothes?*, I wondered. I love clothes and shopping for them as much as any woman. But I thought about the problems of keeping stock fresh and trendy, what to do about the items that didn't sell, and juggling all the size options. Nope, that sounded like a pain to me. Definitely not clothes.

Books? After all, I'd been an assistant manager for B. Dalton Booksellers for two years out of college, and I'm one of those book nuts that is always reading something and usually reading two or three somethings at a time. But there were already more than enough sources for books in town. One more duplication of a bookstore would not have enough market share to make a go of it. Scratch books.

Jewelry, purses, other girly accessories? Again, many sources, too much competition. Artsy home accessories? Maybe, but they were in every furniture store in town. What about a small restaurant? No, I knew I didn't want to do food service. I think you have to love food and recipes and have to have a real talent for cooking to run a successful restaurant. I'd worked in restaurants in high school and college and hated every minute of it.

So, I was back to retail, and looking for something that was a good fit for me. I knew it had to be something that added to the greater good. A product that was good in every way and even healthy for people. Something that made people's lives better.

Hmmm. I was a big believer in herbs and natural things. But there were already several large health-food stores in town. What about a specialty shop with herbs and a variety of products that were all natural and made from herbs? *Yes, yes, now we're getting somewhere,* I thought. I liked that idea. It fit perfectly with my love of nature and my humble farm beginnings.

So, I started to make a list of all the things I would carry. Of course, I would start with healthy herbal capsules and extracts. And herbal teas, all targeted to support a natural approach to better health. Herbal salves, ointments, creams. Dried herbs and spices for cooking, books on herbs and herbal wreaths for decoration. Kitchen accessories all to help prepare herbs, such as garlic peelers, lemon squeezers, nutmeg graters, mortar and pestles, teapots, and infusers.

I carried the herbal theme so far that I added the Brother Cadfael murder mystery books and videos to the collection, as he was the herbalist for the monastery. I loved that he could always figure out whodunit from his knowledge of herbs, which told him such things as which toxic substance had been used to off someone or what field a certain trace of poisonous plant came from, always somehow leading to the killer. I loved the character so much, I decided to name the shop Cadfael's.

I thought it was clever. It was so clever, it turned out, that few people knew who Cadfael was, and certainly couldn't spell it when it came to writing a check. (At least a few people actually wrote checks back then.) And I got really tired of people who weren't familiar with the series mutilating the pronunciation of the name.

A while later, when the spellings came out so bad I thought my bank would start to refuse to deposit my checks, I decided to change the name to Elaine's Tea Shoppe on the advice of my marketing agency. I didn't think it was very clever and didn't really want my name for the shop, but it would be easy for people to remember. And people could just say, "Let's go to Elaine's for tea." That sounded nice, so that became the final name for the shop.

My easy-to-spot teapot sign, before the name change to Elaine's Tea Shoppe.

When I had made the decision to become an entrepreneur and open my own business—I mean, having abandoned the fantasy stage and moved solidly into reality, the absolutely, for sure, I'm-gonna-do-this-thing stage—I started pondering the mechanics. What were the pieces of the puzzle? How many pieces were there? How would I make them all fit to match the picture in my head of "my own business?"

I spent weeks. I sat and ruminated, searched and studied, trying to get just the right mix of product to attract customers to my new venture. Finally, the general outline emerged with all the pieces, and I was satisfied with the picture now coming into view.

To my amazement, I found that the largest piece of the puzzle would be tea. Not herbs, but specifically tea. I had, of course, included herbal teas, or more correctly, tisanes, the proper name for an herbal infusion. But that added up to only thirty or so blends.

I had no idea that there were so many "regular" teas available now, and that loose-leaf tea had blossomed into such a rapidly growing interest. My only knowledge of tea up until then had been the five classic black teas—Assam, Ceylon, Darjeeling, Keemun, and Yunnan—and of course, English Breakfast, which was often the only tea available in most restaurants. My tea world, like many, had been pretty limited.

With the addition of "regular" teas on top of the herbals, it was like a rapidly growing snowball. What started as a collection of a few herbal teas, after I added the must-have list of around seventy regular teas, turned into over one hundred teas in total. That was in the beginning. At the peak I lost count but had at least 130 teas in all on the menu, and around 150 on the shelves.

Tea and things related to tea had now become the major focus of the shop, composing about two-thirds of the total inventory. And that seemingly slight change brought on the avalanche.

I never originally intended to get into food service, but it sounded nice to have a place where people could sit and have a nice cup of tea. *Let's throw in a few tables and chairs while we're at it*, I thought. *And if customers were going to have tea, they'd need some delectables to go with*, I surmised. *Tearooms always serve food, but keep it simple*, I told myself. *Just desserts. It will be easy*, I reasoned. Little did I know what I was getting into. Food service is never a simple undertaking, even when you do your best to keep it simple.

So, like a moth to the flame, I dug in and created my tea biz. I really knew nothing about business. My background was in education, biology major, chemistry minor, and medical technology. I did have exposure to retail from my assistant manager stint at the bookstore: running a cash register, waiting on customers, receiving and maintaining inventory, scheduling staff. But I knew nothing really on how to run a business or how to build it from the ground up, including marketing and advertising, procuring a loan, hiring and managing employees, payroll, leasing property, keeping books, taxes, insurance, and sourcing inventory. I knew I'd go into full-blown panic if I pondered the immensity, so I didn't really allow myself to go there. I just kept telling myself that I'd figure it all out as I went along.

What would be the overall character of the shop? While many tea rooms in America tend toward the Victorian English version, I don't much care for that atmosphere and décor. Tea is so much more than that lace, bone china teapots, scones, and the dainty tea sandwiches notion. I wanted something that was more neutral and could encompass the whole world of tea, including honoring its Asian origins.

I didn't want an Asian theme either, for the same reasons. While the Victorian theme is froufrou and feminine, Asian seems starkly masculine. While the Victorian was too soft, the Asian seemed too unadorned and hard-edged. I wanted, like Goldilocks, something in between, something "just right."

French country, I decided. It seemed like it was fairly neutral and would be comfortable to a wide range of customers; not too froufrou, where men might be put off, and not too harshly modern or Asian, where women could still enjoy that coveted, serene, tea room experience.

That led to the hunt for lots of old hutches, bookcases, and anything that would make for a charming display of goods. I found and repurposed tiered plant stands that showed off teapots and other wares in a most beautiful way. I do admit to an obsession with doilies, and they were everywhere. I suppose that came from my childhood, where my Hungarian grandmother's occasional placement of them gave her house a most serene and comforting atmosphere in my eyes. Besides, they provided a suitable underlayment for the teapots especially, enhancing their beauty and character. It was the most fiercely creative time of my life, and I enjoyed every moment of it.

Colorful tea ware on tiered plant stands
made for enticing displays.

I kept working until the concept was solid, and little by little, the pieces started to come together. Before long, the initial simple idea had grown into a huge snowball. I'm smiling to myself now at the naiveté. If I'd known more of what I was getting into, I'd never have ventured. So, I think sometimes a little naiveté is a good thing. But it has to have a big dollop of guts mixed in if things are going to work out. I guess along the way I grew some guts.

Within the first year, my focus had shifted away from all the herbal variations on a theme, as I found that herbal products didn't sell all that well. In a more progressive town like Ann Arbor or Columbus, my herbal-themed shop would probably have thrived. But in Toledo, Ohio, well, not so much.

So, I made changes and brought tea solidly to the forefront. It was *the* hot commodity I'd been searching for all along that I could put my whole spirit into and indeed contributed to the greater good. It truly is good in every way. Health benefits galore, flavors and varieties in abundance, and lots of fun paraphernalia for creating your very own tea rituals.

With what I felt was a solid plan and a well-organized structure for the business, the first major hurdle would be to procure a business loan. I had some of my own retirement money that I would risk on this new venture. I would need to ask for $60,000 from the bank to start. I figured that would cover initial inventory, fixtures, office setup, etc., and give me enough to draw from until I'd built a steady monthly income. This was the step that took my venture from dream into reality. Things got real serious real fast.

My loan request was accepted by the first bank I'd presented to. Let me repeat that: *My loan request was accepted by the first bank I'd presented to.* That is virtually unheard of. For anyone. But especially for a woman. I'd been warned by the county's small business adviser that it would be a discouraging process, that I'd for sure have to go to several banks before getting one to accept my offer, *if then.* Being a woman and first-time business owner were two strikes against me, and odds of even getting a loan were not in my favor.

I'd worked with a couple of wonderful gentlemen from S.C.O.R.E., the Service Corps of Retired Executives. One had given me a disc on how to write a business plan. *Holy crap!* I thought. *This is worse than any term paper or research paper I've ever had to write.* Not having any business education was staring me boldly in the face, but I followed the format to the letter, did my research, and apparently came up with a sound business plan.

The county's small business adviser accompanied me to the bank meeting to hold my hand and comfort me when I got my first rejection. She kept emphasizing all that I had against me. First was that I was a woman. Yup, that was a point against me. This was only the first of numerous times I would run across that drawback throughout the years. The second strike was that I had never been in business before. No history of success to make them more willing to risk their money with me. That I was both a woman and had no business history at all meant my chances of getting a loan were slim to none, which the small business adviser annoyingly kept reminding me.

I presented my business plan to the president of a bank in a small town outside the city. I think my adviser knew him, at least from business dealings, if not personally. I think she thought he might let me down more softly than an unknown bank loan officer from the city.

But, when he looked over my business plan, he nodded and muttered, and grunted in places. Like he couldn't believe I'd done that thorough a job on researching my product. He seemed quite impressed with my plan. He kept looking at her with eyebrows raised. It was a look that read, "I wasn't expecting something so well put together."

The county business adviser was tripping over her jaw as we left the meeting. I was smiling ear to ear. I got accepted! Against all odds, I got accepted for a business loan on my first try. A woman. With no business experience. It was a possibility that they could have reduced the loan amount, but they had approved the loan for the full amount I was asking. This was another sign to me that I was in the right place, on the right track.

One great thing about this initial loan was that the bank made available to me an interest rate reduction program through the State of Ohio. I would get a three percent lower rate, as long as I hired at least two employees. I qualified, and as interest rates were outrageous at the time, somewhere over eight percent as I recall, it really helped bring down my monthly loan payments.

Worried that my initial cash would not be enough as opening expenses quickly added up, I'd heard about monies available for small business through the city's small business development program. So, I got in touch with the small business development director who helped me procure another $30,000. Now I was comfortable. I had enough money in hand, I could begin to actually bring my dream into reality, and the buffer to get me through the first three growth years.

Pressure was on. There was a short lead time before payments would become due. I had six months before loan payments and a two-month lead time on rent. It helped, but there was no time to waste. Everything had to be put into place in a very short period of time; I had to get some sales and money coming in.

Under the fierce pressure to get up and running so as to get an income stream flowing in a few months, I dug in and created my shop. In just three short months I found a location, contracted workmen and directed renovation, painted walls, scrubbed floors, bought fixtures, put in a second bathroom, sampled many teas and decided on the tea line to carry, decided on and purchased all other merchandise, created a simple inventory system, set up a register and bookkeeping system, interviewed and hired two employees and set up a payroll system, set up a commercial kitchen, got it approved by the health department, sourced the food and created the first menu, found used tables and chairs, sanded and painted and stenciled herbs on thirty chairs (with generous help from my niece Rachelle), designed the store layout and purchased tables, shelves, and bookcases for display, got a logo designed, had signage made and mounted, business cards printed, and informational materials produced, set up a receiving and pricing system, hired and trained new employees, set up my office and files, designed a check-out area for ring up and packaging merchandise, and advertised for the grand opening of my new shop and tea room. Whew!

We were off and running. It was an arduous uphill climb, but I'd made it and was cresting the peak. I felt like I was at the top of that first steep hill on a mean-spirited, runaway roller-coaster. I was now $90,000 in debt and my retirement money was essentially vaporized. I was tied to the shop six days a week and for much more than a regular forty hours. I was responsible for paying two employees' wages. And I had to figure out how to get customers in the door.

If I thought about it for too long, my head ached, along with my soul. So, I tried not to think about the awesome responsibility I'd gotten myself into. I set myself on autopilot and buckled in. The way I saw it, there was nothing else to do at this point but sit back and get ready for the most intense ride of my life.

They say that love moves mountains. Well, corny as it might sound, I know now that it is love that carried me through. The more I learned about tea, the more enamored I was. There was always more to learn, and I loved everything I discovered about tea. This love, early on, turned into my true passion. Sometimes passion burns, but I tell you this: passion is what carries you through the fires of hell if necessary. It is the force that carried me through my sixteen-year venture into the American dream: My Journey into Tea.

Chapter 3

Location, Location, Location

'd been cruising the streets of west Toledo looking for the right location for about six months before I applied for my loan, so I had become well informed on commercial rental costs in the area. One spot in particular that was tucked in a corner of a small strip on one of the city's busier streets, Secor Road, seemed to have adequate parking, plenty of square footage and a nice layout. It was the one, I finally decided, that would meet my needs.

The landlady who owned the strip with three suites ran her gift shop from the one in front by the street. She seemed nice enough. I thought it was a good fit with her shop and that we could both benefit from each other's customers. The layout of the suite seemed to fit my vision with a raised area in the middle that would be perfect for the tearoom tables and chairs, and I didn't think it would take too much alteration to get things up and running. I couldn't have been more wrong.

I found out that my city, a place I'd always been proud of, had been its biggest cheerleader and defended its merits to any naysayer, was simply not friendly to new business. Especially small business. The list of demands that had to be met just to open the doors was atrocious.

At one point, they had inspected the electrical to find it was out of code. It had half-inch conduit and current code called for three-quarter inch. The city was going to make me upgrade the whole suite. *But I'm renting*, I thought. *This isn't my building. Why should I have to upgrade something that should have been presented to me in suitable condition?* There are no laws or regulations addressing this in Lucas County, so the property owners were free to pass along all costs to upgrade their buildings on to the renter. It didn't used to be that way.

According to previous business decorum, buildings were maintained to code by owners with a moral scruple or two. The landlord would also pay for half of any leasehold improvements, the idea being that the tenant paid half since they were adding improvements according to their needs, and the landlord paying half since they would get to keep any improvements enhancing their property.

Not anymore. Of all the places I looked at, only one offered to pay for part of the improvements and in sixteen years since, I never heard another such offer. In fact, in general, buildings were always out of code in one way or another and landlords passed the costs of upgrading on to the tenant.

This is where I started to learn about local politics and government. I learned that corruption has infected every level of government in this country even down to local. It was my first concrete exposure to the reality that governments write laws and regulations to favor those who donate to their campaigns and do not necessarily function to protect and improve the interests of their citizens.

I also learned that a little schmoozing goes a long way, and with frugality and principle as motivators, I finally got the chief electrical inspector to grandfather in the electrical, since it was basically safe with the half-inch conduit. That was a couple thousand that didn't have to come out of my pocket. First of many bullets dodged.

The health department demands were the worst. I was not against making sure things were safe. After all, I had a background in microbiology and knew more about germs and safety than any minimally trained inspector in the health department. But it was all about enforcing the codes, I was learning, and the petty power trips that most of the inspectors seemed to be caught up in.

I was also learning that I would be treated like an unknowing idiot since there were those idiots out there, trying to do business and skirt the regulations. The codes were written by bureaucrats, and the codes were sometimes ridiculous, having been written to prevent those idiots from giving someone food poisoning.

The first health department inspector I'd worked with was very nice and really quite helpful. I knew nothing about the requirements, but she very quickly brought me up to speed. I would need a three-compartment sink: one for washing dishes, one for rinsing, and one for a disinfecting bleach dip. And specific open drying racks above the sink. Not bad, I thought. I can handle that.

Then came the mop sink. Can't pour dirty mop water down the kitchen sink. I wouldn't have even thought to do that, but I didn't understand why the toilet wouldn't suffice. Oh no, the code says . . .

And if that wasn't enough, there were the food-prep and hand-washing sinks. Really? Why couldn't we wash our hands in the bathroom sink? On that one she conceded, since the code said bath sinks could be grandfathered in for hand washing; she wouldn't make me buy and install a separate one, since the bathrooms were just a few feet away from the kitchen. But I would have to have a separate food-prep sink just to rinse a grape. Which was literally the extent of my food prep at that time.

Next were the refrigerator and freezer. I had priced them out at a local appliance store, and quickly learned that everything commercial had to have NFS on it, meaning it was certified for heavier duty use. Commercial refrigerators are made to hold the temperature even with many door openings a day. It didn't matter that I was only a small tea room serving a few desserts. My refrigerator would get less use than the typical home refrigerator, but rules are rules. So, instead of the $199 one I'd budgeted for, I had to get a commercial one for over $1,000.

The freezer I'd already bought, which was not NSF, was OK'd, since one bright inspector deduced that freezing is freezing, and any freezer would keep the foods frozen. Subsequent inspectors, every one of them, would always question the freezer, and it always took a go-around to get them off my back about the freezer.

I already had a blender that cost me only $24, but of course, since it was not NSF, I had to buy another for almost $100. It didn't, in truth, work as well as my $24 one did. But rules are rules, and common sense, it seemed, had no place in our local health department regulations.

Then came the restroom issues. There was a nice restroom there, big enough for handicap accessibility, so I thought all was good. All was not good. The inspectors told me I would need two restrooms, one for men, and one for women. They said that since I had seating for over fourteen people it would be required.

I knew this would cost a bundle, so I tried to reason with them. I was just a small tea room. I would undoubtedly serve 99 percent women. Wouldn't a unisex restroom suffice? Of course, the answer was no. I said that I would reduce the number of tables and chairs. I'd originally planned for thirty, and I said I'd reduce it to fourteen, which would make the one restroom fit into the regulations. But no. Logic was simply not permitted. They said that since I had the square footage for more than fourteen seats, I would have to put in the second restroom no matter how many seats I had. The power was in their hands, and they seemed to take great pleasure in wielding it. This totally unnecessary requirement would cost me greatly.

The plumbing required tearing up the flooring, digging through the concrete to lay the pipes, putting up walls, buying fixtures (toilet, sink, faucet, mirror, towel dispenser, wastebasket) and a second door, and repairing all flooring. After all was said and done, I had spent $5000 to give my landlady a second restroom, thereby improving her property.

That "baptism by fire" thing I'd gotten myself into was really starting to burn.

Right around this time, I was becoming stressed beyond anything I'd ever experienced before. I'd borrowed a large chunk of money. All these delays were pushing back my opening date. Bills were coming in with no income yet with which to pay them. I'd have to live on the starting capital until I built enough business to cover expenses and with payroll starting the day I'd opened and then rent payments hitting in the third month, I got even more nervous.

Then one day, when rushing back to the shop after lunch, I was rear-ended by a woman who was driving with a broken leg. She was driving with a cast on one leg, high on pain pills, with her dog in the car, and rammed into me, pushing me into the car in front of me, who also hit the car in front of his. After the police came, I pulled over into a parking lot and the migraine hit me. I hadn't had many migraines in years, having gone through a treatment regimen that brought them pretty much under control. After that day, and for the next sixteen years, I had at least a migraine a month, and more often, two.

The accident also exacerbated my fibromyalgia. I'd worked very hard over previous years to get it to a manageable level. It was worth whatever I'd gone through to have it under control and be able to live a relatively normal and active life. But the accident, coupled with the long hours and physical work to get the shop open ASAP, topped by the intense stress of it all, put me into a worse bout of fibro than I'd ever had.

The night before opening, my husband had to practically carry me out to the car. My muscles were so exhausted and burning with pain I could barely walk. The pace of running a small business and the physical and mental work involved has caused it to progress over the sixteen years until I ended up on 24/7 pain meds to enable me to just get through the day.

Much of the rest of the work to get the shop up and running was fun and creative. Gathering and painting antique tables and fixtures for display, choosing the color scheme, logo, and the whole theme for the shop, designing the layout, and decorating the shop were all tasks right up my artistic alley.

I found some old heavy wooden chairs at a fraction of the cost of new ones and with twice the character. These had come from a university cafeteria, so they were quite sturdy, but the curved seat and curved, arched back made them quite comfortable and very fitting for the shop's character. A little sanding ... well, a lot of sanding, painting, and stenciling made them into the perfect chairs that brought the tea room to life. Thanks to my niece, Rachelle, for all her hard work on this major task.

The first tea shop incarnation, with the largest
tea room area of all the shops.

Somehow it all came together in the end. The shop was beautiful, and I was very proud of what I'd pulled together. We opened our doors, and I worked on getting our name out there, letting people know that we had high-quality products at a reasonable cost, and provided a lovely, quiet atmosphere to find a bit of respite from the world.

This was a time of much tweaking. If it didn't work, it got

dropped or replaced. I was constantly looking for new products and any ideas that would bring in more business. I was growing, building a clientele of regular customers, and happy enough with the location that I'd planned to stay there for the duration. That, however, was not to be in the cards.

My landlady, that lucky woman to whom I'd given a beautiful new bathroom and many other improvements, was stealing electricity from me. I'd found out about a year and a half into my tenancy that she had half of her suite's electrical wired into my electric box. That resulted in me paying half of her electric bill on top of my own. When I approached her to suggest some compensation, her answer was equivalent to "meh," and when I pressed the issue, it was more like "bite me!"

So, I had my electrician, who had been there installing my new street sign, take all her circuits off my box and reconnect them to hers, and send her the bill for it. She wasn't happy, but she knew there was no way for her to get out of it because what she had done was improper, to say the least.

This is also the woman who my attorney had come to refer to as "the landlady from hell!" She had been coming into my suite at night, unbeknownst to me, or so she thought. I'd find the ceiling tiles moved over and not put back in place. I don't know if she was trying to find a way to hook her electrical back into my box again or what. But she was the only other one with a key and the only one who might have an interest in what was going on above the ceiling.

I soon changed the locks on my door and didn't give her a key. I didn't tell her about it either, waiting for her to find out when she tried to get in again. She was understandably upset at that move, but I explained to her that the only way she could know that I'd changed the locks was that she had tried to enter my suite without my knowledge or permission, which she was not allowed to do. I stood my ground and didn't give her the key until I moved out. Needless to say, things were pretty icy between us by then.

After all I'd done to improve that suite—cleaned up the disgusting filth it had been when I took it over, paint and new flooring throughout, given her a second restroom, added a kitchen and a beautiful service counter with an arched window—she was plotting to get me out of the building at the end of my three-year lease. Every time I approached her about signing the renewal, she just put me off and said we'd address it later.

It was getting on to the end of October, and the lease ran out at the end of the year. Even though I had a "right to renew" in the lease, if she refused to sign it, I didn't want to put my business in the precarious position of not having the protection of a lease. I didn't really want to move as my business had grown substantially over the first three years, but I realized that I had to find another location fast. I could not allow myself to be kicked out with no place to go.

I drove around the areas in my end of town where I thought there would be potential new locations. I spotted a "for lease" sign in the window of one of my favorite strips in a suburb at my end of town. It was named Saxon Square. I'd always loved driving by that strip in winter when it was snowing, where the beams of light shining down from tall floodlights in the parking lot would highlight the dancing snow. It was magical. The strip was viable, rarely having any vacant spots, had a reputation of only renting to small locally owned businesses, was well maintained, had the right square footage, and plenty of parking. It was also on a busy street for good visibility. Bingo. I'd found my next tea home.

Within a week I'd met with the realtor handling the property and had signed a new lease. The rent per square foot was higher at Saxon Square, but the suite was smaller, so the rent per month came out almost the same as I had been paying. My first really important retail lesson—NEVER rent more space than you absolutely need. I didn't pay my December rent, as I knew that the landlady from hell would keep my security deposit, and the suite was pristine when I left. She was, as expected, quite miffed, but could do nothing since the suite was left in such good condition. My time on Secor Road had come to an end.

With renewed hope in new surroundings, I set out to prepare the Saxon Square location for business. It already had two bathrooms, so that was not a problem this time around. I had to wall off the back part of the suite to create kitchen, office, and storage areas. I was now working with the Sylvania township inspectors, as opposed to the City of Toledo. In some ways they were better and seemed more friendly to new business, but one thing they insisted on was the drawing of a simple L-shaped wall in my plans being submitted by an architect. My clear drawing was not permitted, and that added another unnecessary cost of over $500. Regulations, you know, and power. We must exert our power over these little guys.

I'd hired a private contractor who was recommended by a friend. More lessons learned: *don't take recommendations from friends who know nothing about business and are suggesting using "a guy I know."* He turned out to be a manic-depressive con artist (one of numerous cons I'd meet over the years), who never finished the job. I had to have my brothers and husband finish the last details because money was tight. Money is always tight in small businesses. I felt so bad asking, especially my older brother, Dave, since he was recovering from a heart attack several months before. But as he is the carpenter in the family, we needed his expertise. And as brothers and husbands do, he and my younger brother Denver and my husband Phil stepped in and got the suite finished on time.

While this location was maintained pretty well, it had been occupied by a pizza shop previously. The basic suite had been "white boxed," meaning painted all white to give the impression it was clean and ready for move in. We painted one accent wall melted-chocolate-ice-cream brown to give the suite some warmth, just as I had done in my first location. This became a feature in all of my four shops.

Then there were the bathrooms, which had not been touched by the landlord. How could someone get so much pizza dough splattered on all four walls and including the ceiling? It took days to scrape and repaint walls, scrub and rewax the floors, so they were suitable for customers. New flooring was needed throughout the rest of the suite, and reinstallation of all those sinks for my kitchen, plus building all new counters to fit the new space, and finally we were ready to move in.

Packing up a shop with several thousand small items, much of it breakable, is no small undertaking. There were also all of the fixtures to move: display tables, bookcases, all sorts of display stands and racks, slat wall, brackets and wall shelves, cash register counters and retail supplies, tea room tables and chairs, refrigerator, freezer, oven, microwave, all kitchenware, my desk, filing cabinets, printer, reference books, office supplies, receiving table, and supplies. The merchandise, when all packed, probably filled a good forty to fifty boxes of all sizes.

It was a monstrous undertaking, but I was carried by the excitement of a bright, new location that also carried the hope of a better relationship with the landlord. The financial commitments were always a powerful motivator, as the loan payments didn't stop while I was moving. So, getting reopened ASAP was of utmost importance.

Getting everything up and running was no small task, either. Phone lines, internet connection, changing over all the utilities, making sure I could keep my same old phone number, letting all my vendors know of the new address, getting new signage in place so customers, old and new, could find us as soon as we opened for business. Finding the right configuration for all the display furniture and wall displays and giving the new shop a bright and inviting look was a creative challenge I took on with relish. We had a fairly customary lead time of two months before rent payments kicked in, and we were ahead of schedule, reopening two weeks before the beginning of the third month.

Saxon Square, with a smaller tea room area. This shop brought the wall-mounted shelves for our expanded tea wall.

There was just enough space in the landscaped area out front of the shop to put in a small patio, so in the spring we decided to add one. It was pretty simple to do, but leveling the ground for the patio stones was the most labor intensive and accomplished again with the help of my husband and my carpenter brother, Dave. We then surrounded it with a white picket fence, added new outdoor tables, umbrellas, and chairs, and the front of the shop was even more inviting. The tables, chairs, and umbrellas had to be taken in every night so that they wouldn't be stolen. I was prepared for that, and found collapsible tables and light, stackable chairs. A bit of a pain to do every day, but it worked.

The patio area, later turned into a garden.

At first business was booming at this new spot. It seemed everyone in Sylvania was out to discover the new kid in town. It brought a few new regular customers, but many fell off after their curiosity had been satisfied. We kept many of the old regular customers, but surprisingly lost some to this new location that was only about seven minutes away from the old one, and apparently too far for them to drive. Lesson number I'm losing count—*some people are just lazy, and you'll never be able to please them all.*

Business evened out to a bare-survival level, and I was always scheming ways to bring in new business. I'd worked with an ad agency in my first three years, but I wasn't bringing in enough to keep paying their fees. They were a good firm, and their creative ads did bring me some new business, but I wasn't sure that much of my growth hadn't really been from people just discovering by word of mouth that there was a new shop in town. Some of both, I'd guess. And after a couple of years, the newness of my shop to the Sylvania area had worn off, too. This is where my marketing skills became more refined, but it seemed no matter what I tried, business wasn't growing. For every couple of new customers I'd gain, I seemed to lose a few. I was getting by, but barely.

At my first location, I survived 9/11, which took a toll on

all businesses, and that was on top of the building of a new hospital just down the street, which made people avoid Secor Road like the plague for months. But I grew and was thriving during those first three years. During my six years at Saxon Square, I was always at a stubborn plateau. Then when the Bush economy tanked, and brought us to the crash of 2008, I knew I was going to be in trouble if something didn't change.

The arched service window where,
"It's always tea-time...," said the Mad Hatter to Alice.

I really didn't want to leave the location, but it was becoming clear that I'd have to if I didn't do something to bring expenses closer to income. I hadn't been able to pay myself a paycheck in several years. So, I got my courage up to approach the landlord about reducing the rent. Desperation is a great motivator to help you find your courage. It was good timing, as the lease was coming up for renewal. I did actually get them to come down a very small amount as we negotiated a lease for the next three years.

There I was, tied into this location, which I loved, for another three-year term, and it was probably the most intensely creative time in my life. Besides all the classes I taught, I'd expanded our food service to casual luncheon and more formal afternoon teas. I held special tea events, such as our lovely Mother's Day tea, came up with new tea blends, new packaging (several times!) and labels for the teas, improved décor and landscaped the patio out front of the shop, added new items to the menu, reworked the menu with everything being made from scratch and mostly organic and even some gluten free.

But by the end of the next lease term, the struggle had taken a serious toll on my health. So did unreliable employees and an unscrupulous business partner. I knew then that change was an absolute necessity. Again.

With all that looming over me, I still really loved my location and didn't want to move, even if I could find something more affordable. Then, in one of my many brain-wracking sessions, which I did often to try to find the solution to my dilemma, I didn't exactly find a solution, but I did find powerful motivation.

The landlord at Saxon was a large conglomerate and while they kept the building in good shape, I knew that I was paying for every light bulb they replaced, and painting the building had already been added on to my Common Area Maintenance (CAM) charges. The painting charges were so exorbitant that they had to be amortized out for five years among the fifteen or so tenants in the strip. I thought, *I could have found someone to paint the building for a fraction of what they had apparently paid.* But that's not the way these big corporations work. I'm sure they had someone they knew, or a family member, do the job for that hefty price.

Wow! I thought. *How the heck is THAT fair?* Well, it most certainly is not fair, but as it turns out, it is not illegal. Lesson number one million and two—*if it isn't written in law that a business, landlord, contractor, bank, or whoever cannot do something that doesn't seem right, someone will definitely do it.* Landlords were smart and cagey enough to bury things in thirty pages of small-print leases that they got away with whatever they wanted.

Buried in that small print was a clause that said that if anything had happened to the front windows of the building, like someone driving through them, I would have to pay for repair and replacement. I only found that out one day because an elderly customer who was parked right in front of the shop hit the gas instead of the brake. He came with such momentum that he went up over the very wide sidewalk and stopped just short of my picket fencing and thankfully, did not end up going through the window. The tea room was almost full that day, and there were over a dozen people sitting at tables right inside the window. My lucky stars were shining hard that day.

At one point, Saxon decided they wanted to replace all the front doors from the old English Tudor-style wooden doors to glass doors in their efforts to make the building look more contemporary. Of course, tenants would have to pay for it. I'd learned the art of dragging my feet by then, so I never did put in a new door. Instead, I learned to endure the constant nagging from the landlord to get it done and how to simply let it roll right off my back, while I kept the money it would have cost in my pocket instead of his.

I approached management again about working with me on the rent, but they were unwilling this time. They were, apparently, completely willing to lose a good tenant who was never late on rent and added much character to their plaza. While I was looking for ways and reasons to stay, in browsing through the lease one day I found the bit that tipped the scales in quite the opposite direction. Among that laundry list of CAM charges, I found something called management fees. What? I was being charged management fees by my landlord?

When I'd finally thought it through thoroughly, I realized

that my landlord was charging me for him to "manage" the plaza. So, let me get this straight. The landlord was charging me a fee to cover his job, which was to rent out his buildings to tenants. In other words, not only did the tenants pay every red cent to maintain his buildings, making the rents he collected pure profit with absolutely no expenses for him, he was collecting money from the tenants to cover his costs to run his business, which was to manage properties like Saxon Square.

Wow, again! How the double heck is THAT fair? This man has absolutely no expenses! His rent is pure profit. ALL of his expenses are paid for by the tenants, including all building maintenance and improvements. And, again, since there's no law saying he can't do that, he gets away with it. It is no wonder how he can donate $100,000 here and there to entities like local hospitals, no doubt donate to local politicians, and come out smelling like the proverbial rose. He took it from my pocket, so he can get his name in the local papers as a good and generous businessman.

That would be comparable to me charging my normal profit for the tea, plus a bit to cover my rent, my electricity, my payroll, my office supplies, my food, and ALL my expenses. So that every penny of my cost of doing business came out of my customers' pockets and none from mine. Sounds nice, huh? But if I actually tried to do that, each cup of tea would cost more like $10 instead of $3. It simply wouldn't fly.

It didn't take long to conclude that it was simply too costly to stay at Saxon Square. With that one heart-sinking realization, I made the decision to move. Lord knew I didn't want to go through that expense and mountain of work again, but it was now, to my mind, absolutely necessary. The rent was too high in light of what 9/11 and the recessed economy had done to my revenues.

This conundrum forced the situation, and I'd soon be on

the move. I'd done it before, I knew what needed to be organized to make it go as smoothly as possible, and so, I thought, *Here we go again!*

Surprisingly, it didn't take too long to find another suitable location, and I really couldn't believe my good luck. It was a smaller suite, but downsizing again felt right. Rent would be less with less square footage but adequate for a more streamlined shop. Exactly what I needed. This was almost too good to be true.

Everything on the list of desirables was possible at this location. I would end up with three tables instead of six, but that was OK. I'd already decided to give up the bulk of the food service, reducing it to just tea and homemade scones, which seemed to be the most popular menu item. Check. I would now need fewer employees than my full luncheon and afternoon tea service required. Check. The suite needed little build out. Check. It was a prime location on the main drag in Toledo, Monroe Street, across from a popular and well-known restaurant. Check. And it was all of two minutes from my home. Checkmate.

I got set up in this new location very quickly, having been through it all before. I loved this space even better than Saxon. The heavy burden of out-of-line expenses was off my shoulders. The simplification of the food service alone seemed to take the weight of the world off of me. I was recovering and relaxing into this third incarnation, making a reasonable go of it, and enjoying running my business again.

There was no room for a patio out front, but the truth of it was that almost nobody used it. Most of the time, someone would give it a go, decide it was too hot, and then ask to be reset up inside where the air conditioning was. No more dragging tables and chairs in and out every day.

A smaller storefront, but in keeping with our character.
The service window area expanded to include a tea bar,
and the "Tea Cottage" was built to house the
tea tins for daily tea service.

I don't really think Murphy's Law was in play here, but just when I was sure I would finish out the next couple of leases and cruise into retirement from this great location, something I could not have ever imagined happened. I had started contacting the landlord about renewing the lease but got several put-offs, saying that he was out of town and the agency would get back to me when he returned. I was about a week over the three-month notice of intent to renew, but I didn't think there would be any problem as I was told repeatedly that he would be signing a renewal as soon as he got back in town. That was not to be the case.

Soon after, on one fine day as I drove into my parking space facing the back door, I saw that there was a large note taped to the door. It said something to the effect of "Please be here on xx/xx date for an important meeting with the landlord's representatives." While I didn't know exactly what that meant, I knew it probably wasn't anything good. And, as it turned out, it was horrible. We (all three tenants) were told about a week later that the building had been sold, and the new owner would be taking over the whole building for his own use.

Things that are too good to be true usually don't show up in reality, or don't stick around long if they do. This perfect location I'd found and loved doing business out of, vaporized within three short years. Like it or not, we would have to vacate the building. This was in early fall.

I met with the new owner and begged him to let me stay through the holiday season, including January. In small retail, well, in all retail, but especially very small businesses, you make a huge portion of your yearly income over the holidays. Like a quarter of it. It would crush me out of existence if I had to leave before then. He was understanding, explained that he had much planning yet to do, and that there would be no problem with me staying through January. A fatal bullet was dodged, but I wasn't sure the wounds I'd already received from having to move again wouldn't do me in anyway. And they almost did.

On top of getting through the last holiday season on Monroe Street, I was madly looking for another new location. It was a real challenge. I knew the area I needed to be in. I knew what worked best for my city. Many strip malls were just too expensive for a small, independent business like mine. They wanted chain businesses like Subway and AT&T phone centers, who take in such high profits that they can pay a disproportionately high rent and not blink an eye at that long list of CAM charges. I found one place in an older strip. I offered a rent comparable to what I'd been paying, only a little under what they were asking, and they turned me down. I simply couldn't take on higher rent.

Then I found what looked to be another great location, a bit further down on Monroe Street and in the center of my target area. Good visibility from the street and prominent signage, perfect square footage, good layout, great parking and a patio area, and it was very near the most successful mall in town. The rent was higher than I would have liked, but the location and layout were so perfect, I knew it would work. I talked to the owners, and we came to an agreement. We shook hands, and since I wouldn't be ready to take possession until February, they indicated we would sign papers after the first of the year. I breathed a sigh of relief and went on to prepare for another hectic retail holiday season.

After the holiday frenzy subsided, I attempted to make contact with the new location owner in order to get a lease signed. In January, the most dreaded task of inventory has to be completed. We'd sold more than usual, as we started mark-downs in anticipation of the move. As soon as that was under control, and since I'd not heard back from the new landlord, I made more serious attempts to meet to go over the lease. When I finally got the owner on the phone, he informed me that he'd changed his mind and was going to use the location for his own business office and would not be renting it out after all. It was mid-January, and having to be out by the end of the month, I suddenly had no place to go.

Besides the horrible sinking feeling in the pit of my stomach, I also realized that not having any place to go would require moving everything twice. I would have to put everything in my garage and storage shed until I could find a new location. While rent and utilities would stop, loan payments would come due every month with no flow of income until I found another location. So, in the midst of this dreadful situation, I did what I always did before. One foot, then another, and I would simply march on.

I moved out of the suite after having a huge sale and reducing merchandise as much as possible. Everything had to be stuffed into my garage at home. We tried to label and organize all the merchandise and fixtures to facilitate an easier move in when I did find a new space, but moving is such a chaotic experience, everything got all mixed up.

At least I got out on time to meet the new building owner's needs and could now concentrate all my energies on finding yet another location for my shop. The pressure was off somewhat. I still had loan payments to make, but all other expenses stopped. No rent, no electric bill, gas, phone, internet, and no merchandise purchases, and no food to maintain. It also gave me a little break from the regular baking of scones. I'd baked so many batches of scones, I thought I could probably do it in my sleep. I enjoyed the reprieve.

I scoured my target area for weeks and weeks. My emotions vacillated between dread, hopelessness, and out-and-out despondency. I started to look farther out of the area but always came back, knowing that it was crucial to be located in the central area I'd defined. Then one day while driving around with my brother Dave, he spotted a building only a few short blocks out of the target area on Sylvania Avenue, another main street in Toledo with a high traffic count. It was actually just around the corner from my original shop on Secor Road. It looked about the right size and had minimally adequate parking, so we decided to check it out.

The owner of the building just happened to be there, as he occupied the back suite with his own business. He gave us the key, and we went in to have a look around. It had been white boxed, poorly, the carpet was old and dingy, but the square footage was minimally right, and the layout was open, meaning we would have few changes to make it workable for the tea shop. It was small, but the rent was only a bit above the last spot, so I decided I'd find a way to make it work. It had been three months already, and I need a place to get the income flowing again.

The final incarnation on Sylvania Ave.
gave us room for a patio again.

As with these smaller and independently owned buildings, the leases are much simpler than the thirty pages of fine print of Saxon Square. I negotiated the two-month lead time, hurriedly read the simple lease, signed it, and got to work. Every minute was critical now, and I had to get reopened as soon as humanly possible. But, by this time, I was a practiced pro at moving. I was beginning to think of my shop as the MASH of retail.

Pretty much rote by now, we built out the service counter, figured out kitchen layout, and added as many storage shelves as we could fit in as the footprint was so much smaller than previous locations. My brother and husband were right there again, helping me every step of the way. They installed a slat wall along the whole length of the suite, which turned out to be perfect for my hundred-plus varieties of tea.

By sheer will and a bit of luck, in the end everything fit, the new flow of operation was designed, and we were again up and running. I'd managed to skirt the general building inspectors altogether, since the changes needed didn't warrant an inspection. I did have to have the plumbing inspected, but my plumber did a good job of installing all my sinks, and it passed with no problems.

The tea wall was the foundation for each shop.
Customers could easily browse for tea by color-coded category:
Black, Green, gold for Oolong, red for Decaf, silver for White
teas, and purple and blue for Herbals.

There were a few things about this location that I was nervous about. Although only a few blocks away from my prime area, it had higher crime rates, and the liability insurance went up. My worries about that were lessened when one day we got a visit from the new neighborhood foot-patrol police team. That gave the whole neighborhood a different, safer feel. It was one of the things I loved about this neighborhood, and I loved it every couple of weeks when they would come in for a chat. It didn't lower my liability insurance, of course. Nothing ever goes down these days, does it? But the sense of security it gave us and our customers was worth more than any amount of money.

Another thing that troubled me a bit was the age of the building and the obvious signs that it had not been very well maintained. I shrugged it off until about the third time we noticed some sludge-like grunge in the bottom of the three- compartment sinks in the morning. I had noticed it but thought my helper who had covered the previous day just hadn't washed out the sinks well. Then she noticed it but had not said anything to me because she thought the same—that I had not rinsed out the sinks well from the day before. Finally, I said something to her, and we put two and two together. Something was backing up into the sinks.

I called the landlord and asked him if he had been doing anything on his end of the building that might have caused this back up. He played dumb and said he knew of nothing that could have caused such a problem. He suggested it was sludge backing up from my grease trap under the sink. I explained that the grease trap was almost new, and there would be no sludge in it to back up. Besides that, I explained that there had to be some pressure coming up from somewhere else in the building to cause that kind of backup. Again, he poo-pooed my concerns and said it must be my grease trap. When it continued to happen later, I insisted on him getting a plumber in to check it out.

He did, and the plumber tested all my sinks and water lines, and indicated there was nothing wrong with my side of the plumbing. He tried to check in the landlord's suite, but there was no access panel to get at the plumbing—something required by code, but obviously not enforced by the city. The plumber recommended a clean out and offered to install the proper access panel and do the necessary clean out for only $400, but the landlord refused. So, this building, which had been built around ninety years ago, had never had the plumbing cleaned out. Lesson number one million and three—*the city imposes the letter of the code on small business owners but lets the building owners get away with not keeping their buildings up to code. Especially if they donate to their political campaigns.*

I stopped paying my portion of the water bill, attempting to put some leverage on him to fix the problem. Every time it happened required a thorough bleaching out of the sinks, and

I lived in perpetual fear the health department would come in for one of their surprise inspections and shut me down because of this unhealthy contamination that kept occurring in my dish washing sinks. I could see them telling me that I had to pay to get the building plumbing fixed, or I would not be permitted to operate my food service. It was another situation of me having to upgrade a building I was renting, and being a little older and a little wiser, I was not about to do that this time. The landlord, of course, ignored it, but kept insisting I pay the water bill.

Months later, suddenly one day, the floor drain under the sinks started to back up. Gallons of sewer water were oozing out onto the floor of the kitchen/storage room, into the hallway and tea service area, and even went as far as the carpeted retail area. I called the landlord, explained what was happening and asked him to get a plumber in to address the problem. He said that as he was vacationing in British Columbia, and he couldn't do anything about it from there. I explained that as he had a cell phone, he could call his plumber. He laughed and said that since I wasn't paying the water bill, it was my problem, and promptly hung up on me.

On top of all this, the water bills started to escalate. They should have run around $185 to $200 max per quarter for the three suites in the building. Then, one quarter they went up to more than $600. After that, they hovered between $300 and $600. We had several other floods from the floor drain.

I'd checked with the city water department to see if there was any problem in the city lines that might have caused the problems. They came out to the building and checked the lines. No problems with pressure, plugs, or surges that might have caused the backups. Something was clearly wrong with the plumbing in the building. But no matter what evidence I presented, the landlord (read: slumlord) refused to do anything about it.

I examined this situation from every angle I could. I was

actually loving this location and all the new customers I was getting. The visibility from the street was superb, and it was a neighborhood that supported its local businesses. Plus, the central location helped me retain most of my old clientele. I wanted to stay at this location until I was ready to retire. I didn't really want to retire yet and hoped to sign at least another three-year lease, and possibly five. For the first time in years, my business was growing again.

But I simply couldn't continue to deal with the smelly floods of sewer water, the potential risk of damage to my products, and the constant threats from the landlord over the water bill. I tried in earnest to meet with him and his attorney, but I've never met anyone quite as unreasonable as this man. No agreement could be reached, as he refused to even meet with me. So, after serious contemplation, and increasingly absurd threats from the landlord, I decided that I had no choice but to close up shop.

I simply could not move forward into territory where there was no lease to protect me, and if I was going to close, I had to make that decision in time to sell off as much as I could before the closing date. Sadly, after having just moved twice in the past six years (costing me around $15,000 each time), I simply didn't have the income, nor did I have the stamina in my sixties to go through that arduous experience again. So, the decision was made to close for good. I still had around $25,000 on my loan to pay off and didn't want to enter retirement with a debt over my head. Luckily, I did sell enough in the end to break even.

That became my final brick-and-mortar location. My shop now resides on the World Wide Web. I have to say, my stress level and overall health have improved greatly with this move to the virtual world. Well, not entirely virtual.

A neighboring business offered to be a local pick-up spot so that local customers don't have to pay shipping. That was extremely generous of them, but they understand that it will help us both. Every one of my customers that comes into their shop to pick up tea, also gets exposed to their wares. Business helping business works markedly better than any cutthroat competition model ever will.

And as I am still at least a part-time TeaLady, I may yet be able to fulfill my wish to keep going until finally one day, I drop dead, face planted in my last pot of tea.

Chapter 4

The Cheers of Tea – Communion of the Spirit

When I was a clerk and then assistant manager at the bookstore years before, I learned the art of customer service. I loved it. I took it as a personal challenge, because I loved books so much, to put a book in the hand (and a sale out the door!) of every customer I waited on. I loved picking their brains on what their likes were, or details about a friend so that they could find the perfect birthday gift if that's what they were after, or find some dreamy novel to get lost in while on vacation.

That's probably why the very favorite part of my shop was waiting on customers. Just like with the books, it was a joy for me to help them find the perfect tea. That meant developing a more-than-average depth of customer service than you find these days. And, in order to accomplish that, I had to converse with customers to a degree that would reveal things like their level of tea experience and their likes and dislikes as far as flavors. It worked to keep customers happy with their tea choices and coming back for more. Often it led to a willingness on their part to try something completely new. That was great fun for me.

After only a year or so in business, we had a growing list of "regulars." Those people who loved the shop and came back repeatedly. We got to know all their names. We would even sit and have tea together sometimes, and consequently, I got to know a bit about their lives. Somewhere along the way, it began to feel like we'd become the *Cheers* of tea– "Where everybody knows your name, and they're always glad you came. You wanna be where you can see, our troubles are all the same. You wanna be where everybody knows your name."

It is a comfort to be among friends. It is a comfort to be able to share your troubles over a cup of tea. It seems the world has become so fast paced, impersonal, and overloaded with technology and information. We loved being this comfortable respite for our customers.

It's what I like to call a communion of the spirit. It's about connection. It's what we all yearn for. To be connected with others, not so alone in the world. Sometimes our society seems to be sadly inept at this. There seem to be so many lonely people. Maybe that's just the way it will always be, but I was proud for at least the duration of those shop years to be a conduit for that communion with others.

We made those connections with every one of our customers. And some of them made connections with each other. There were so many wonderful people over the years, and some were real characters. I could tell tales all day, but I'll just share with you some of my very favorites.

Here are some of these stories from my tea blog, *Tea-Time Tales*.

Good Afternoon, Mr. Spielberg!

One of our lunch time regulars was Stephen Spielberg. OK, not THE Stephen Spielberg, but that was his real name. He was always alone but got to know two other lunch regulars, Suzanne and Carolyn. He'd sit at the table next to them, so he could chat with them throughout lunch. It was nice to have a bit of the Y chromosome in the shop on occasion. We had a growing number of regular male tea drinkers who would come in to resupply their stashes, but it was almost always just the ladies at lunch.

He informed us, after about a year, that he would be moving out of town to be nearer to old friends and family as he was getting older and needed their support. We really missed being able to say, "Good afternoon, Mr. Spielberg" when he walked in the door and watching all the heads turn to see if it was the real Stephen Spielberg. Life moves on, however, and we wished him well. One of the many who would come and go over the years.

Carolyn, the Elder, and Most-Regular Regular

We had many single ladies who came in for lunch regularly. There was Suzanne, who came about twice a week to escape the dull assisted-living lunch menu and swap stories with us. And Barb, who'd lost her husband recently. I remember how sad she looked and could barely talk without tears. I was so happy to see her return to her normal happy state over time. She came in for so many years that, now that I've closed the shop, we still meet for lunch on occasion.

Then there were the two Carolyns who came into the shop on a regular basis—one to shop for tea and one pretty strictly for lunch. In order to keep them apart, the shopper who was in her late twenties became Carolyn the Younger, and the other who was around seventy was deemed Carolyn the Elder.

Carolyn the Elder was our star lunch customer. She discovered us shortly after we moved to the Saxon Square location, as it was in her neck of the woods. She could no longer drive, so she kept to places near her where she was familiar with the bus routes. I honestly cannot remember a day where she did not come in for lunch except once, when she went on a vacation. One day, she even came in with half her right-hand fingers bound up in a massive amount of gauze and medical tape. We asked her what happened. She said she'd broken a finger the night before. We were aghast and urged her to get to urgent care or an ER right away to have it looked at. She agreed, but said, "Well, I have to have lunch first, don't I?"

She's an amazing character. She loved to talk, and sometimes, I admit, it cut into our ability to get our work done. But it was usually worth listening to her ramblings, as she was very well informed on a whole host of topics. I've always found old people to be a great source of wisdom if we just listen. She read every word of the newspaper daily, so was more up on current events and politics than most of us. Much of the time that's how I got my news!

She was still driving when she first started to come to the shop. We all wondered, with her slowness from age, whether she should be driving. But then, when she got into a fender bender, and other health problems cropped up that prevented her from being a safe driver, one of her sons took her keys away. Not to be deterred, and determined not to be grounded, she always found other ways to get around.

She was highly motivated to visit her other son, who I think had Down syndrome and lived in an institution. She went every day across town to make sure he was getting proper care, and to let him know, I'm sure, that his mother would never forget about him. So, she searched and found senior shuttles and city bus routes that would take her wherever she needed to go.

Carolyn the Elder was a fierce model of caring and perseverance. Her tenacity was a lesson to us all: one must never give up.

Tea & Sympathy

I first met Barbara when she and a friend came into the tearoom for tea and scones one afternoon. When they finished, it was pouring rain outside. So, they laughed and said what the heck, they'd have another pot of tea. Then, another. Hours later, it was still raining, so they ordered another and even a second round of scones. I don't remember how many pots they'd gone through, but I'll never forget that rainy afternoon where those two ladies drank pot after pot of tea.

Barbara became a familiar face, but I noticed at one point that she hadn't been around for quite a while. I knew Barbara was hooked on a couple of our teas and replenished her stock about once a month. It had been long enough now that surely she had to have been out of her tea for months. I thought that perhaps she'd just stopped drinking tea, but as much as she loved her tea, that didn't seem right.

Then one day, I was pleased to see Barbara walk in the door. She looked fabulous, always dressed to perfection. Something underneath the surface was different, though. I could sense the heaviness she was carrying. As we caught up on events of the past six months, I shared how my husband and I had lost our entire animal family within a few months' time: a beautiful Siberian Husky, Kira, and two lovely cats, Chelsea who was almost twenty-two, and Eykis, our sweet, deaf, long-haired white. She was totally sympathetic and recounted her own sad losses of these past few months.

One day, coming home after running some errands, she found her elderly husband dead after apparently falling down a flight of steps. And, if that wasn't shocking enough, a short time later she found out that her only son, in his early thirties and just getting a hold on life, was diagnosed with cancer and died soon after.

My heart broke for her! I couldn't imagine how difficult that must have been to bear. I asked how on earth she was even still standing? She shared that she simply decided that she must move on with life. With one foot in front of the other, she managed to move into a new house to distance herself from the horrible memory and begin to put her life back together.

She became a very independent woman. She loved to travel, and she didn't let being alone stop her. One year near Christmas, she decided to take a tour through Europe and was able to share her holidays with some lovely people instead of being alone. She would always recount her travels with me over a cup of tea, of course, and I enjoyed hearing about the many adventures she had.

Another thing she did was to give elaborate tea parties in her home. She always had a theme and would come in to discuss ideas and details with me. One time, she gave a historically accurate "High Tea." High Tea is actually the evening meal that the working class takes at a regular dinner table. "Afternoon Tea" is actually "Low Tea," where ladies sit in parlors with the tea and culinary delights perched at low tables beside their chairs.

But everyone mistakenly thinks that high tea sounds loftier and must be a fancy event with lace and doilies. When Barbara served her guests the soup, heavy meats and cheeses, and heavy desserts that would entail an evening meal in Victorian England, they were shocked to find out the real meaning of "High Tea." I loved how she had sort-of punked her guests, and I loved being a part of the planning for her stunning events.

She was the embodiment of our shop motto, the famous quote from Eleanor Roosevelt: "A woman is like a teabag. You never know how strong she is until she gets into hot water." I was truly in awe of Barbara's strength.

We shared a few more sips of tea, now both perhaps better understanding the meaning of "tea & sympathy."

Biker Rik

I will never forget the first time Biker Rik walked into my shop. He'd pulled up to the front of the store on his beautiful candy apple red Indian motorcycle. Decked out in leathers and a skull ring, he looked very much like a typical biker. Not so much like your typical tea drinker. But I was soon to find out what a serious tea connoisseur he was.

He was a merchant seaman on the Great Lakes—First Mate, to be precise. He was stationed out of Cleveland at that time, and on one of his leaves where he visited friends in Toledo, he happened upon the shop. He came in, sat down at a table, and ordered a pot of tea and made himself at home. We started to chat, and the next thing you know, we were deep in conversation to solve as many of the world's problems as we could. I couldn't remember when I'd had a more enjoyable afternoon, certainly not with a stranger. He then wandered around our tea shelves and did some serious tea shopping.

Since he was on board ship for long stints of time, he bought enough of each of his favorite teas to get him through. Manly teas, like Lapsang Souchong and Scottish Breakfast, along with a cast iron Tetsubin teapot. He had his well-worn wooden tea chest with him, and he carefully packed his tea wares to make sure they would all fit for travel aboard ship.

The other appreciators of tea on the ship all knew the

path to his quarters—that's where the good tea was to be had. So, it gave him occasion to pull out his heavy cast iron pot and perform his sea-going version of tea ritual. He complained that everyone was drinking up his stash of good tea, but I could tell that he very much enjoyed the ritual of sharing tea and life with his shipmates.

As he was about to leave that first day, I mentioned that I was starting my first tea tasting series that evening. He not only came to the class that night, but as it fit into his time on shore leave, he signed up for the entire four-week series. I think some of the ladies in class just couldn't make him fit into their conventional image of a tea drinker. But, in the end, his warm and outgoing personality won out, and they all came to enjoy his company and participation in class.

So, he became a regular and stopped in whenever he was in the area for pot after pot of tea and long, spirited conversations on any and every subject under the sun. The ship line he'd been sailing on has since been sold and may not even be in operation by now. Rik moved out of the area, last I heard. I miss those leisurely and most entertaining afternoons. The seaman's version of 'Afternoon Tea'.

The Stars Align around Biker Rik

Rik's warm and friendly ways did win over most of the ladies in class, except one—"Suzie." She was a regular at the shop at that time, and whenever she came in, we'd sit and have a nice cuppa. She often had her daughter with, and she was a sweet girl and pleasantly well behaved. Suzie was the role model of a good mother: just the right mix of discipline and love, and it showed in her delightful daughter.

If the subject of the tea class came up, she would always

mention "that motorcycle guy" who made her nervous and fearful. I questioned why she felt that way, since I was quite familiar with his gentle nature. Her description went something like this: "He has the eyes of the devil! Have you seen them? They're black!" and "He wears a ring with skulls on it!" I just had to laugh every time she ran through her litany of fear.

I tried to convince her of his true character, but she remained convinced that he was the devil himself. I told her that she just needed to meet him someday, and she'd see his true and gentle nature. And, I added, if she looked closely, she'd see that his eyes are really a beautiful blue!

Well, as luck would have it, and the stars were properly aligned one day, Suzie and I were whiling away a late afternoon over tea and who do you suppose waltzed casually into the shop? Biker Rik, of course. I thought Suzie would die! She immediately took on a look of horror, and I grabbed her arm to reassure her. I said, "Now, I'm inviting Rik to join us, and I want you to look closely at his eyes."

It took all the strength she could muster, but she forced herself to sit and join in conversation with Rik. After about five minutes I could see her begin to relax. We were joined by various others as the afternoon wound down.

Her hubby came in with their daughter after running their shopping errands. My husband came in after work for a late afternoon sip. My friend Margaret, who was like a surrogate mother or aunt to me, and another friend whom I have known for many years also straggled in and joined our table. After about an hour and a half and the magic of many cups of tea, this cacophony of souls had solved most of the world's problems and we were laughing like a circle of old friends who'd known each other for eons.

As I've said many times: "Behold the power of tea!"

The Teacup Story

One day a middle-aged couple came into the shop and when they saw the tables at the front of the shop, asked quietly if they could sit and have a cup of tea. I said, "Of course—have a seat and I'll bring you a menu," in my normally cheery voice. They sat, ordered tea and scones, and said how much they appreciated this opportunity for respite from their weary travels. I didn't probe but garnered that they were here in town because of a family illness or possibly even for a funeral.

They chatted softly with each other over their tea, and within their time there, seemed a bit more relaxed by the time they had finished. As they got up to leave, they said how appreciative they were for the opportunity to relax and refresh in our serene environment, and said that this teacup story, which is in one of the pages of our menu, had deeply touched them and was so comforting to them at this juncture in their lives.

I love what I can bring to my community through the sharing of tea. I make very little money doing what I do, but this, fellow tea-lovers, is what it is all about. On this particular day, I was richly rewarded.

The Teacup

There was a couple who used to go to England to shop in a beautiful antique store. This trip was to celebrate their 25th wedding anniversary. They both liked antiques and pottery, and especially teacups. Spotting an exceptional cup, they asked, "May we see that? We've never seen a cup quite so beautiful."

As the lady handed it to them, the teacup suddenly spoke. It said, "I have not always been a teacup. There was a time when I was just a lump of clay. A potter took me and rolled me, pounded and patted me over and over, and I yelled out,

'Don't do that! I don't like it! Let me alone!' but he only smiled and gently said, 'Not yet!!'

"Then—WHAM! I was placed on a spinning wheel, and suddenly I was spun around and around and around. He spun me and poked and prodded and bent me into a shape he liked. 'Stop it! I'm getting so dizzy! I'm going to be sick!' I screamed. But the potter only nodded and said quietly, 'Not yet.'

"Then, he put me in the oven. I never felt such heat. I yelled and knocked and pounded at the door. 'Help! Get me out of here!' I could see him through the opening, and I could read his lips as he shook his head from side to side. 'Not yet.'

"When I thought I couldn't bear it another minute, the door opened. He carefully took me out and put me on the shelf, and I began to cool. Oh, that felt so good! 'Ah, this is much better,' I thought. But after I cooled, he picked me up, and he brushed and painted me all over. The fumes were horrible. I thought I would gag. 'Oh, please, stop it. Stop it!!' I cried. He only shook his head and said, 'Not yet!'

"Then suddenly he put me back into the oven. Only it was not like the first one. This was twice as hot, and I just knew I would suffocate. I begged. I pleaded. I screamed. I cried. I was convinced I would never make it. I was ready to give up. Just then the door opened, and he took me out and again placed me on the shelf, where I cooled and waited . . . and waited, wondering, 'What's he going to do to me next?'

"A few hours later, he handed me a mirror and said, 'Look at yourself.' And I did.

I thought, 'That's not me; that couldn't be me! It's beautiful. I . . . I . . . I'm beautiful!' I said.

"Quietly he spoke. 'I want you to remember . . .' Then he said, 'I know it hurts to be rolled and pounded and patted, but had I just left you alone, you'd have dried up. You'd still be nothing more than a lump of clay. I know it made you dizzy to spin around on the wheel, but that is what has given you your magnificent symmetry. I know it hurt and it was hot and disagreeable in the oven, but if I hadn't put you there, you would have cracked and crumbled. I know the fumes were bad when I brushed and painted you all over, but if I hadn't done that, you would not have had any color in your life. And if I hadn't put you back in the second oven, your colors wouldn't have become so bright and beautiful. Now you are a finished product. Now you are what I had in mind when I first began with you.'

So, when life seems hard, and you are being pounded and patted and pushed almost beyond endurance, when your world seems to be spinning out of control, when you feel like you are in a fiery furnace of trials, when life seems to "stink," try this ... Brew a cup of your favorite tea in your prettiest tea cup, sit down and think on this story and then, have a little talk with the Potter. (Author unknown)

The Honorable Wu De

In my constant search for all things tea, I had stumbled upon a new online tea magazine, *The Leaf*. It has since grown into an entire worldwide online tea community called the Global Tea Hut.

This community is the brainchild of Aaron Fisher, originally from Sylvania, a suburb of Toledo, where my shop was located for six years. He lives in Taiwan now, after traveling the globe for ten years, and has made it his life's work to "live" tea. That becomes abundantly clear from his writings, and his presence is that of a serene, reverent "tea man."

On one of his visits home to see his parents, he and his father discovered the shop. He was thrilled to find a real tea shop in his hometown, one with real, high-quality, loose-leaf tea. He goes by Wu De now, and he and his father sat down to enjoy some tea. As it was my habit to greet and chat a bit with all customers, I did so with them, and upon finding I was the owner, he invited me to join them for tea. He offered to share some of his tea treasures he'd brought from Taiwan with me.

I was thrilled! It isn't often one gets to taste such fresh and high-quality teas in America. He also carried his traveling tea box, much like Rik, the sailor. In it he had his well-used Gong Fu tea set, for tea preparation anywhere. All that was needed was some hot water.

What he presented were a couple of absolutely lovely oolongs. Oolongs can be quite green if only very lightly oxidized, or they can be darker and richer if more heavily oxidized. The heavier ones are my personal preference, and I was pleased to find out that they were his as well. The reverence with which he prepared his tea (the essence of the true Gong Fu tea method) was a joy to watch.

We sipped and talked, talked and sipped. So many wonderful cups of tea! I have no idea how much time passed. It was like a meditation, where one is fully present in the moment and oblivious to all else. It reminded me of the flow one reaches when doing Tai Chi, where you are somehow not bound by time, nor concerned with all of the stress and "stuff" of daily life. All that just falls away, and you just *are*.

He showed me some of his brush and ink drawings, which were beautiful in their simplicity and serenity. They evoked the very essence of tea, I'd told him. So, much to my surprise, before he went back to Taiwan, he dropped off one of his drawings for me to keep. It is one of my most favorite tea treasures.

Random Acts of Kindness

One day, a customer came in for a quiet afternoon break. She sat down for a relaxing glass of lavender lemonade and cranberry scones. While she was here, another regular customer, a young college student named Angela came in for tea and a quiet place to study. These two only customers sat at tables across the tearoom from each other, each quietly enjoying their goodies and a respite from the hectic outside world.

The first customer had finished and came to the register to pay with a sort of pleading look on her face. She paid her bill and then handed me a piece of paper upon which she had written, "Random Acts of Kindness—I have $20. Please use it to pay for your other customer's bill." I smiled and rang up hers and Angela's bill, and then she indicated for me to keep the change, a bit more than a normal tip. She smiled and thanked me for such a wonderfully relaxing place and said she'd be back to enjoy it again another day.

After she'd left, I took the paper over to Angela and handed it to her. She read it and smiled broadly, being a typical college student with limited funds. She looked up at me and asked who the other lady was. I told her I didn't know her name, I think it was the first time she had been in the tea room. Angela expressed disappointment that she did not have a chance to thank the woman for her kindness. While normal social graces are not to be discarded, I explained that the whole idea behind random acts of kindness was that one just did them for the pure sake of being kind to another. That anonymity was key, and thanks were neither expected nor needed.

Another time, another day, we witnessed another one of those random acts. It was moderately busy and the tea room was almost full for lunch. We loved those days.

Carolyn the Elder was, of course, there in her usual corner

table, and across the room was another single woman eating by herself. For whatever unknown reason, something moved her to buy Carolyn's lunch, even though Carolyn, who was always well dressed, didn't look like she *needed* anyone to buy her lunch. As I served her apricot scones, she revealed her plan to me and instructed that I was not to say anything to Carolyn until she had left the shop.

I guess there's something about that randomness and anonymity that inspires some people. Every time I get to observe such events of kindness, I am inspired to conjure up one for myself on some unsuspecting lucky victim. I admit I don't do it as often as I should, but it is incredibly gratifying when I do.

Carolyn was so surprised when I told her that her lunch ticket had been paid for by the other customer. We often feel sorry for those more impoverished than we are and are willing to give to those who look needy. But I think the well-dressed folks, those who can and do take care of themselves without much struggle, are rarely granted such gifted grace. I only wished that the other customer could have seen the smile on Carolyn's face.

One more such act stands out in my memory. The chef was making a batch of yummy chocolate something-or-other for one of our favorite customers, a sweet woman named Betty, who we knew would be celebrating her birthday with us that day.

All of a sudden, she realized she was out of condensed milk, which the recipe called for. I was out at a doctor appointment, so I was not there to make a store run. Being quite the self-talker when she's in the kitchen, she exclaimed out loud something to the effect, "Oh no! I don't have any condensed milk! What am I going to do?"

It so happens, a nice, pierced and tattooed young man was in the shop searching for a new tea to drink, and he overheard her. He asked what the problem was, and she explained the birthday surprise she wanted to make for Betty, and that since she was alone in the shop, she couldn't leave to go to the store.

He promptly offered to go get some condensed milk for her. She said that it was too much, but he insisted, explaining that he had plenty of time and absolutely didn't mind. So, he went to the grocery store a mile down the road, brought back the milk, and wouldn't take a penny for it. Thanks to his kindness, Betty got her birthday surprise that day.

These are the riches beyond money that are there in life for all to receive, if only more people would invite them in.

Pamper Thyself

I'm a firm believer that before taking care of others, we must first take care of ourselves. When I got my first good-paying job as a med tech, on every payday I would take myself out shopping. It was such a treat, pampering myself with a new sweater or shoes, or whatever I wanted. I just think it's a good thing to pamper yourself once in a while.

Carolyn the Younger was the shopper, although she'd stay for lunch on occasion. She loved the pretty bone china teapots and tea sets, and would eye them every time she came in. I got the impression she was on a somewhat limited budget but always went away with a few modest treasures or a bag of new tea to try.

One day, she mentioned that one fairly expensive tea set was something she'd been coveting since she first laid eyes on it. She really wanted to buy it but clearly couldn't afford to. She had obviously been scheming ways to get this pretty tea set into her life and asked me if I would be willing to do a layaway plan with her.

I said that of course I would. It worked for me, and I kept the set on display with a sold sign on it. Sometimes seeing something has sold is an incentive for other buyers. And it worked for her, so that, in about four months, she was able to bring in her final payment. I swear she was like a little kid in a candy shop that day, almost jumping with excitement over the treasure she'd finally be able to take with her. I packed it carefully so that it would safely make the trip home. She'd told me several times about the empty spot on her buffet that she had prepared for her new tea set. Today that spot would be filled.

Gratuity with Heart

I'd been in full throes of the summer doldrums on the day that Julia came into the shop for tea with her daughter. It gets downright lonely in July and August, when customer flow slows to a crawl while everyone is getting in that last summer vacation and going through all the preparations for "back to school." This summer had been the worst I'd seen in seven years, and I was fretting about even being able to pay the rent. So, I was delighted when they came in, and especially so when Julia invited me to have a cup of tea with them, since I wasn't particularly busy.

We had a lovely chat about this and that, how slow business was all over town and how many businesses in the area have closed. She shared how this economic downturn had impacted her, and we got to know each other just a little bit better on that otherwise dull afternoon. I always feel so privileged when someone shares a part of their life with me.

They left the shop, and when I went over to clear off the table, I found one of the dollars from her gratuity folded into an origami heart! That just made my day! It was like she was saying, "Take heart, it'll get better." What a lovely gesture— one which I will not forget for a very long time.

A Bite of Tea

A delightful gentleman came in the shop yesterday and, as people often do, started telling me tea tales from his childhood. The one that made me laugh was this. He often spent time with his grandfather, an avid and daily tea drinker. His grandfather didn't like anything too hot, so he would always take the first sips of tea by scooping out a teaspoonful and blow on it, then take it like one would take a bite of food from a spoon. The child, wanting to mimic and enjoy tea like his grandfather had, finally asked, "Can I please have a bite of tea?"

To this day, every time he takes a sip of tea, he is taking a bite of tea with his grandfather.

Lovely.

A Sweet and Peaceful Tea

Sunday, yesterday, was a sweet and peaceful day. I had the great pleasure of taking tea with a friend at Sweet Shalom Tea Room in Sylvania, Ohio. As always, Chris, the lovely proprietor, and her partners-in-peace had prepared a charming themed tea based on the 1950s. Chris served as "Aunt Bea" for the day, from *The Andy Griffith Show*. It took us all back to a saner, more peaceful time. The menu was right out of the simple food of the fifties. Plain cream scones with butter and apricot jam—warm and melt-in-your-mouth good. Second course of quiche, followed by third course of tea sandwiches—ribbon, chicken salad, and cucumber cream cheese. Plus, banana nut muffin with cream cheese frosting and peanut butter chocolate chip cookie. The place settings were so lovely, as usual, perhaps a bit simpler than normal but as they would have been in the fifties. The tea menu allows for a different tea with each course, so my friend Karen and I chose our favorites for each. Never too much tea, and the variety offered in one setting was heavenly! Karen had never been to a formal "tea," so it was a real treat for her. It's always a treat for me, too, as this is where I get to relax and enjoy being served instead of serving customers myself. That magic, rejuvenating power of tea in a warm, inviting setting—one can hardly ask for more! One of the touches I particularly enjoyed was the fireplace mantle in our room, decorated with hats and hankies from the era. For those of you not old enough to remember days pre-Kleenex, a lady always had her hankies. I remember ironing them with my grandmother and always enjoyed the variety of prints and patterns they came in.

And then it came time to bid farewell to this retreat to the serenity of the fifties. It was a most lovely day, filled with good food, good tea, and good company. As we left, Aunt Bea stood at the front door, wishing us a "Sweet Shalom."

I could swear I heard Andy whistling his tune as we sauntered back to our 21st century lives, sated and filled with marvelous memories of sweeter days gone by.

A TEArful Farewell

My art teacher and dear friend, Joe Ann Cousino (Jody) was my very first customer on my very first day of business. Not only did she teach me how to be a better sculptor, but she gave such an incredible gift when she came in for that first cup of tea. She's the one who had encouraged me to connect with customers. I cannot begin to put words to how much her advice changed my life.

When she died, the six regular students from the Thursday night sculpture group got together to hold a memorial for her. She meant so much to all of us. I think it'd been about seventeen years for me, and one of her students had studied with her for almost thirty years. A few other students came and went over the years, but the six of us shared a comfortable and special camaraderie.

Jody had been gravely ill and in much pain for some months, and we all took any time we could spare to visit, bring her flowers, massage and pamper her, read to her, and comfort her in any way we could. Oddly enough, it was she who comforted us in our grieving her impending parting and our impending loss. She would tell one of her many travel stories, invariably filled with some tidbit that would have everyone laughing. The thing that was so wonderful about that horrible time of waiting was the love that just poured out from every quantum dot of space and being.

After she passed, just before Christmas, her son had decided to put off her memorial until the coming June. This afforded him time to put together a slide show of all her work and more appropriately gather the many people who would no doubt want to share in the celebration of this great lady's life. I looked forward to that celebration, but that left me and the other five students in an odd sort of limbo. We just had to somehow mark her passing sooner than June.

So, we decided to meet on New Year's Day under one of her most loved sculptures, *Woman with the Birds*, which graces one of our city's lovely garden spots. She stands comfortably, comfortingly, on a high platform surrounded by the greenery of Toledo Botanical Gardens (a.k.a., Crosby Gardens). She's stout and wears a big-brimmed hat, and it's the serenity she emits that attracts the birds (sculpted and real) and anyone who passes by. We couldn't think of a more fitting place to hold our ceremony.

I had prepared a poem by Kahlil Gibran, which so beautifully talks of death and dancing. I thought it so appropriate as Jody loved to dance, and I can remember on many occasions during class where the music, which was always playing in the background, would move her to dance around the studio while we sculpted. Since it was a very cold and snowy day, I had also taken an insulated pot of my Wild Blackberry Hot Chocolattea, a comforting blend of wild blackberry tea and hot chocolate.

We read poems and cried, told stories and cried: funny stories of things that happened in the studio; stories of how she touched our lives; stories of her body of work, and we each told the story of how it was that we came to be in the sculpture class and how grateful we were to have been chosen.

We lit a candle and toasted our cups of tea to this wonderful lady under her comforting sculpture, with giant snowflakes gently falling all around us. It was so cold we all shivered and sipped, trying to keep warm, and by the time we were ready to leave, losing feeling in our fingers and feet. Not one of us would have missed this celebration of life for all the tea in China.

I could go on and on. About Bob, the guy who bought his wife's favorite teas for her every month or so (still does through our online store), smelled wonderfully of pipe smoke, and always splurged on the more expensive teas for her birthday and holidays. Or of Karen, a local who oddly enough found out about the shop from her sister, who lives in Florida. She came regularly, and we shared many wonderful pots of tea together. She is an avid runner and, in a touching gesture, gave me one of her medals after I'd completed my radiation treatment for breast cancer. She said I was her hero as a cancer survivor and that I deserved a medal for all I'd been through. So, since there are no medals for survivors, she gave me one of hers. How sweet and kind.

Or James, the chemistry professor who would share tidbits about the chemistry of tea with me, as he knew that I had a biology/chemistry background and might be curious about the chemistry of tea. And all the young guys who were just getting into tea. Their passion and joy in learning about this jewel they could afford, even though they were poor college students, was delightful to me. One student came in regularly and went straight to the display with a particular tea set that she coveted. It was a very common clay set, but it held some special beauty to her. She'd pick up each piece and lovingly cup them in her hands every time she came in. After several weeks, I couldn't take it anymore. I knew she couldn't afford it at the regular price, so I casually approached her and her tea set. I told her that I was just about to put that set on sale, and would she like it for half price? She was ecstatic, and it made me feel good to know that someone would treasure that tea set for a long time to come.

There were couples who would come in regularly for a special quiet time together. There were even those who were meeting for the first date. Those were always fun to watch from behind the counter. Love's potential blossoming.

People would come in to get their center aligned again or unwind from daily stresses. One woman was the assistant county coroner, who had more stress than I could imagine to deal with every day. Another was a woman working on her doctorate. Our environment was so calm and quiet with only soft new age music playing in the background that she would often come to work on her thesis. One more very frequent patron was a regional manager at McDonald's. She would come in to unwind from the pressures of corporate life.

I watched children grow up. Maddie was so sweet at five when she first came with her aunt, who spoiled her at my shop. I hardly recognized her at sixteen, the last time she came in. And little Anna, who was the daughter of a high school friend, was so cute trying to run the cash register for me. She's a grown woman now, and I keep up with her on Facebook. Sarah was only about four when she and her mother first became regulars, and she's probably finished college by now. I was so tickled to get a Christmas card from her mom with a college sophomore photo of Sarah. I'd have recognized her, but my, how she's changed, as we all do when we grow out of childhood. Not having any children of my own, this was a joy for me to watch these young ones grow up and blossom into a life of their own.

There were lots of ladies who came in, rushed, frazzled, stressed, or otherwise overwhelmed with some aspect of life. Even with the ones who were so closed off that they would snap at me after offering to help them find something. "No, I'm just looking." They might as well have said, "Just leave me alone." I would put a tea sample in their hands and wait a few minutes. Until the atmosphere and tea had a chance to work on them. After a bit, I'd reapproach them, and gently start to chat. Then they'd relax. That was as much success to me as money in the till.

I developed dozens of techniques for working my way in, thanks to Jody's original urgings, so that I could give them some comfort and a dose of friendly connection, which seems sadly so rare these days. With the ones who were grumpy at first, I might just go near them and make a light comment about the weather or news of the day. With those who seemed sad, I'd compassionately ask how they'd been lately if I recognized them from previous visits, or just compliment them on their hair or clothing or complexion or shoes.

I could always find something to genuinely compliment anyone on. And I could tell by their reactions how rarely people receive compliments and how welcome they are. Right away, the sadness or weariness would melt away. And often, someone who came in a rush would decide to stay and linger over a cup of tea. If I sensed they needed an ear, I would sit and listen. I'm a good listener and firmly believe a little commiseration is good for the soul. Everyone needs relief from their burdens from time to time. That's why I often thought of the shop as the *Cheers* of tea.

The atmosphere was of supreme importance to me. I am

so tired of places with fake plants, weird commercial/industrial odors, and tacky, cheap décor. It was a goal of mine to be different. Genuine, warm, comforting, and pleasant.

So, all my fixtures were antique cases, tables, hutches, and wall shelves. Their history gave off an energy of real depth of character—the complete opposite of cheap, fake, plastic, or wood composite. We had naturally scented candles, which give off a subtle pleasant fragrance, unlike the overpowering over-scented fake scents some places use. Plus, we sprinkled lavender oil everywhere once a month or so.

And all our plants were living, not artificial. We had two huge hibiscus, which were like two faithful guardians who stood watch over the shop. I love it that one of them was my mother's. She died in 1997, unfortunately, four years before I opened the shop. She would have loved the shop and would have been there frequently to man the register and tend customers. She loved selling, and we shared some wonderful days schlepping her handmade wares to craft shows and chatting with all the nice people all day.

Two huge hibiscus plants graced each shop location for over sixteen years.

Whenever they blossomed, which was an amazing thing, considering their age and pot bound status, I always felt like it was my mom saying "Hi!" from the other side. They must be over forty years old by now, which has to be some sort of record for indoor hibiscus plants.

Besides the subtle energy or chi of "real," the plants give off oxygen, which has more than a subtle effect on people. Many people gave lovely comments over the years, but I was always so pleased when men, who usually don't notice that sort of thing, would come in and within minutes be moved to remark on how nice the atmosphere and aroma were.

But, the one thing I most enjoyed was helping customers find the perfect tea. Obviously, that was the number one item customers were seeking. So, I'd find out what they were looking for. Was it just for flavor? Did they have a physical condition they hoped to remedy? Were they looking to branch out into new teas they'd never had before? Did they like fruity flavors or were they a tea purist? If they'd only ever had black tea, I'd see if they were open to green tea or an oolong. Had they read an article or watched Dr. Oz rave about a particular tea? Did they need to restrict their caffeine intake? If they were looking for relaxation, I'd direct them to my favorite white teas, which are highest in relaxing L-theanine. I loved every minute of it, and I loved the endless variety of situations it presented.

Just like I had done in my bookstore days, I took great joy in fitting every customer with the perfect tea. Well, almost everyone. It was an irresistible challenge to me when someone came in who announced that they weren't a tea drinker and might even go as far as to say that they didn't like tea. Invariably they simply hadn't ever tasted anything beyond a common tea-bag cup of tea. The first thing I would do is put the sample tea in their hands and gently urge, "Just try it. You've probably never had anything like this before." And, when their eyes opened wide in surprise and a subtle smile emerged, I knew I had them. Not every time, but when it did happen, it was a victorious day.

The prime directive to all employees was to make customers feel welcome, make them comfortable, keep them happy, and make sure they walked out with a tea they would love. It was probably the first thing a new employee was expected to do, even before learning other details of the job. I knew that it was a constant struggle for small businesses to attract customers in the first place. We weren't going to lose any precious one due to lack of exemplary service. And if they found a tea they loved, I knew they'd be back for more.

From the numbers of loyal regulars we built by the time I'd closed up shop, I'd say I was successful in accomplishing a loyal clientele. And, judging by how many people call years after closing and are thrilled to find our tea is still available, we did a good job of offering a high-quality product. Happy customers, loyal customers are the true measure of success.

It wasn't all rainbows and roses with customers. They were thankfully few and far between, but the nasties would show themselves from time to time.

Sometimes customers would try to bring something back that they had ruined themselves. One lady put her entire French press in the dishwasher. It ruined the screen at the bottom of the plunger, and there were no replacements available. She tried to pawn the loss off on me, but it clearly said on the box, "Not dishwasher safe," so she lost that one.

Another lady brought in a bag of herbal tea that was infested with bugs. Now, I was absolutely OCD about how we kept our stocks of tea, especially the herbals. Early on, I had received a bag that must have had a few bugs to start with from the vendor. We kept the herbs in large storage tubs, so there were about twenty different herbs in one.

When the bug population in that one bag took off, it eventually contaminated the whole tub. I lost a large chunk of stock in one blow. We carefully checked every other bag of herb and tea, and that's when I became obsessive about taping bags shut tightly. We switched to smaller storage drawer bins to prevent such a huge loss in the future.

When the customer came in with her infested bag of herbal tea, I immediately checked the stock bag hers would have been filled from. It was clean. So, I knew the contamination had come from her own kitchen. I took the bag from her, mostly so I could triple bag it and sequester it in the garbage ASAP. I gave her a new one just to make her happy but emphasized that the contamination had not come from our stocks.

We isolated our stock bag for about two months just in case. After eight years in a microbiology lab, it raises your germ and contamination consciousness to acute levels. Not exactly a bad thing in my book. With regular checking, we were confident that there was nothing wrong with our supply of that herb and could again use it for tea blends.

Once in a rare while, we'd find something broken that no one had owned up to. We only ever asked that we'd be compensated for replacement value, but some folks just can't be that honest. And I can't fill one hand with the number of times we knew something had been stolen. In sixteen years! That's pretty rare in retail, where shoplifting is a rampant problem. I think it was because of our smallness, our connection with every customer that kept that nuisance to a bare minimum for us.

And that's about it. I've wracked my brain to remember other problems with customers, but we simply didn't have many. I think the nature of the shop just drew a different crowd than the general population. Tea drinkers tend to be more sedate, more cultured, and generally nice people. That's why, what I miss absolutely most about the shop is that daily interaction with my customers.

Chapter 5

Employees: The Good, the Bad, and the Downright Ugly

B ecoming your own boss is an appealing goal for many people. After going through such a nasty corporate-America downsizing, it became absolutely compelling to me. No more demanding bosses. No more difficult coworkers. No more idiotic corporate regulations. You think you will finally have to answer to no one. As it turns out, you now have to answer to everyone.

You answer to your landlord for rent and upkeep of the building, to the city, making sure utilities are paid and code requirements are fulfilled, and to the state, making sure taxes are rendered on time and employees are documented. The city also dictates everything from your signage and what you can put in front of your shop to what you can put in the windows. Both city and state wanted permission and license fees for everything.

You answer to your vendors because you have to meet their minimums, or you don't get to do business with them. You would think that they would be anxious to sell their wares to any legitimate retailer, but profit is always the name of the game. One way they increase their profit is to require a minimum amount to purchase. Usually the opening order is higher, and subsequent orders a bit lower. Frustratingly, I found that some were so high I couldn't purchase their goods. And sometimes even reorder minimums made it challenging to keep the right mix of merchandise stocked.

And of course, most importantly, you must answer to your customers. When you are a very small business, there is little leeway in what you can do with customers. They want you to do what *they* want you to do and be whatever *they* expect you to be. I can't count the number of times a customer threw in my face "The customer is always right." in order to get their way. On an occasion or two, I did have the pleasure of informing them that they were wrong, but usually I bent to whatever they wanted. Bad word of mouth was a potent power they held, and they knew I just couldn't risk it.

The one arena in which I thought I'd really have some control was with employees. After all, I was the boss, right? And their paycheck depended on them meeting my requirements. I'd managed employees before in the corporate world and thought, *How hard can it be?* I thought that since I would also be the one choosing my employees, I'd find the best, most capable, and loyal people to work for me. I thought that they would appreciate having a nice boss like me, and everything would be rosy.

Hold on for a minute while I recover from a hysterical fit of laughter. Another lesson I learned early on—*Small business runs nothing like large corporations.* Compared to them, you have no power and no leverage over anyone.

My first mistake was to hire the sister of a friend. I didn't know her, but as I knew her sister to be a hard worker, competent and capable, I thought she would be similar. I thought that connection would bring a loyalty above that of a complete stranger.

Not quite. She was good with customers but became increasingly emboldened to do whatever she wanted, regardless of my instructions. She would sell anything that wasn't nailed down, so to speak. More than once she sold a display stand or an item that was part of my décor because a customer wanted it and set a price off the top of her head, usually far below the replacement cost to me. *What else was she doing behind my back?* I wondered.

She wanted to wear her high-heeled boots in winter for fashion reasons, which were very slippery on the tile floors. She'd almost slipped several times, and so I requested that she wear safer shoes with some grip to the sole to reduce the risk of a fall. She did not heed my request, and one day she did not recover from a slip and fell hard on her keister. She got up and appeared to be OK, so she finished out the day. I told her she was never to wear those boots for work again.

In a move that I thought displayed an astounding impudence, a week later I got papers from a workman's comp claim she'd filed. Needless to say, the air between us was pretty icy after that, and coupled with strong suspicions that she was lifting things from the kitchen and possibly some merchandise, I decided to confront her. The minute she realized I was not going to put up with any more nonsense, she hurled an indignant "I quit!" and stormed out of the shop.

In the end, I did not get charged with any liability from her slip and fall once I'd responded to the state with my side of the story. I had long ago learned to document important work incidents, and I had it on record that she had been warned not to wear those boots again at work.

I had two part-time employees in those early years, and my second employee, Margo, was an absolute joy to work with. Margo was always coming up with great suggestions to add to the shop or improve our workflow. She'd found the Lavender Lemonade recipe that we added to the menu and it became a big seller for us. While I didn't mind losing the first employee, I was devastated when Margo had to quit a week after boot lady because she was moving out of the state to Florida for her husband's new job. Suddenly, I was working by myself. Yikes.

I'd put an ad in the paper right away and thankfully had rapid responses. I hired a nice young woman named Angela. I thought she really was an angel to come rescue me at that time of need. She was sweet and capable, and customers loved her, but it took a long time for someone new to learn everything. There were over one hundred teas alone, and there were fifteen different merchandise departments.

Although the food service was simple compared to most restaurants, it was riddled with lots of regulations and particulars. Tea Rooms are notoriously labor intensive; even if I was just serving tea and desserts at that time, everything had to be just so. Doilies, pretty plates and glasses, artsy garnishes, and much attention to every detail, which you won't find in most average restaurants, are essentials in tea room service.

I had just opened the shop in January, and by September, on Labor Day, fate handed me another curve ball. Angela had only worked for *two days* when I fell while riding my bike that holiday weekend. I had crushed my left foot under the bike with my entire weight pinning it down and by the time I got it out, I'd realize it was broken. I'd never had a broken bone before, but I learned when you get one, you pretty much know it.

When X-rays finally came back, it turned out I'd basically crushed my foot. I had fractures in most of the bones of that foot in places that were TNTC, as we used to report in the lab. Too Numerous To Count.

I ended up in a boot and on crutches for months. And in a wheelchair during the day, so I could scoot around the shop with ease. Well, not exactly with ease as I was constantly bumping into any protruding table, chair, wall, or corner, but it was easier than hobbling on crutches all day.

With only two days under her belt, Angela couldn't handle the shop by herself, and my husband ended up taking a month off work to help cover. He didn't know much about shop operations, but he helped to keep things going by handling anything physical I simply couldn't do. It was the blind leading the blind for the two of them, but two functioning bodies were better than none, or the prospect of closing the shop for a while. And I was still there most of the time, pumped with pain pills. I had to be, since I was the only one who knew operations.

I was in the wheelchair for over a month, and during that

time I got pretty good at tooling around the shop. I was not happy that I had to ramp the steps going into the shop when I first opened. I saw it only as another expense. But this experience gave me great awareness of how difficult it is for someone with a handicap to get around and enjoy all the things in life.

Another event happened during this time that changed everything from that moment on. Eight days after I broke my foot was 9/11. I'll never forget, the employees from the shop next door had come over and asked if we'd heard anything about a terrorist attack in NYC, that a plane had hit one of the twin towers. I first thought, *Oh my gosh, there goes everyone overreacting.* I thought for sure that it was just some quirky accident. But, of course, it was a horrific terrorist attack. That moment changed this country for good.

Moving along as we all learned to slowly get back to normal, I kept looking for another part-timer to become fully staffed again. After a few duds, as if to answer my great need, in walked a very attractive woman named Diane. She was dressed very appropriately, and a total charm, compared to most. Well spoken, eager, competent, and willing to learn. So, I hired her on the spot. She was a gem, one of the few. She never called in sick and was never late for work. She did a great job and was exceptional with customers. I couldn't have asked for more in an employee.

We eventually became friends, as Diane was closer to me in age, and it was nice to have a coworker to socialize with outside of the shop. Diane and Angela were so pleasant to work with, and it was a good period for me and the shop. I still treasure the little lit-up tea cottage they gave me one year for Christmas, and it sits on my mantle every year throughout the holidays.

Another woman of great boon to me was Beth. She was young, still in college, and in the interview, I could tell she knew almost as much about tea as I did, which was very surprising. She was an absolute delight to be around because she was incredibly intelligent. She was creative and interesting, and I could tell the customers were responding very positively to her, too. I could hardly believe she was real, after some of the useless ones that had passed through my doors.

She brought me many new ideas on how to streamline the way we were doing something or came up with recipes to make our food selections better. She graciously shared her mother's scone recipe with me when I'd decided to start baking my own. It was a drop scone recipe, which turns out much moister than most traditional scones. I liked it because it was different from the usual ones, and customers loved how soft and moist they were. I came up with many variations on the theme by adding cranberries or blueberries, cherries, apricots, chocolate chips, or cinnamon chips. They became a cornerstone of our food service. I had many regulars who came back time and again for a plate of our delicious scones.

Like me, Beth had migraines. I remember more than once, when I really needed her, she would work through the headache to fulfill her duties. I was so appreciative, as there was always more to do than I could handle. Her perseverance made it possible for me to get my work done and not have it pile up because she had to go home.

That strength and loyalty is rare anymore, and I cannot begin to express how impressed I was with this exceptional young woman. We also kept in touch long after she left the shop, and she became a baker, something she's really good at and enjoys. I'm happy for her. I carried some of her tasty delights in the shop until I closed. Her salted caramels still make my mouth water just thinking about them.

Marsha was another excellent employee who gave me loyalty and her full efforts every day. She was great with customers, but really shined in the kitchen. She was there when I decided to add our own sandwiches to the menu and start lunch and afternoon tea service. I thought chicken salad was a must and had a great recipe called The Best Chicken Salad Ever. But it was curry based, and I thought some customers might not like curry. It was also a laborious recipe.

So, Marsha was gracious and shared her favorite chicken salad recipe with me, which was incredibly easy to prepare. I can't tell you how many customers begged me for that recipe over the years, but we decided to keep our recipes proprietary to entice customers to come in regularly. It seemed to work. To this day, I still make this chicken salad over any other recipe, and I am ever grateful to Marsha for her kindness.

And there were a few others, like Heather, Tina, Donna, Courtney, and Tanya, who were quick learners, always great with customers, and dependable. It was difficult to see them go, but this kind of job was always just a steppingstone or filler on their way to something more fulfilling and financially rewarding.

Sadly, there were many more who were mediocre at best, and some unbelievable nightmares on the other end of the spectrum. Those were the ones who I was always glad to see go.

A puzzling one was Brooke, the youngest one I'd hired, who was right out of high school. She seemed bright, and I thought she would be an eager learner with her first real job. She, on the other hand, thought her only job was to wait on customers and would sit and do nothing in between. In those early days, it could be an hour or two or three before someone would come in.

When I found her just sitting behind the register despite my instructions not to, I sat her down in my office and explained to her that she must be working at all times unless she was on break. I gave her the laundry list of things she could do, like straighten and dust displays, price and put out new merchandise, bag tea, prelabel tea bags, prep work in the kitchen, clean out the refrigerator, sweep floors, wipe counters, organize or clean the stockroom, tidy restrooms, etc. There was always something to do.

I had to call her into my office a few days later when she still was spending most of her time sitting, doing nothing. I gave a very stern warning again, but apparently my message just wasn't sinking in. By the third time, just a few days later, I'd lost all patience with her. My decision was to let her go. She cried all the way out the door, and I scratched my head at her lack of responsiveness to the simple duties required. All I could think was that she had an awful lot to learn if she was ever going to succeed in life.

Looking for new employees became a dreaded task. It took a long time and tedious effort. Advertising in the paper. Collecting and reviewing applications. One time, I had to advertise all over again because I didn't get one suitable applicant out of around twenty interviews. I had one woman tell me that she could only work for me if I paid her under the table. I told her that I paid taxes, and if she didn't want to that she could take a flying leap. This happened right when I was first hiring, so I really think she was a plant from the state government to make sure I was going to hire properly, though I'll never really know for sure.

One young applicant brazenly told me how much I would pay him, as he guaranteed he would make my business a raving success with his great marketing ideas. Another woman came in to apply at my tea shop missing teeth with uncombed hair, wearing a red plaid flannel shirt and ratty jeans. Obviously, she had no clue to the grace and civility generally expected in tea rooms.

Interviewing candidates was always an interesting study in human nature. One woman looked like she would be a good bet because she was older, retired, and had a totally flexible schedule. Perfect, I thought. No more young, irresponsible employees. I'd try this more mature, presumably responsible woman.

She told me she totally understood the horrors of the hiring process as she and her husband had owned a business and had experienced it firsthand. I explained that reliability was most crucial to me and that as a very small business, vacations or time off would be on approval as the scheduling permitted. I emphasized that I could not be left hanging without a proper two-week notice whenever she decided to move on to full retirement. She assured me she would never do such a thing, so I hired her.

After a few months in my employ, she informed me that a friend of hers had a spare ticket to Florida and that she was going because "How could she pass up a free ticket to Florida?" And, by the way, she added, it would be for a month. It took around two months for me to get a new employee up to speed, and she had just gotten to the point where she could function independently. I did not want to go through the hiring process again, so I bit my lip and struggled through a whole month being an employee short.

Then a few months later, she wanted another month off to go to Florida again. Yes, really. Starting the very next day. I had finally planned a week off for myself at exactly the same time she wanted to start her second month of leisure. I explained that I just couldn't do it this time, and that since I hadn't had a vacation myself for about two years, I desperately needed this one. She said that if I didn't give it to her, she would have to quit. I didn't, and so she did. No two-week notice. Just quit on the spot, like she said she would *never* do.

I didn't get my vacation, but I didn't have to put up with her any longer. Sometimes you just have to choose the lesser of two evils.

"Sherrie" was a short-lived employee who was a real piece of work. On the surface, she was a well-dressed, poised and pleasant woman. In reality, she was a bit off in the head. I had started to get reports from my customers that one of my employees was being nasty with customers. I was puzzled, as exceptional customer service was the first rule at my shop. Several complained that they were treated with disdain if they asked a few questions about tea, something all employees were trained to answer.

I would ask for a description of the employee, and all I ever got was that she had kind of short blonde hair. Sherrie had short, very light-brown hair, and so I didn't think they were describing her. Sheila, another employee, had short-ish very blonde hair, but I was again very puzzled as Sheila always seemed great with customers when I was around. But, whenever I was around, Sherry seemed good with them, too.

After several more complaints, I felt I had to do something. Since the description seemed to fit her best, I called Sheila in and questioned her about it. Of course, she denied it, but I doubted anyone would actually own up, so I felt I had no choice but to let her go. I felt terrible, but this was something I could just not tolerate. Customer service was the most important element in customer retention and growing new business.

Then one day I sat down to chat with one of my regular customers, who was a small-business owner herself. We'd often trade stories on the challenges of small-business ownership. She pulled me over and quietly said that she perhaps shouldn't say anything, but since she was a business owner herself, she would want to know. She proceeded to tell me that one of my employees wasn't very nice with the customers. I was truly puzzled since I thought Sheila was the one who had been the culprit, and Sheila was now gone. I questioned her further, and she told me that this employee, the one who always overdressed for the job and wore high heels every day, was also telling customers that she owned the shop!

My heart sank. I had fired the wrong person! It wasn't Sheila but Sherrie. I thought I'd die right there on the spot. I'm a very sensitive person, and I just couldn't stand the thought of having wronged someone like I obviously had done to Sheila.

I could have called her, but I just didn't know what to say and didn't want to handle this over the phone. She had actually, surprisingly, been in the shop with her daughter a short while after I had let her go, and she told me she had another job working for a vet with animals, which I knew she loved. I was relieved, but I still felt terrible about what I'd done. So, I made up my mind that when she came in the very next time, I would give her the sincere apology that she deserved. That gave me a little time to bolster my courage.

I'm guessing it wasn't more than a month or so, and Sheila came in to shop with her daughter again. And so, I asked her to come back into my office where I apologized. Profusely. Amazingly, she took it well, gave me a hug, and thanked me for being honest with her. All this time, she had puzzled over what she did so wrong as to get fired. I couldn't have been more impressed with the rare level of emotional maturity and kindness of spirit she displayed.

The very next day, after I'd found out that she was being so nasty with my customers, I called Sherrie into my office. I told her what had been reported to me by numerous regular and trusted customers. I told her that I now knew she was the culprit, and that I was completely disappointed in her. She did not deny anything. She knew she was guilty, and she showed it when her face turned a few shades of red.

She would become indignant next, when she realized she was being fired. She started calling me names, screaming at me, and telling me what a horrible person I was as she edged her way toward the back door. *What a horrible person I was?* She was the one not helping customers, treating them poorly, over-dressing for the job so that she could tell people she owned my shop, and adulterating products.

After she left, my other part-timer confessed that she had seen Sherrie mix up the flavors of the hot chocolate powders and had blended some in with another flavor, so that if a customer ordered Raspberry, they might get Raspberry contaminated with Mint instead. I could never figure out why the other part-timer, who had otherwise been a good employee, had not told me about the ruined chocolate powders before. When I asked her, she told me she just thought it was funny. I didn't quite expect that from a seemingly mature, responsible woman, but there you have it.

Another one of the doozies that stands out is "Dolly," a woman who had applied who was right around my age in her mid-fifties. At that time, the tea room was in full swing, offering luncheon sandwiches any time as well as the fancier, three-course Afternoon Tea with reservations. On a busy day, we'd turn the tables over a couple of times, and we were hopping with business for a solid three hours over lunchtime.

Working the tearoom kitchen was the most demanding, exhausting physical work I've ever done. Lots of running, and lots of tasks to juggle. Taking orders, serving the tea, preparing the food with all the special garnishes and touches a tea room is expected to supply, delivering it to the table, cleaning up the kitchen, clearing tables, doing dishes. It wasn't always serene and pretty like it looked from the customer side of things. So, I told Dolly that I just wasn't sure she would like the work. I didn't say it out loud, but my other reservation was that I wasn't sure she could physically handle the work. I knew the toll it took on fifty-some-year-old feet.

I left it at that and continued to interview other candidates. She came back a couple of days later and begged me for a chance at the job. She assured me she would love it. She said she was not afraid of hard work and could stand being on her feet and doing the running required and that she just loved the atmosphere of the shop so much; she was begging for the job. So, I thought, *Anyone who wants to work for me that badly must be a good bet.* I finished several other scheduled interviews, but no one came even close to Dolly's enthusiasm. I hired her.

The first day was hectic. Not as bad as it can get, but busy. She was quite frazzled at the end of lunch, needed to sit down, and looked miserable. I wasn't sure she would show up for work the second day, but she did. We got our normal hectic lunch crowd, and again, I could see she was having trouble keeping up with it all. Then, in the middle of the rush, she'd cleared a table and came back to the service counter with a full tray of dirty dishes. She slammed it down on the counter, looked at me with eyes fuming, and said, "What were you thinking? This is crazy! I quit!" And she walked out.

What was I thinking? I couldn't have been more up front with her as to the difficulties of the job. There I was, left holding the bag, or teapot, again. Back to square one, after wasting a month on the hiring process in what turned out to be a bad bet. So, there I was advertising again, waiting for applications to come in, sorting through and setting up interviews. Hoping against hope that I'd find a decent employee *this time*.

Another one that has always puzzled me, and knocked my view of humanity down a notch, was "Kitty." Another one who told me how perfect this job was for her and how badly she wanted it. She seemed very positive and friendly in the beginning. She was eager and learned everything very quickly. But at one point, she started calling in sick, or feigning sickness at work. It was obvious she was faking it. Every story was some nonsense that didn't quite seem to add up.

One story was that her mother was very sick, and she had to go up to Michigan to stay with her until she got better. I'd given her most of the week off already, and she then called to tell me that she needed the weekend, too, as her mother had fallen, and she couldn't leave her yet. She was scheduled for work on that Saturday.

I said OK, as I always did, but was tipped off when she came back in with a fabulous tan. Then, in one casual conversation, she slipped up and mentioned an event that she and her husband had attended on Saturday in Toledo. I questioned that and told her I didn't appreciate being lied to. She danced around and kept denying that she'd ever said she had to be with her mother all weekend. So, then why wasn't she at work on Saturday as scheduled? It didn't add up, and she knew it.

One sunny day shortly after, she decided midday that she wanted to go home again. I'm guessing to lay out in the sun to keep up that deep tan she sported. So, she came up with this convoluted story about how nauseous and sick she was. When I suggested she sit and perhaps have some peppermint or ginger tea to calm her stomach, her symptoms mysteriously started to magnify.

She was so suddenly so weak and faint that she insisted that she could not finish out the day and had to go home right away. So, I turned her lie right back at her in a way I knew she hadn't thought through. I told her that I could not, in good conscience, allow her to drive herself home if she was so lightheaded. The look on her face was priceless! I said the only way she could leave was to have someone else drive her home.

She begrudgingly called her husband, and he came to get her. She was steaming at the inconvenience that they would have to come back and get her car later. It wasn't long after that when she came in and, while I was waiting on a customer, waltzed over to the service counter, slammed her shop key down, glared at me and indignantly shouted across the shop "I quit!" mumbling all the way out the door how I was so unfair to work for.

I was becoming very tired of being called the bad guy for simply wanting an employee to show up for work and do the job. You know, all that stuff they promised me in the interview they said they understood and were happy to do. I tried to bend, to accommodate employees' whims as much as I could. But in the end, I always got to a point where I had to request that they simply fulfill their duties. Then I'd be met with indignation and ire. I will be eternally puzzled at this behavior. I was brought up to have a sense of responsibility and work ethic. I was learning just how many people weren't.

The last straw came about nine years in. I'd hired an exceptional young college student, "Sarina." Another employee had just quit, and shortly after hiring Sarina, the second part-timer had quit, too. I explained to her that I was looking for someone long term, that it took too long to get someone up to speed, and I literally asked her not to take the job if she couldn't fulfill my needs. She was eager, her school schedule allowed her to work three days and every Saturday, which was what I needed, and I decided I would fill in the other two days by myself. I was so tired of unreliable employees; I just didn't want to go through the hiring process again. I'd gone through upwards of thirty-five employees by this time.

Sarina was great with customers, learned all about the teas, how to handle customer calls, and could run the kitchen proficiently. It was just coming on to two months, and I was thinking I might be able to finally take a long weekend off. She had demonstrated enough competence, and I knew she could handle the shop for at least a short stint by herself at this point. I breathed a sigh of relief. I started to relax.

Shortly after that, Sarina came in one day and by the look on her face, I knew my relief was going to be taken away. My stomach sank again. She informed me that she had changed her whole college program to one that required her to be there most every day, and that she would no longer be able to work. At all. Not even Saturdays. She was sweet, and very apologetic, but that didn't ease my angst. I now had no one, not one person I could depend upon, and I just didn't have the strength or drive to go through the hiring process again.

I was positively despondent. No vacation or time off again, and I really needed one. I had already cut the shop hours from 10:00 a.m. to 6:00 p.m. to 10:00 a.m. to 5:00 p.m. after realizing hardly anyone came in after five o'clock. I'd also cut from six days a week down to five, closing on Sundays and Mondays so that I had at least some semblance of a weekend with two days off in a row. Six days a week was just too much for me to handle, and five was bad enough.

With no other alternative at the moment, I steeled myself to handle the shop alone, while I again regrouped to figure out what to do and where to go next.

What I saw of human nature from being an employer was disappointing more than rewarding. There were those few good people I had the pleasure of working with and am still friends with today. But for the most part, being an employer was an eye-opening and disheartening look into the ugly side of human nature.

I was at another of those crossroads where I knew I had to make a serious change or I would not survive. I started thinking along the lines of a partner. I know, I know, there are nothing but horror stories about partnerships going sour. But I was desperate. I needed someone who had a vested interest in the business, and I saw clearly that employees just don't have that. I had to get off the merry-go-round of hiring and losing and hiring and losing employees.

So, as often happens, when you put something out to the universe, it responds. You have to have your eyes open for it, of course, and I sure did. I considered every possibility and every person I'd encountered as a potential partner. Women would often come into the shop saying that they always wanted to open a tea room. So, I was on the hunt for that woman. Hunting for someone to specifically take over the food-service portion, since that was the part I did not enjoy, and tea rooms are often more about the food and ambiance than the tea.

I was going to a sculpture group at a friend's house, enjoying getting my hands back in clay again. It was a great stress reliever for me. Several members were from my old sculpture class, which I missed terribly. One night, a new woman showed up. Let's call her "Griselda." She was friendly, and as we chatted while working the clay, it came out that she was looking for work and had mentioned that she loved to cook. So, I gently presented my idea for someone to run my kitchen for me, and she liked it. We made plans to meet at the shop the following day.

I explained what I was looking for. Not an employee, but

a partner. Someone to take over the food service and be fully responsible for that side of the business. She told me that she had always wanted to open a small restaurant, as she loved to cook. Bingo.

I offered a fully functioning tea room with an established clientele, a fully equipped kitchen, all my recipes, and she would be free to change or add to the menu as long as she got my approval. After nine years in business, I knew what our customers expected, and she did not know anything about tea rooms. So, for someone with no capital and no means to acquire any, this was a dream come true.

I was basically handing over half of my business to her. For no initial outlay. That is unheard of. But I needed help, and she loved food service. So, it seemed like a solid solution. I only required her to pay half of the overhead (i.e., rent and utilities), since I was basically giving her half of my business.

It should have worked. Had she learned from all my years of experience, learned anything about running a business, it could have. She didn't understand marketing at all. Her idea of marketing was giving away the store. She needed to make at least a meager profit from the start, as she was living off this income. But she would do things like make a huge basket of food for a doctor's office a couple of miles away, which brought no new business. She gave every customer free dessert on more than one occasion. She did nothing to build the tea room back up to those days of a solid lunch rush almost every day. In fact, it dwindled to a sporadic few and Carolyn, who came in every day. Many days, she'd be the only lunchroom customer.

Shortly after she'd taken over the tea room, we held one of our event evenings. On this particular night it was tea leaf readings by a dear woman named Retha. She was one of those incredibly intuitive people, thus her ability to read tea leaves, and I knew that what she saw and felt was usually right on the money. She took one look at Griselda and shook her head slowly back and forth: NO!

My heart sank. But by then it was too late. We'd signed a year contract and were in full swing of her running the tea room. All I could do at that point was hope for the best. Hope Retha was wrong. But, of course, Retha was rarely wrong.

When her lack of organizational abilities caught up to her, she started to make noises that she shouldn't have to pay half the overhead because she wasn't making enough. She wasn't making enough because she was doing absolutely nothing to grow the business. She thought it was totally unfair that she should pay for any kitchen breakage, even though that was in our signed agreement. She did much damage over the year to my kitchen and never compensated me for any of it. After she was gone, it took many hours of scrubbing over a two-day period for me to clean up the crud on my convection oven, which looked like new when she had taken it over.

She simply didn't seem to understand that she'd gotten a fully functioning business handed to her with no outlay of cash on her part. I didn't charge her to use my fully functional kitchen, supplies, and utensils. I bought all that, paid for the construction to build out the kitchen, designed the menu and recipes, provided the tables, chairs, and tea room space for her to serve her customers, and created and scheduled special events, which brought in more business. What she just didn't understand was that half the rent was for the opportunity to take over half of an already existing business, with a basic customer base from day one. And she thought that was unfair.

The icing on this deteriorating cake was that I began to suspect that she was also stealing from me, which, sadly, was only a couple of months into our agreement. I had children's tea sets, which sold occasionally, and a dozen would usually take a year or so to sell. I went on a week-long vacation and, with nine on the shelf when I left, there were only three when I got back. I asked her about it, and she hemed and hawed around the question. I'm sure they ended up on eBay or at one of the craft shows or summer festivals where she sold her tie-dye clothing, with her also taking profit from the selling of my merchandise.

I decided to show up at one of the festivals where I knew she'd have a booth. It was about an hour from our town, so I also knew she'd never expect me to be there. When I found her booth, she had another table aside from her tie-dye clothing, which had various and sundry items, half of which were from my merchandise. I confronted her and picked up all my things and left. After that, I watched her very closely.

Not long after taking on a partnership with her, I was diagnosed with breast cancer. It turned out I needed two surgeries and seven-and-a-half weeks of radiation. For each of the surgeries I took only a week off, less than I should have. On radiation days, I'd go to my appointment directly from work, and come right back to the shop. All the time I had to be out of the shop, dealing with the horror of breast cancer, I was also worrying about how much she was lifting from me.

Toward the end of the year, I got an opportunity to travel to Sri Lanka to visit tea estates that one of my vendors was hosting. This was the trip of a lifetime for me, having never traveled outside the US, except for a couple of short trips up into Canada. By that time, I had videotape evidence of her pocketing cash sales when I was not in the shop. I knew I'd not have much of a shop left by the time I came back if I left her there alone.

So, I paid a friend of mine to come in every day, pretending to be there to help out greeting customers and answering the phone, but she was really there to monitor my cheating, thieving partner. I remember Griselda pleading with me on several occasions before I left for my trip, to not have my friend come in. I insisted, and she was not happy.

She had all the skills of cajoling and charming people, a trick which is often employed so that if caught, no one would believe they are guilty. She actually got over on my friend, as she kept telling me what fun it was to work with Griselda and that she didn't think she was as bad as I thought.

I found more merchandise gone than sales indicated when I returned. She got my friend to trust her (i.e., have "con"fidence in her), so that she would drop her guard. I was heartily disappointed that with all the fair warning, my friend couldn't see through Griselda's games.

I lost some sales and merchandise, but not as much, I'm guessing, as if my friend hadn't been there at all. I had such a good handle on my business that I knew things like what percentage of sales were usually cash vs. charge. During the two weeks I was gone, mysteriously, almost the only sales recorded were the charge sales, as there was no way to pilfer those. The cash percentage was far below usual, and most days oddly none. I'd already made my mind up that there would be no second year contract with this horrible "partner."

In the end, she had, of course, made me out to be the bad guy. I guess that's another tactic of scammers. It was somehow my fault she didn't get more customers. It was unfair for her to pay half the overhead, although she agreed to these routine terms and signed the contract. She denied breaking and taking home lots of my kitchen wares. She got caught in her false denial one day when I accused her of taking some glass bowls we used every day. I'd started out with about thirty when she took over, and there were less than half a dozen left in the kitchen.

Her own son, who she forced to wash dishes for her every day after school, heard my accusation and her denial. He had just embraced Buddhism, and one thing important to Buddhists is total honesty. He butted in the conversation and said to her, "That's not true, Mom. You have a couple of those bowls at home in our refrigerator right now." A look of fury took over her face. She was clearly one who blamed all her failures on someone else. And justified all her wrong-doing because she didn't have enough money, even when her own son couldn't justify it.

She just quit one day, about two weeks before our contract was up. By that time, I had decided I was moving to another location—without her—and she wanted us to stay in business together. She begged me. In other words, she wanted my money to set up another kitchen for her in another location. I refused. I said I was looking for another smaller location and would only serve tea and scones, which I could handle myself if I had to.

So, with only two weeks to go, and customers on the books for one last tea experience at Elaine's—customers who had been coming to me for years and wanted to come one more time before I shut down the luncheon tea service altogether—she called them all and canceled on them. How petty.

When she did find a location for cheap, she set up her own tea room. While I can't positively say how much of her merchandise was stolen as I never went there, I saw several photos she posted on social media of my glass dishes, upon which she served her lunches. And, there was some of my merchandise perched boldly on her shelves for sale, including a pricey designer teapot.

I didn't go after her. I probably should have, just so she would have this thievery on her record, even if I never got any compensation from her. But, people like that are clever, know how to exist on the fringes, and worm their way out of things. Or at least muddy the waters so thoroughly that you can no longer see the light of day.

And so, I learned the hard way that what they say about partnerships is absolutely, positively, and unfortunately true.

The last year or so at Saxon Square brought me help in the form of welfare back-to-work programs. They would send me part-time employees in exchange for their work experience, and I would teach them basic employment skills like productivity, being on time, working with customers, accuracy, etc.

It was a real boon to me in one way, in that I didn't have to pay wages. These were welfare-to-work programs, where the work experience was required in order to keep getting welfare payments until they found a job. I was tasked with teaching the candidates how to hold a job.

I would spend lots of time explaining the basics. Things like showing up for work on time, not calling in more than the allowed times, learning the job and becoming proficient at the tasks required, developing people skills to work with customers, etc. It turned out that I could only use them to bag tea behind the counter. None of the candidates had the requisite people skills to trust them with handling customers, but there was always plenty of bagging to do, so I was grateful for that help.

I was really thrown for a loop when one young woman, whom I'd just lectured the day before on how important it was to show up for work, didn't show up and didn't bother to call to explain why. The very next day. I'd spent an hour with her explaining that in the real world you would get fired if you just didn't show up for work and didn't call your employer. I emphasized how important it was to be responsible and reliable. She said she understood.

Unbelievably, the very next day she didn't show up again. I was so annoyed by this; I kept calling her cell and her emergency contact number, which turned out to be her grandfather. He finally called me back later in the day to explain that she just couldn't come in for work that day because her sister-in-law had a baby and she just had to go to the hospital to see the baby that morning. Seriously? Their work hours were only until 2:00 p.m. She couldn't go to see the baby after 2:00 p.m.? Apparently my teaching had not sunk in.

Another young girl, who had two kids and had just gotten married, came in with a lip ring. At that time, tats and body piercings weren't as prolific as they are now, and we had a clientele with a lot of older, conservative women. So, I explained that the ring would have to come out when she was at work.

She looked very distressed, and said it was possibly too early to take it out as she had just gotten it before she got married two weeks before as a wedding gift from her mother! What the heck happened to gifting toaster ovens and other useful items to set up a household? She'd shared that she didn't know how to bake, so I guess a toaster oven would have been pointless. I felt sorry for her in that it really wasn't her fault, since no one was teaching her the basics of life survival. Her first life lesson with me was that she'd have to take the lip ring out for work.

So, I'd also spend time trying to teach these girls some of the stuff of life. I'd explain things like how to organize their time to be able to show up for work on time, and shop for groceries to stretch their food dollars to last the month. I'd seen them run out more than once.

They were scheduled for five days, Monday through Friday, but only four hours a day. They were *allowed* five call-ins a month before they would be penalized. These requirements were so lax and easy, it was so dismaying that of the three clients I worked with over the period of a year or so, not one of them *EVER* showed up for the minimum required days of sixteen a month. When the social workers wouldn't let me record the delinquencies on their worksheets, always let the girls off, it made me realize how hopeless our system is. We are several generations into this thing, and the system that's supposed to help fix the problems is quite broken.

These welfare programs eventually dried up in our area when the grant money ran out, and I was back to looking for help. I tried a few more part-time hires, but had the same problems as before. Luckily Sheila and daughter happened in a couple of weeks before closing for the next move to a new location without Griselda. She shared that she was again needing work, and I offered her a job on the spot. I was almost surprised that she would trust me enough to work for me again, but I think she knew how sincere my apology was.

So, she came back and stuck it out with me until I closed the shop three years later. She was so great with customers, and the customers loved her. I'm sure she brought me more business using her superb people skills. We worked well together, and that was a joy. It was great to fill out the last days of the shop without a problematic employee.

That's why, in the end, I'd shored myself up to just work by myself until Sheila thankfully showed up. In retrospect, I'm not sure I could have handled it by myself totally. It's just too much work, especially because by then, I was in my sixties.

Covering all the shop hours, which, I admit, were sheer joy for me, on top of all the management work I had to do would have been too much for me. Until you've seen that side of a small business, you have no idea how much time is spent doing books, paying bills, managing accounts, running to the bank for deposits or stores for food and supplies, searching out new product, ordering product, designing/printing all the graphics—brochures, certificates, display graphics, signage, and labels—inventing the next marketing scheme, designing ads, and baking scones. Ad infinitum.

It was a never-ending list of tasks. There was never much time to rest. But I have to admit; I loved it all. It was the greatest creative outlet I've ever had. I could get lost for hours in designing a new brochure or creating a label for a new product. It satisfied that intense artistic urge to create that I was born with.

I just wish I'd had better health throughout. It would have helped immensely if I'd had the energy of a thirty year old. Still, with all my deficits and debility, it has been a rewarding venture. I was so determined that through it all—working weeks that should have been vacations, working days with a raging migraine or bad cold or sprained foot, stealing a lie down on a cot in the back room when no customers were in the store so that my migraine medicine could kick in, dragging my tired fanny in when an employee called in sick when I was planning on a much needed day off, my motivation never wavered.

In the end, the love for the little shop I'd created was great enough to get me out of bed and carried me through each day. I learned to take it a day at a time out of sheer necessity. I felt like Scarlet O'Hara bravely saying, "After all, tomorrow is another day!" If I hadn't gotten to that determined place, I'd have crumbled and lost it all. My husband and I could very well have lost our house and spent our retirement eating peanut butter and jelly on soda crackers. I simply wasn't going to let that happen.

Like most things in life, my experiences with employees were some good and some bad. Some richly rewarding, and some horrifyingly ugly. As many times as I was disappointed in the whole of humanity, I was encouraged by the kindness, respect, and loyalty some granted me.

That's just life, I guess, with all its ups and downs. It's best when we learn to hang on and simply enjoy the ride. And that I did. Screaming at the top of my lungs in frustration sometimes, like the terror experienced at the top of a monster roller coaster peak. Sometimes the ride was so intense, all I wanted was for it to stop.

But there were also many times of smooth sailing. Times where the ride was truly enjoyable, peppered with lots of intangible rewards. Those are enduring treasures no one can ever take from me.

Chapter 6

The Agony of the Leaf

There is a moment, an almost sacred event in the making of tea. It is that moment when the hot water rushes over the dry leaf and the leaf begins to sacrifice its essence to the water. It is called *"the agony of the leaf."* It is this agony, suffering, passion that gives rise to that magic elixir we call tea.

This process is a perfect metaphor for running a small business, if not life itself. The moment you dive in, take the risk, open your doors, you begin the manifestation of your passion. This is where reality sets in and where you begin to feel exactly like that tea leaf, sacrificing your essence for the perfect cup of tea or in this case, for the fruitful manifestation of your vision. It is nothing like that fantasy of being your own boss, where you get to call all the shots and are the one in control. You have just entered the joyride of your life. Sometimes exciting, sometimes terrifying, and everything in between.

Greg Levoy, one of the most enchanting writers I've ever come across, talks about this process in his book, **Callings: Finding and Following an Authentic Life.** He brilliantly discusses finding your authentic self and your true passion. When you are truly passionate about something, it ceases to be just a job or task, it becomes your "calling."

The very definition of passion, he points out, is suffering. So, when we enter our passion, it is often beset with painful events or encounters, unpleasant tasks, oppressive workload, and weighty obligations. The whole endeavor can become unbearably oppressive, unless you have a true passion for what you have taken on.

Thankfully, I did. I knew the time was right. I was old enough with enough life experience under my belt. I knew that I had the personality to be the one in charge. I had an intense desire and ability to create. The year of planning was pure joy. Creating the framework for this shop. Deciding what items to carry and imagining how all the pieces of this large puzzle would fit together. Sourcing the original product line and tasting all the teas.

As I moved out of the planning, scheming, and fantasizing phase and got deeper into the active, bringing-into-reality part, the joys began to subside and transitioned into the agony. I had no education or training in running a business or in the art of tea, so I had a steep learning curve to surmount; so much to learn in a very short time. The business plan had to be written, and it had to be good enough to enable me to procure a loan. Learning how to hire employees—interviewing, fulfilling paperwork requirements for my records and the state of Ohio, learning how to do payroll and submit payment of payroll taxes was all new to me, except I had done some initial interviewing of couriers for the lab. Setting up a bookkeeping system was something I'd never done before. Managing a food service, basic as it was, was also completely foreign territory.

Interestingly, it all fell into place in spite of the pressure. A friend recommended a friend of hers who understood bookkeeping for small business. Between her and my accountant, I was able to get a handle on it pretty quickly. The bookkeeper also filled me in on the employee requirements. Whenever I needed it, it seemed like with a little bit of sincere effort, I found what I needed to solve each problem.

Searching for the right location was fun, but dealing with leases and landlords, well, not so much. At the moment the lease was signed, a heavy reality set in: rent and utilities would be due every month. As soon as I put two employees on payroll, another weighty burden sat on my shoulders: every two weeks I had to meet payroll. Purchasing fixtures and the many varieties of product I'd decided to carry was great fun, but all that money going out and nothing coming in yet added another level of stress.

I was too busy tackling my enormous to-do list to notice what was happening to my body. I was carried along by the excitement of opening and the pressure to get income flowing. By the night before opening, I was so physically exhausted and so stressed that my husband had to virtually help me walk to the car. I remember it was about 10:00 p.m. when we got the last detail finished for the grand opening the following day. It was a surreal moment. I was so incredibly excited that I'd done it, and clearly that excitement carried me through until every detail was in place, and I was looking at my dream manifest.

When all the final preparations were finished, and we packed up to go home, the reality set in. I was in so much physical pain that I was ready to drop. Literally. My passion had carried me like a drug. I had been functioning in an other-worldly state, and didn't even realize the damage to my body. Then the drug wore off, and I crashed.

All that stress, exertion, and pain made me feel like a tea leaf in agony. I was giving my very essence to create something bigger than myself. I was realizing my passion and experiencing firsthand the suffering that goes along with it. I got a taste of what the phrase "being in hot water" means. Get it? Tea pun.

My most favorite tea quote is the one from Eleanor Roosevelt: "You never know how strong a woman is until she gets into hot water." So true. So apropos.

Interspersed with the excitement of opening was the realization that my fibromyalgia, which had been quite well controlled up to this time, had reared its ugly head and was in full force again. Fibromyalgia makes you feel like you don't have enough energy to get through an average day. For the next 16 years, none of my days would be average. Almost every day would present some sort of challenge, sometimes physical, sometimes emotional, and usually a mixture of both.

One of the t-shirts I designed for
the shop with Eleanor's famous quote.

It was a mental blow that the fibromyalgia was back, but the migraines, which went from one or two a year, had now increased to often two a month. That was a difficult pill to swallow after all the work I'd done over the years to get both conditions under control. I cannot count the number of times—days upon days—I had to work through a migraine because an employee had let me down. But when you live with a chronic disease, you have two choices. You can check out, go to bed, and find as much comfort for yourself as possible. Or, you can decide you don't want to miss out on life. You can teach yourself to persevere through the pain. To keep moving in spite of it. Sometimes movement helps you lose consciousness of it for a brief reprieve. Like going for a walk in a park on a beautiful summer day, where the full bloom of nature and intoxicating aromas of the flowers can distract you for a bit.

Other times, you end up pushing yourself past your limits. You learn to focus on what has to be done, on the goal, the end point. You teach yourself to not take your eye off the goal, and do whatever you need to do to get there. I did that second one a lot. And then I'd pay a price. My physical coffers were often empty, and I must have borrowed into deficit, because, no matter what, I kept going and my passion carried me through. But in the end that price to be paid would present itself with a hand out, demanding its due.

I'd gone to a doctor for the fibro who had me taking all sorts of meds that tore up my stomach. I endured several series of painful injections into the nerves or tendons of my back. It didn't really help. After that, I took it upon myself and looked into every natural thing I could find that might lessen my pain.

I started to do things like yoga and very regular exercise. I studied the nutritional aspects and found that larger doses of Vitamin C, plus CoQ10 and acetyl-L carnitine helped the metabolic side of things as well as the pain, and I'd have more energy to get through my day. I meditated every weekday without fail for years.

I read everything I could get my hands on about fibromyalgia and ran across something that said aspartame was very bad and could be particularly harmful for fibro. So, I immediately stopped taking anything that contained aspartame. People can poo-poo all they want about the warnings on harmful substances, but I honestly felt markedly better within days.

I worked with a physical therapist who specializes in myofascial release, deep muscle massage to break up scar tissue and the knots that form in the fascia. To use the word massage is a bit of a misnomer. It hurts so bad sometimes; I'd be in tears. It also causes emotional release, which is good in the long run, but bursting into tears while driving home from the PT appointments was disconcerting, to say the least.

Little by little, I got it to a manageable level. I knew I'd been diagnosed with a disease they say there is no cure for, but it truly was like I was in remission for many years. Until I took on my passion.

After the rear-end car accident two months before opening and the intense work of getting the shop open, I was no longer in remission. The fibro was back with a vengeance, far greater than I'd ever experienced before. Probably being older had something to do with it, too.

Eventually, I could no longer function through the constant pain. I discussed it with my primary care doctor, who put me on pain medication. I started taking it and found I could function again. I have to pop a pill every four to six hours, every single day, but I could function again without debilitating pain and agony, and have only a milder version of the discomfort to contend with. Unless I overdo. Then, I pay a price for the next few days.

I'm also sure it was the auto accident two months before opening that caused my migraines to come back. I'd had those under control, too. But while sitting in my car waiting for the police to come after the accident, I got a brutal migraine headache. From that moment on, they came like clockwork. It was beyond frustrating. It hampered my ability to get my work done in the timeframe I needed. It clouded my thinking on those headache days.

They persisted for the entire sixteen years the shop was open. Thankfully, they have subsided somewhat since closing, but I have more work to do to get them under good control again. I refuse to believe I will be unable to get them controlled, if not totally gone. I just don't give up, and I won't give in. Life is malleable, and we have much more control over things than we sometimes think. I've learned to seize that control. Life gets better when you do.

I was determined to not let these setbacks and all the pressures spiral me down into an irreversible course, and I realized there was a huge mental/emotional component that needed attention. So I got myself into therapy, where I could talk through the mounting stresses. One of the things most helpful about the guidance I received was to realize that, as a businesswoman, I would need to learn how to better handle some of these constant challenges—most specifically, the encounters with people who seemed to want to make my business fail.

The landlady from hell, as my attorney called her, was a constant nuisance. At first, things weren't too bad, but she was actively seeking to rent the third suite in her little strip. She had an antique dealer look at it and then a bridal salon. Either would have been a perfect fit for her gift shop and my tea room. I encouraged her to work with either of them to sign a lease.

But she didn't, and in the end, she rented to a mortgage loan shark, and I do mean shark. That was my first close encounter with unscrupulous business. I would go into his suite to deliver some of his mail I'd gotten by mistake, and overhear his telemarketers trying to talk old ladies, whose homes were paid off, into taking out a mortgage for remodeling or to take a trip. Offering people money far in excess of the value of their homes. Anything they could come up with to make a mortgage. Around 2004, this is what was going on in our country, setting us up for the crash to come in 2008.

So, all these telemarketers took up all the parking spaces in the lot, leaving me none for my customers. Their constant diet of fast food and junkfood brought cockroaches into the building. Complaints to the landlady fell on deaf ears. When she decided to have the parking lot redone, I redesigned the spacing in the lot to angled parking, which would have given us four more spaces. When I came in to work the day after she had the lot resurfaced and parking lines painted, imagine my dismay to find that they were in the same old configuration as before.

I eventually had to get signs made and mounted on the wall in front of the three spaces directly in front of my shop, threatening to be towed if anyone other than tea shop customers were to park there. And I had to get regular pest control to keep the bugs out of my kitchen.

I had no respect for the loan shark neighbor. Partly it was because of what he had decided to do with his God-given talents: talking people into loans they didn't need. But beyond that, he was a truly nasty person. He would come into my shop every week or two and insult me. He would say things like, "I can't figure out what kind of business you are—a destination or a happenstance. You're not gonna make it by being so undefined. You don't know anything about business." This was from a man on his umpteenth venture with a string of previous failures.

I would go in and week after week complain to my therapist about this guy. How cruel he was. In my idyllic world, people should just be nice to each other. I'd done nothing to bother this man, and I was a good neighbor. It just didn't make sense to me that he would be so nasty to me. I found out later that he wanted to expand into my space. It all made sense then, but I was determined to make sure that he would not push me out before I was ready to leave.

It helped to have a sympathetic ear to listen to all the mean-spirited things, but I was really there to figure out how to deal with this by myself. And, one day, as sometimes happens when therapy is working at its best, he hit on something that clicked. I was relating the latest horror story, and when I finished, he looked at me intensely and sincerely said, "Elaine, I don't know why there are such mean people in the world. I don't know how they get up out of bed every morning and decide that they are going to be mean SOBs every day. It's beyond my understanding. But I do know this: they do. And there will always be mean people.

"Now, the way I see it, you have two choices. You can come here every week, and I'll listen and take your money for as long as you want. I mean, the guy's an a$$h@!e. I'll listen and try to make you feel better. But you'll probably lose your business. The other option is that you can learn how to deal with these people. And, you might just save your business, as well as be better off for the rest of your life. Because there will always be people like this."

Well, that gave me much food for thought. On the half-hour drive home, his words kept churning in my head. Then, suddenly, the lights went on! Choirs of angels sang, and the waves of epiphany washed over me. It sunk in. If I wanted to be a successful businesswoman, I would, like it or not, have to learn how to deal with these people. I knew the neighboring tenant was just one of many I'd be encountering in this journey.

So, right then and there I decided. I was going to learn how to stand up to these mean, abusive, controlling bullies. Before I got home, I already had a plan.

I remember an episode of the *Dr. Phil* show, where he was talking about how to deal with bullies. His words were still with me. "Bullies are the weakest people on the planet. I guarantee you, if you stand up to a bully, they will always tuck tail and run." I decided right then and there that I would do just that. Shaking in my boots, probably, but one way or another, I would stand up to this nasty guy and get him off my back.

I started thinking, *Who do I know that's a really strong person? Someone who stands up to people?* I immediately had a vision of a friend who I used to work with, Linda. She was strong. Not afraid of anyone and capably handled any situation. I would be like her. I had to muster up some courage, because the one word that described her was *fearless*.

Then, I thought, *How am I going to handle it when he comes into the shop and stands in the doorway of my office, cornering me in that tiny room?* I remembered learning about "personal space." That comfort zone everyone has, where whenever someone comes too close, inside that zone, we want to back away and get to a comfortable space again. I rehearsed and rehearsed these ideas until one day, only a week or so later, he came into the shop.

As usual, he came to the doorway of my office and started right in, trying to intimidate me, spewing insult after insult. I was ready. I slowly got up out of my chair and faced him. I cut him off with a tirade of my own. I just let fly whatever came to my head. I admit, I must have sounded more like a sailor than a polite businesswoman, but I thought a little shock value would be a good thing.

I started to move toward him, ready to get inches from his face, if that's what it took. As I got about a foot away from him, he started to back up. Out of my office doorway, down about fifteen feet of hallway, backward up the ramp to the front door, and out the door! I kept the tirade coming the entire way, and by the time he got to the door, I had told him, "How dare you come into my shop and insult me? When I want your opinion, I'll ask for it. Until then, keep your abusive remarks to yourself. Get out and don't ever come into my shop again!" Of course, that's the cleaned-up version.

After he'd left, I was visibly shaking and sat back down in my office to settle myself. *That was pretty awesome*, I thought. Dr. Phil was right! After that, he wouldn't come anywhere near me. Victory!

Going to therapy and having someone in my corner to talk things through with was a lifesaver for me. I'm really not sure I'd have made it without that help. With this one very large victory under my belt, I got stronger and was able to eventually handle things without that crutch. I kept working on that skill, as I knew there would be many more bullies to come.

After that, I wasn't surprised when what surfaced over time was that there was always some new struggle to overcome. It seemed like I was always having to fight with someone to get something I needed. None of these were things that I should have had to waste vast amounts of energy on just to run my business. But, they surfaced constantly and had to be contended with, like it or not.

Health Department regulations, while I welcome efforts to keep our food safe when eating in any restaurant, were often things I'd have to comply with just for the sake of uniformity. The department inspector was often a rookie and all full of their new-found power and an attitude that their job was to be a pain in the neck.

When these interpretations of the rules cost you a thousand dollars here and a couple hundred there, it gets beyond irritating. Like having to spend about $5000 for a bathroom for men in a suite I was renting, for a business that only seated thirty people max, that served 99 percent women, where a unisex bathroom would have completely sufficed. That was an outrage that not only cost me in dollars but set back my opening by about a month. That lost time cost me a month of revenue and a very important one. It was December, and I missed the first Christmas season, where revenues are quadruple other times of the year. Thanks, Toledo.

It also left a bitter taste in my mouth every time I'd go to a restaurant to eat where, in spite of all the rules, it didn't look clean or safe. Obviously, a mindless imposition of the rules wasn't all that was needed to keep things safe. Who hasn't gone to a restaurant and ended up with vague flu-like symptoms the next day that lasted a day? Well, guess what? There is no such thing as the twenty-four hour flu. That's food poisoning.

The thing that always grated on me most was that there was absolutely no consideration for my background. Having a past work history as a med tech with eight years of experience in microbiology, I knew much more about bacteria and contamination than even the most experienced health department inspector. If I dared even bring that up, there would be hell to pay for threatening their authority. It got tiresome.

One day, a particularly young and very green inspector came in, and I could tell she was pumped on that full-of-her-newfound-power high. It was in the middle of a hectic lunch rush. That's their version of a "gotcha!" As if, during a lunch rush, you'd be too busy to cover up all your violations.

So, she's snooping around and getting in everyone's way. She kept interrupting me to ask me where this or that was. I tolerated it, for a bit. I'd already explained to her we were in the middle of a lunch rush and that I really didn't have time for all her interruptions. She then pulled me aside to tell me that I had a violation that would need to be corrected immediately. It was that one of the bathroom wastebaskets didn't have a lid on it.

Now, I'd been in business for at least five or six years by this time. I'd had two inspections a year, and no one before had ever even brought that up. So, I explained that it had never been a problem before and asked why it was now. She said that she didn't know, but maybe it was a new rule. She started to get in my face with all that power just begging to be wielded and told me that I'd need to take care of it within thirty days or they could pull my license.

Well now, that did it! I took a deep breath, and I think even she, in her naiveté, could see that I was using every fiber of being to remain calm. I resisted grabbing her by the scruff of the neck, which I admit I thought about, and instead backed her into my office area and parked her in front of my desk. I told her to either have a seat and wait for the lunch rush to be over, or come back later, but that I had no intention of signing anything or giving her any more of my time until I had met my customer's needs.

She sat. I chuckled to myself and reveled in one of those small victories.

When the rush was under control, and my employees could handle the rest, I went back to talk to little miss "wet-behind-the-ears" inspector. I finished my dissertation to her with a controlled but stern lecture explaining that, as she was a state employee, my taxes paid her salary. That meant that she was there to serve me and the people of Ohio to make sure their food was safe. And that, as her employer, I didn't like the way she was talking to me. I explained that she needed to change her tune, get polite real quicklike or I would send such a seething letter of complaint to her boss that she might lose her job.

I'd like to think she learned a thing or two that day. Or maybe she didn't. I never saw her again, so that job might have been too much for her. I rarely remember seeing the same inspector twice, although they always kept the same assigned territory. I guess people didn't last long at that job.

That felt really good! And lesson number "I've-lost-count"— *When you're right, stand up for yourself. It feels good, and you won't have to take so much crap from people.*

Perhaps the most important parameter for any business is appropriate and effective signage. People have to be able to find you. If signage is inadequate or not visible, it can be doom for a small business. An easily read sign when you are located on a busy street is a critical marketing tool, and it's essential.

Signage was another arena where the city got their jollies by dishing out grief. One would think that a city would welcome any new business and even be supportive. The more successful a business, the more revenue for the city. Unique and interesting small businesses add much to the character of a city. There just seems no good reason for impeding their efforts to simply do business. But that's exactly what I found.

Toledo seems to be obsessed with imposing every ridiculous letter of every ridiculous regulation. Now, don't misunderstand me. I completely understand the need for regulation and the importance of safety, as well as aesthetics, when it comes to signage. But imposition of poorly designed rules for the sake of imposing rules is absurd, nonproductive and can add unnecessary cost.

Two years in, I ended up changing the name of the shop on the advice of my marketing team, which meant I had to get new signage again. The most effective signs tell the customer what you are about, at a glance. I came up with the idea for a huge teapot shaped sign. It was a great visual cue that told customers right away that this was a place for tea.

When I moved to a new location, just after the first three years in business, it was to a large strip mall. The strip was well established, always full of tenants, and the property well maintained. But, as they were trying to update the façade, they had just made a new requirement that all new signage had to be the individually lit letters. That was a huge blow.

These kinds of signs were much more costly. Instead of being able to reuse my beautiful teapot-shaped sign, which I could have moved and mounted over the new shop front for a couple hundred dollars, I had to invest over $4000 in a brand-new sign. More expense, and quite a big bite for a small business, but in the long run there were some real advantages to this sign.

It was electrified, and so keeping it lit every evening gave us potential notice to people driving by every night of the week. It was much larger than any other signage I'd had, and so much easier to read while driving past. And, I was at this location for six years, so that's much more mileage than I'd gotten out of my first two signs.

As it turned out, I was able to take that sign with me to the last two shops as well, so I used it for a total of twelve years. It fit perfectly over the front façade of the next two locations and gave me continuity as well as great visibility. That softened the initial $4000 outlay, and I felt this was one of my best investments. Thankfully, it was well made and none of the lettering ever went out, which I often notice on individually lettered signs. I got lucky on that count.

While my large-lettered sign fit on the last shop façade, the building was set back so far that no one noticed it. That made for the necessity in putting the teapot signs in the front yard, which brought me lots of grief from city inspectors. There was, in reality, no good reason to not let me place them where they were needed to be seen by customers.

They also had a problem with my white picket fence. I'd had one at the previous two shops and neither were questioned. This time, the city insisted I have a permit in order to put it up. Well, I'd already put it up, but they wanted me to pay for a permit and fine me for the offense. The city continued to take their petty stance and were a thorn in my side the last three years of my business.

It is such a shame that Toledo wasn't more helpful to a small business. At my last location, I tried to get the city to force my landlord to fix the faulty wiring in my suite (and no doubt, throughout the building). It was like pulling teeth to even get them to come out and inspect. What I saw plenty of was the city protecting the building owners from having to put money into proper upkeep on their buildings and passing it on to the renting small-business owner. That's just not right.

I was not the only small business affected. I spoke with scores of other business owners over the years and heard many similar stories. I never understood why a city, always struggling to grow, would exert such hostility toward small business, when it is those unique small businesses that bring so much color and character to our cityscapes. Seems counterproductive, but it was the reality I had to live with. Perhaps that's one of the reasons Toledo has so much trouble growing into a big city and has been referred to as the biggest small town in the country.

Now, don't get me wrong. I love my city. It really is a great place to live. Lots of wonderful metroparks. Easy and manageable in many ways. Plenty of culture to experience, and its downtown is on a riverfront, not to mention kissing the west end of one of the Great Lakes. It's just such a shame that it can't ever seem to reach its considerable potential. Being a stubborn hindrance to many businesses is at least one reason why.

It was so satisfying when I first opened, and I was so proud and pleased with what I had created. I was rewarded with the real, physical materialization of what had been for so long just a dream in my mind. It was now something tangible, beautiful, new, unique, and refreshing. At least that's how it struck me. And many people confirmed my own impressions.

But soon there was what seemed a constant litany of suggestions that came from customers. Beyond suggestions, really. It was as if all this work I'd done was cast aside. It was as if my dream had been absconded by everyone who hadn't had the courage to manifest their own dreams but didn't hesitate to tell me what they thought was wrong with mine.

"You know what you should do?" I had only been open for a couple of days when a guy came in and said, "This is a nice shop, but you know, the lighting is all wrong." Another woman offered, "Your menu is so bland. You could really spice it up if you served a truly English peasant ploughman's menu with roast beef sandwiches and chutney." I'd hear, "You need more . . ." or "You should carry this . . ." It was as if they didn't even see what was in front of them and took the liberty to distort it into their own vision.

But it wasn't their dream or vision, was it? It wasn't their blood, sweat, tears, pain and exhaustion that went into creating it, was it? It was mine, and in that exhausted state that never left me throughout the duration, it was so disheartening to hear. Emotionally draining, when I was already exhausted beyond my limits. That's perhaps why I couldn't shake it off at first.

I had employees who wanted me to make changes in line with their visions for the shop. Suggestions were always welcome, but not always doable, nor were most of them what I wanted to do. I made many tweaks of menu or merchandise, created new tea blends, and anything else I felt would make the shop better. It always puzzled me when one would insist on something that simply wasn't doable. It is like they had no concept of finances, and some of the things they were proposing were simply out of budget.

At the Saxon Square shop, my partner had worked and worked on me to put a garden patio in the front of the shop. It did have potential and would make a great outdoor tea area. She talked me into it with promises to provide all the plants and landscaping, which was a side business of hers. So, I thought I would only have to put in the patio stones and the picket fence. Seemed like a fair deal, so we went forward with the plan.

As it turned out, she lied. She only planted about two flats of flowers in a space that needed six. She'd removed a large bush without the landlord's or my permission, which left more empty space needing flowers. I kept bugging her about adding more flowers, and while the promises were plentiful, the flowers weren't. I finally figured out that she'd probably stolen the two flats she put in from another landscaping job, and she had no other jobs to siphon from, so more plants never came. I finally couldn't take it anymore, and I bought four more flats, which filled out the garden nicely.

The patio was beautiful, and I was glad I'd done it, even if it turned out to be an unfair bargain. After that, I'd adopted a "put your money where your mouth is" attitude. Since I ended up footing the bill for all the changes, I would make all the decisions from then on. No one would sway me into costly territory again.

By the later years, I was so planted in my garden of dreams that I guess it must have come across to customers when they came in the door. It became commonplace for them, even the men, to exclaim how beautiful and comfortable it was ... what a relaxing atmosphere ... how lovely the aromas. Customers were always amazed at our huge selection of teas. Our prices were always fair, and customers would tell me how they would never go back to the mall and pay the exorbitant prices there. They loved our homemade scones, and many people came in for them regularly, raving about how delicious they were.

All of that was anything but disheartening. It was lovely and rewarding. Another one of those intangible benefits. Not a financial reward, but something immaterial and ethereal. Warm memories that will be with me until the day I sip from my last cup of tea.

Another bit of agony that seemed to last throughout the sixteen years was what I like to call the everybody's-got-their-hand-in-my-pocket-before-I've-even-made-a-dime phenomenon.

It started very early on. I'd expected to spend a lot just to get open, and I did. I expected it to level off and then turn around into the "money coming in" part. It did start to come in, slowly. But expenses were high, and I wasn't making enough to cover them from profits until my second or third year.

I found that when you have a business, everybody thinks you have lots of money to throw around. You become a target for donations to schools, charities, and even private parties' "family-member-got-in-an-accident," or "help-we-can't-afford-to-bury-uncle-Harry" funds.

I was still novice to all of this when the first affronting woman walked in the door, after having been open for only a month or so. She walked across the shop to the back wall where my most beautiful and most expensive dried herb wreath was hanging. I walked over and asked if I could help her. She said with a most definitive tone, "This one is perfect. I'll take it." I was elated at the thought of selling my first wreath and started to take it down from the wall to box it for transport.

Then she continued with her spiel. She said it would be perfect for their auction for whatever charity she was representing, and it was so kind of me to donate it. Wait. What? Donate? I mean, it was one thing to ask for a donation, but to be set up and misled like that. Well, that wasn't going to work with me!

I had just taken it off its hook, and once her con had sunk in, I turned back around and put it right back on the wall. I explained to her as civilly as I could that first of all, as I had just opened the shop and was still getting my feet on the ground, I wasn't prepared to part with my most expensive wreath for her charity. She wasn't a customer, I didn't know her and so there was nothing moving me toward meeting her request. Secondly, I also explained that I didn't appreciate her technique, which felt very much like a con routine. She didn't like that much but we were even on that score.

Another customer came in one time and was eyeing a particular teapot at the front display. She'd been in before with a friend of hers, and I knew they were from Ottawa Hills, Toledo's most exclusive neighborhood. She'd looked at the pot the first time, but decided not to buy it.

When she came in the second time, she again pawed at it, inspecting it, and hesitating. Then she asked for me to reduce the price. Again, I hadn't been open very long. This was one of my finest bone china pots, and I wasn't about to reduce the price. I told her so, and so again she declined to buy it.

She came in at least two other times, always expecting me to buckle and reduce the price for her. I honestly think it was just a game for her, as she could well afford the reasonable original price I had on the pot. I never did, and someone else eventually got to own that lovely piece of china.

This is where I began to find my voice. I'd been pretty timid about speaking up about things, especially if it was a complaint or something I didn't agree with. I didn't want to upset people. But, somehow, putting my heart and soul into this business gave me the courage to stand up for myself. Nobody was going to walk away with a part of my dream. Many tried. But I got better and better at protecting what I'd given so much to build.

When I was closing the shop, I had many people come in whom I'd never seen before, looking for something at 75 percent off. Most in the final weeks went for 30 to 40 percent off, with a few things at half off. But, I just wasn't about to feed those vultures who'd not supported me in sixteen years, so I refused to drop my prices any lower.

I did have some merchandise left, but ended up selling that to another tea room in the area at 75 percent off, so they could make a good profit on it. I lost half of what I'd paid for it, but that was more than made up for by getting it into the hands of someone more worthy than those greedy vultures.

The banks were the entity that tried to screw me over the most. That's what I think of banks: entities that screw people over. Their fees are outrageous and out-and-out theft, in my opinion. A nifty little statistic—the three largest banks in the US made about $6 billion from overdraft fees and ATM charges in 2015. Understand that this is $6 billion taken from people in order for them to obtain their own money from an ATM machine, and overdraft fees from people who don't have enough money in their accounts. An overdraft fee can be upwards of $35 these days, and that might be on a bounced check of $23! They're nothing but scoundrels, in my humble opinion.

When I got my first business loan from a bank in a small town outside of Toledo, interest rates were very high. As I'd mentioned in the beginning chapter, the State of Ohio had a program where, for every person you employed, you could get an interest reduction of 3 percent on every $25,000 borrowed. With two employees, this almost covered my whole loan, and the bank president was good enough to give me the reduction for the entire loan.

Payments were high, but at least I got a significant reduction. That is, until the president of the bank left his job, and the vice president took over. All of a sudden I started getting notices of payments hundreds higher than they had been. I immediately made an appointment to meet with the VP now president.

I explained how the program was supposed to work. The State of Ohio would give banks 3 percent lower rates on money for them to pass along to loan customers who employed people. It was an incentive to increase employment, and the bank got the discount from the state regardless of how many loans they gave or did not give.

The new president, all full of his power, proceeded to explain to me that he completely understood how the program worked, but that he was under no obligation to pass the discount along to me. So, let me get this right. The bank got a discount from the state because I hired employees, but they did not have to pass it along to me? Surely this can't be right, I thought.

So, when I got back to my office, I immediately called the state of Ohio. That was always such a pleasure. Sometimes it took days to get through to the person or department you needed to talk to. And, as I recall, it took two days to get through to the department handling this employee loan reduction program. When I finally did, I couldn't believe my ears. "We loan this money to banks at a 3 percent reduction in hopes that they will give out more loans to businesses who employ them, but if they don't pass it on to the employer who took out the loan, there's nothing we can do to force them."

Nothing you can do to force them? What the heck did they mean by that? *You could make it a requirement for the reduced money to them in the first place. You could require them to show their subsequent loans with the reduction passed along to the employer where it was intended to go in the first place. What do you mean you can't do anything about it?* What I learned here was that "can't" actually means "won't" or "don't want to bother." There's always something that *could* be done to promote fairness. I was livid.

But, it was not the last time I would be livid about some gross injustice levied upon me. This was when I really began to learn to fight, and scheme, and come up with workable solutions to the many problems I would have to face over the life of my little tea shop.

I immediately started looking into how I could get out of this loan. A friend had suggested a home equity loan. So, I looked into that and found a wonderful woman who worked at a local Toledo bank who helped me get that in place. The interest rate was much lower, even without the 3 percent reduction, as interest rates were coming down some by this time, and it was a different kind of loan.

This made me nervous having my house up for hock. But over the next five years or so, until my helpful bank lady retired, we were able to make moves to keep my rates and fees the lowest possible.

When she retired, and with no one looking out for me, I got slapped with unnecessary fees again. So, I thought, I'll just look around at other banks and loan programs to see if I can find something better. Coincidentally, and shortly after, two women came in from a different bank and started to tell me about some new programs of particular benefit to women in business that their bank had. I was all ears.

It turns out, there was not really any special program for women. I'm thinking, well then, why did you say that? But while that question seemed quite legitimate to me, the bank's attitude was, "So what?" Business was taking a directional turn that I didn't like at all. It was as if they could say anything they wanted to get you roped into a contract. "All's fair in love and war." Right? And now that seemed to have expanded to "All's fair in love and war and business."

So, the bank duo came in with the contract all prepared, and I took my time to actually read the entire thing. They were very perturbed with that, as if no one ever did that. Well, I'd learned how unscrupulous some people can be, especially banks, so I took my time. Sure enough, there were questions and discrepancies from what we had first discussed. I carefully went over the terms and told them that they would need to make all the corrections on parts that weren't in line with their original promises, in writing, before I would sign anything.

They were, to say the least, not happy with me. They complained that it took days back and forth with their corporate office to come up with a contract, and how could I expect them to do it all over again? They tried to get me to sign anyway, saying that they would make the corrections later on the final copy. I chuckled to myself, *Do you ladies think I was born yesterday?* I was firm and said they would need to make all corrections, and the contract had to be right before I would sign.

The following week, when they returned with what they thought would get them my signature, I again sat and read through the entire contract. Again, they were rolling their eyes at me. But when I got to one part, where a change was supposed to have been made, it hadn't, and it still stated the old, unacceptable terms. They started to fast-talk me. They tried everything they could think of, pleading for me to sign anyway, and they'd try to get it fixed later.

Just then a phone call came in for me. It was my dearest friend from kindergarten on up, who now lives in New York City. I don't usually take personal calls interrupting a business meeting, but I needed a break from these women, and so I let them believe it was something I needed to attend to right then.

I was happy to hear Christine's voice in the midst of the unpleasantries, and right away she could tell I was flustered about something. She asked me to share it with her, and so I summarized the banking fiasco for her. I said I wasn't going to go with this loan because I was just tired of dealing with unscrupulous people. I didn't know what I was going to do, but like always, I'd figure something out.

That was when she offered. My mouth fell open and nearly dropped to the floor. She offered to take over my bank loan, if she and I could come to agreement with interest and terms. I immediately thought, "Don't borrow money from a friend." And what the heck was she doing offering to loan that much money to a friend?

It really worried me on one hand. We had been friends forever, since little kids, and actually even before. I swear we knew each other from a past life. I'm not sure I believe in past lives, at least the neat-and-tidy version, but I have felt many resonances with people I know in this life that it seems like I must have known them for eons. This move was something that could jeopardize this treasured friendship, and I worried if I should risk it.

The first worrisome thoughts quickly turned to *I trust this person completely, and she trusts me. I would* **never** *let her down, and would sell my house before I would ever renege on a loan with her.* I knew this could work. I thanked her profusely. I could now go back out to the meeting and tell the bank ladies to get lost. Christine and I agreed to talk again in a day or two when I had worked out the terms to discuss with her.

So, I then took great pleasure in returning to the table where the ladies were patiently waiting and telling them to take a flying leap. Well, in nicer words, but I let them know clearly that I had given them two chances to get this contract right, and because of their shenanigans, I would not be doing business with them. What an astounding moment of serendipity and victorious relief.

Later, Christine and I worked out an agreement. It brought me great relief to not be under the thumb of any banks ever again. It saved my fanny. And enabled me to keep my shop going for another eight years. I am happy to say that when I sold off most of my merchandise upon closing, I was able to pay off the remainder of the loan in its entirety.

In essence, Christine became a silent partner in my business. And we know what usually happens with partnerships. But, this time, our deep friendship and the honesty and integrity we both garnered from our Catholic upbringing carried us through.

There were times when I was so overwhelmed and that I would miss a month or two of payments to her. Yes, I got *that* overwhelmed with the stressful nonsense of the business that I missed payments. Not only hers but the electric and phone bills. I paid penalties for every other entity, but with our friendship in the mix, Christine just allowed me to catch up on payments.

I'm not sure she will ever know how crucial she was in helping me to get out of this venture without losing my shirt. And probably our house. I can't even put into words the deep gratitude I have for her kindness. I guess that's what you do for someone you've known for lifetimes!

All I know for sure is that we have a deep love and respect for each other and that those things carry you much further than any of the unscrupulous business tactics so common today. Proving old adages wrong, we got through this trial to remain friends forever. BFFs.

Agony is a part of life in general. Ups and downs. Successes and failures. Loves won and lost loves. It is what makes this world work. The whole of our world is held together by the attraction between positive and negative forces. It's what makes up every atom of every thing in the universe. Without those opposing forces this world would not exist. Could not exist.

Without the agony, that tea leaf would be just another green leaf on just another bush. But, when you pluck it, wither it, process and dry it, it now has the potential to become a lovely, replenishing, health-giving cup of tea. Without the agony of the leaf, without it going through the hot water that extracts its essence, there is no beautifully delicious tea to drink.

So, it is with living. Without those opposing forces, life would be mundane and boring, if it could even happen. Sure, every once in a while we need peace and calm so we don't go off the rails. That's when we meditate, pray, play, walk in the park, or go on vacation. Those sweet, rare moments when everything is in sync, where the stars are in alignment, and all goes well.

But the rest of the time, you get back on that roller coaster of life and ride again. Strap yourself in and hang on. You have only two choices, like my therapist explained. You can dread those scary peaks and cower in fear, and you will lose out on much of the intensity, joy, and experience of life. Or you can decide that you're going to get through, even if you have to scream your bloody head off and enjoy every moment of the ride.

Chapter 7

Selling without Selling One's Soul

One might think that selling a popular commodity like tea would be easy. I thought, at the very least, it should not be terribly difficult. After all, I'd done my research in preparing my business plan. Tea was a *hot* commodity. Increasing sales in leaps and bounds, according to the statistics. And projected to be one of the top-growing commodities in the next ten years.

I had no idea that selling tea in this hot market would be so difficult in my city. It seemed that the entire sixteen years was one struggle after another to try to figure out the magic formula. How to get new customers and build enough of a regular customer base to make a profit and build a solid, adequate clientele in Toledo was a never ending challenge. At times it felt akin to selling ice to polar bears. It seems like it shouldn't have been that difficult.

In retrospective analysis, Toledo's a strange bird when it comes to functioning cities. It's sizable enough, with a population a little over 275,000, so there should certainly be enough people to reach that adequate level of business to sustain. Tea drinkers tend to be of the more cultured lot, and Toledo has one of the country's best art museums, a reasonable symphony, a university, a large network of wonderful metroparks, two large hospital networks, and a fabulous zoo. So, it seemed there should be tons of cultured people and serious tea drinkers.

While there may not be as large a percentage of tea drinkers in a more blue-collar populous, the Jeep plant brings Toledo a strong blue-collar element to add to the potential customer base. It seems that everyone, regardless of education, is interested in the health benefits of tea. And still, with all of that potential, a complicating factor is that Toledo never really recovered from the recession. At least not as well as most other cities its size. Selling the commodities of your dream is particularly difficult here.

At the time of my shop's inception, there was no other specialty tea shop in my town, nor were there any tea rooms. There had been one tiny tea room/antique shop, but it had closed before I'd opened. There were also some ladies who were offering beautiful three-course afternoon teas once a month at a local botanical garden. I'd had the privilege of attending one of their teas, which was held on the Maumee riverfront. It was a lovely tea experience but nothing like what I was planning to do. So, I thought, no real competition, and in actuality we'd complement each other nicely. That's a very good thing.

Little did I know, however, that because tea was such a hot commodity, other plans were in the works besides mine.

Exactly one month before I opened, another contemporary tea shop/small tea room opened about five minutes away from my planned location. Yikes! It wasn't exactly like mine. The décor was ultracontemporary—glass and chrome—with large attractive tea tins displayed all along the focal wall of the shop. It looked inviting, I had to admit.

The similarities between our two shops, other than décor, were astounding. He carried over a hundred quality loose-leaf teas and a nice array of contemporary and classic tea wares. He also filled in the shop with a few other lines, such as bath and body care. His wife made homemade scones, and they had a few tables where you could sit and have tea and scones.

One thing they carried, which I didn't have, was a large selection of fine chocolates. *Oh, no,* I thought, *tea AND chocolates!* They might just have one up on me.

When I first opened, I had all the teas and tea ware, but I also rounded out the retail shop with an assortment of bath and body care, a wide variety of herbal products, books, and sundry other things. So, I thought I might have an edge with about twice the merchandise, which, in my estimation, would keep people in the shop longer. Longer browsing meant potentially greater sales.

Then, the ladies who'd held the lovely afternoon teas at the botanical gardens found a permanent home and opened a Victorian Tea Room named Sweet Shalom, again, in the west end of town. I wasn't really worried about them, as I wanted nothing to do with Victoriana, and their shop was very small and, as in many tea rooms, the tea itself was secondary to the food service. A nod to Sweet Shalom, they served a nice variety of high-quality tea, and know how to properly prepare it. On top of that, their food remains the best I've ever had in any tea room.

Then, another Victorian Tea Room opened in the south end of town. After checking them out, I wasn't too worried about any competition from them. They had little tea to sell, and ladies (primarily) only go to afternoon tea once in a while, so I knew they were no threat to my bottom line. On top of that, their food was nothing to crow about.

Several years in, a Teavana opened in the mall that was—you guessed it—in my end of town, literally just two minutes from my shop. At first I panicked, knowing that they carried a large variety of loose-leaf tea. I had never been to one, so before they'd actually opened in Toledo, we decided to check out the nearest one in a mall outside of Ann Arbor about forty-five minutes away.

My husband and I drove up the following weekend, and after sampling about four teas they had prepared for the day, any worries I'd had about them melted away. Never had I tasted such crappy tea. One sample was a chai. Chai is wonderful and the only tea I drink sweetened. Theirs was so sugary it overpowered the tea altogether and, in my opinion, was unpalatable. All their teas were laden with massive amounts of sugar and fruity flavors. They were targeting the young, don't-know-any-better mall crowd. I thought, *Well, they can have them. I'll keep all the serious tea drinkers.*

I even managed to turn their presence and efforts to expose new, young palates to tea into a benefit for me. Once they had turned on to tea, these people would invariably check out the other sources for tea in town. And once they came into my shop, tasted my samples, and compared my prices, they never went back to Teavana. So, I'd turned this potential threat into a feeder of new business for my shop. Doesn't get much better than that.

Competition aside, the main challenge was always getting enough customers in the doors and getting exposure to new customers to build a sufficient customer base. This, of course, is where traditional advertising comes in.

The greatest challenge in advertising is figuring out what you can do that will be effective but fits in your skimpy budget. Unless you've got lots of money to play with, the typical small-business owner just doesn't have much to work with. The dilemma here is that you can't just keep borrowing more money. Bigger loans mean bigger payments, and big loan payments need enough business income to pay them. Borrowing more money to advertise more, bring in new product, or expand service does not necessarily bring in enough business to cover those bigger loan payments. Catch-22, but always a necessary risk.

Word of mouth is simply not an effective way to get your presence noticed, at least at first. So, in the beginning, before you have a solid customer base, you use your capital to spend on advertising to bring those customers in to make enough sales to pay those loan payments. Sounds like solid thinking, but what happens when you spend on advertising and the customer base doesn't grow enough?

At first I tried some advertising I designed myself. One campaign was a coupon to go in a monthly paper in an upscale neighborhood near the shop. Coupons bring the customers in, right? But no. They didn't. No matter how tempting I made the coupon. I'd purchased a year's worth of advertising, twelve ads, one each month, and I'd tweak it every month to try new enticements to attract some business. In the entire year, I'm not sure I got one—yup, you read that right—not one coupon returned. Other ads I'd placed didn't amount to much either.

I realized I was just out of my league in figuring out all the variables in advertising, so, I bit the bullet and hired an advertising agency. They designed some great ads for me. Several, which didn't even have coupons attached but providing a tidbit on the health benefits of tea, came back to me in the hands of customers saying, "I want some of that."

They tried lots of angles. Health was a good one, quoting some statistics for improving risk of heart disease. Another cute one compared the warmth and quality of our tea room to those special times with Grandma where she carefully cut the crust off your peanut butter-and-jelly sandwiches (because tea sandwiches always have the crust cut off.) It was cute enough; it at least brought a few new customers.

They were wonderful guys to work with, too. Stan was so creative; I looked forward to our monthly planning sessions. He'd probe with many questions to learn all about the product I was trying to sell. We'd come up with an angle for the next ad, and he'd get out his sketch pad to draw out design ideas until we got to what we'd all agree would work. And, he always made sure it was something I liked and was excited about. His demeanor, polish, and knowledge impressed me so much that I always thought, "Gee, this guy could be president someday!"

When all was said and done, comparing what I'd spent each month to what new business I was getting, I wasn't even anywhere near breakeven. Now, I'm the cuckoo bird who went into business with no business degree, but it seemed to me that I couldn't sustain their service if it wasn't even paying for itself, meaning I was at a loss every month for the advertising. After a year, I had to cut them loose.

I decided, like with most every other operational aspect of the shop, it would be much more cost effective to do it myself. Well, in monetary terms. It would cost me greatly in extra workload. Tapping into an already strained energy source wasn't necessarily a great idea, but it was my only alternative to take on the load myself.

I'd learned from the ads the agency designed what made a good ad. I was pretty good at graphic arts, for someone with absolutely no training in it. I couldn't get the same frequency that they were able to provide, but I studied the advertising picture in my area and came up with something just as good.

All the newspaper, or TV or radio station, or magazine marketing reps will tell you that frequency is the key. They quote you statistics on how many times someone has to see an ad for it to enter their brain and actually get them to respond to it. Of course, this is so that they will make more money, but it's also true.

What I did to get around the frequency issue, which was just too costly for me, was that I reasoned that shows like *Oprah* and *Dr. Phil* had the largest viewership by far, so if I advertised just during their shows I'd get more people noticing. Less ads to pay for but more people watching. I surmised that these were the kinds of shows that people watched every day, so I knew the frequency would be effective, not hit and miss like an ad campaign spread out all over the viewing times.

I tried that for a while, and it was as successful in getting new business as the ad agency had been. But again, it was not enough to break even with my costs, although it was a lot closer. I tweaked the programming again when I found that the local station's *AM Saturday* news show got even higher viewership ratings than *Dr. Phil* or *Oprah*. Ads during that program didn't cost much more, but I would only have to run one ad a week instead of five.

We were able to cut costs further by making our own ads. My husband was a videographer for one of the local hospitals, so I was fortunate to be able to take advantage of his skills. I designed, and he did the shooting and editing. I have to say, we came up with some pretty dynamic ads, and the satisfaction of producing them ourselves was another one of those intangible rewards. At least that offset some of the energy drain it added to my workload.

That turned out to be one of my most successful campaigns. I had lots of people come in and mention that they'd seen my ad on the *AM Saturday* show, and I could see that my business was growing.

Finally, I had found something that worked.

Until it didn't.

It seemed that advertising now had a shelf life, so to speak. It only lasted so long and fizzled out. I attributed that to the short attention span most Americans were developing from the overload of advertising with which we are constantly being bombarded. We live in what I call information overload. That causes many people with the frustration of too much incoming information to go into shutdown a lot of the time. Coupled with that, social media platforms like Instagram, Facebook, and especially Twitter have trained some susceptible brains to not be able to comprehend more than small bites of information, as in Twitter's 140 characters at a time. Advertising simply didn't work like it used to.

At that point, I stopped TV and tried radio. It wasn't as costly, and I got an offer from a local radio host to feature me on his show a couple of times a month. He would call me and interview me on the air. It was very personal, and I could give out lots more information than a thirty-second TV spot.

It was very frightening for me at first. I got so nervous on the day Dennis, the show's host, was going to call that I'd almost thrown up. Then, gradually, I got used to it. He was really nice, and an experienced radio interviewer, good at guiding me with the right questions to give me the opportunity to really sell the benefits of tea to his listeners. I got to a point where I would actually look forward to it. Experiencing the growth to become a person now able to speak to a large audience of people—live, no less—was another skill I'd acquired by having my own business.

And it was fun. I remember one interview in particular. The building I was in had a mouse or two living in the walls. We found this out that Christmas when I had hung gingerbread hearts on garland strung along the half wall that framed the tea room. I was sitting at my desk one day where I could see the garland right outside my office door and noticed something funny about the hearts. They all seemed to be missing pieces on the corners. Like little bites had been taken out of them. Holy crap! Growing up on a farm told me what that meant—that we had a critter in the building.

Before we figured out how to evict our resident guest, I was chatting away on the radio with Dennis one day, and my employee, Tanya, started jumping around wildly in the tea room. Her eyes were as wide as saucers, and she was holding her hand tightly over her mouth so she wouldn't scream. Apparently, our little friend had decided to come out in the middle of the day since it was quiet, and of course, at the very same time I was on the air. Thankfully, no customers were in the shop at the time!

Knowing that this was going on in the background and watching Tanya jump up on a chair was hysterical. Life on a farm gave me exposure to all sorts of creatures, and cute little mice just didn't bother me much. It was all I could do to keep a straight face and keep my voice steady throughout the interview.

If I started giggling on air and had to explain that to Dennis and the listening audience, well, it wouldn't have given customers a good impression of our cleanliness. Never mind that it was a mouse that lived in the walls. It'd have been too difficult to explain that while we were absolute sticklers about cleanliness, it was our telemarketing neighbors eating candy, fast food, and pizza all day that brought the pests into the building. Thankfully, I got through it with no one the wiser and considered myself a pro after that.

Dennis lost his show after that, as all things, especially in communications, were changing rapidly at that time. The station closed or got sold, I can't remember. TV was just too expensive for me, and so I went back to print ads to keep up my presence in the retail community. I had another campaign or two that did bring some notice to the shop, but I never again felt that it was worth the dollars.

Until Groupon came along.

The traditionals—TV, radio, print advertisers—were desperate, and kept hounding me. I'd turned marketing rep after rep after rep away, telling them that if they could prove to me that their advertising would at least break even for me, I'd buy. No one, of course, was able to show me. "That's ridiculous!" they'd say. "No one can prove the effectiveness of advertising. It's a risk," they'd say. Guaranteed money was in their pockets, and the risk was all mine. "No, thanks," I'd say.

I got to a point where I'd feel sorry for any advertising rep that walked in my doors. I knew what was coming; they didn't. I felt especially bad when it was some young, gung-ho newbie at their job. I had almost ten years under my belt by this time, and I knew what I was talking about. Traditional advertising, in the small volumes small businesses can afford, just wasn't working anymore, and dollars spent on it were a waste.

Then came Groupon. It was new. It was ingenious, in fact. And best of all, there was no outlay of cash for the business. For those who don't know how Groupon works from the retail side, the retailer offers a product for at least half off. That means that for the most part, I'd be selling things at or near my cost. Out of the 50 percent I'd collected, however, Groupon would take half of that. So, in the end, I was giving something away at less than my cost, about 75 percent off.

But the upside to all of this was multifold. First of all, it was a great advantage not to have that initial outlay of cash. I didn't pay a dime until the customer actually walked in my door to redeem their Groupon. No other advertising had ever worked that way. It was ingenious, and the greatest benefit was that it took the risk factor completely out of the equation.

No other form of advertising ever guaranteed bodies in the door. If the campaign wasn't very successful, and you only had twenty people come in to use the Groupon, you'd only pay for those twenty. Not a great reward, but you got those twenty people in the door, and often they were new customers. Without any risk. I doubt any other advertising I did over the years got twenty people in the door. Seriously.

If you had two hundred people come in, you'd have to pay out more, but you got more new customers in the door. Win-win. That small percentage I'd pay Groupon was a drop in the bucket compared to the cost of every other type of advertising. And, since the customer had already paid for the Groupon up front, the great majority of them came in to redeem their coupon. No other advertising could offer that huge guarantee of business.

If the customer never came in to redeem the Groupon, I still had to pay my 25 percent of the value of the deal, but if they didn't come in, they didn't get the tea they'd already paid for. That product stayed on my shelves to sell to another customer at full price.

There were even more brilliant parameters to this new form of advertising. The greatest advantage was that with bodies actually in the shop, there was always the chance of an upsell. Upsell, meaning that they would buy more merchandise, and at full price. Sure, there were those who would search the shop for as long as it took trying to find something that wasn't a penny over the coupon. I'd set my coupon so that it was $10 worth of tea for $5. I believe my lowest priced bag of tea was $5.35 at that time. So, no one could get it to the penny, and believe it or not, I actually had a couple of ingrates who complained about ($10.70 for two bags of tea) that seventy cents!

Groupon was a great incentive for people to try something new. Another one was that it gave that final push to get into a shop they'd maybe been meaning to go to. That was what clicked for us, and it turned out that the majority of our Groupons were purchased by brand-new customers. That meant we got to expose them to our shop, our quality tea, and all of our wares.

For the Groupon customers, it gave them a chance to really get to know us. While they were tasting the sample, it always led to a conversation on how to properly prepare tea. Lots of people who were new to loose-leaf tea didn't have a way to prepare it. That meant we'd get to show them all the easy, contemporary ways to make tea, and also possibly sell a tea infuser or even a teapot. Upsell accomplished.

What that meant in the long run is that we gained new customers who were now hooked on high-quality loose-leaf tea. Not only did this advertising campaign break even, I *always* made a profit from Groupon. Something NO other advertiser could offer or even come close to providing. Customers in the door, new customers, and repeat business. Triple win!

I did three Groupon campaigns over the next three years. The first one sold about five hundred Groupons, the second sold around three hundred, and the third, about 150. I always made money, and I always got new customers. But, by the third campaign, the problems started to crop up. What is it they say about all good things?

The first glitch was that Groupon got greedy and started to change the way Groupon was originally designed to work. At first the offer was only good for one day. Buy in, or the offer would be lost. And, a set minimum number had to be sold that day, or the Groupon offer wouldn't go through. This put the pressure on to tell others about the great deal you'd found and encourage them to buy into it so that enough would be sold and the deal would go through. In retrospect, I think they realized that wasn't really working. People didn't like being pressured. People also were getting too many emails, and weren't necessarily checking them every day anymore.

So, Groupon quickly changed in response to this, and they'd make the minimums so low that a Groupon would always go through. Next, they extended the time from one day to a week or so to purchase the Groupon. Making those changes were actually beneficial, as it usually resulted in about twice as many Groupons being sold.

The second set of changes is where the greed started to ruin this good thing. Groupons were coupons with an expiration date. You had to redeem them by a certain date, usually a more-than-adequate six months, or they were void. I don't know about other states, but in Ohio, some irresponsible person who couldn't remember to redeem by the due date actually went to the Attorney General and got it made law in Ohio that these coupons had to be honored *after* the due date for the amount they paid. In perpetuity.

I didn't have to give them $10 worth of tea anymore, but the state had deemed that they could never lose their $5 they originally paid, redeemable in merchandise any time after the due date had passed. The difficulty for me was that I now had to keep the records on all Groupons forever.

Sometimes years after the campaign, someone would

come in and want to use the Groupon, which they'd usually lost their copy of. I'd have to dig through all of the records to be able to keep track of it all. That was quite a nightmare for me, with hundreds of Groupons over three campaigns. All over $5 that adults could not be responsible enough to redeem within the ample six-month period.

I even had one person insist on using the coupon after I'd closed the shop. They also went to the Ohio Attorney General's office—over $5! When the AG's office contacted me, I explained that the Groupon was an advertising campaign for my brick and mortar shop, now closed, not my online business. They let the customer know that this time, it was simply too late.

Then Groupon started offering lots and lots of other coupons, not just local businesses. In their greed, they lost the power they once had in an ingenious and highly effective advertising tool.

I saw the diminishing numbers with each successive campaign. Within three campaigns, I'd exhausted the local area of those potential new customers interested in tea. And so, as with other forms of advertising that reached their effective limit, Groupon had burned out as well. I sadly stopped using it altogether.

They say all publicity is good publicity, even if it's bad. Publicity, being where someone else talks or writes about you, and so, your name gets out there, and it's a real bonus when it's free! Over the years, I had many articles written about the shop in local papers and in some national publications.

The local newspaper gave me lots of free publicity when my sign fiasco was going on with the city inspectors. They tried to paint me as an "offender" and one who wanted to skirt the rules. But I always had the support of the customers.

They wanted my sign up so that they could spot the shop easier and could clearly see that it was causing no harm. I even got a photo of me by the sign in question in our major newspaper. That was great. I smiled ear to ear.

The local rag also had a great cartoonist who made a cartoon about the sign issue in Toledo. He joked about the "Toledo" way to get signage up in front of your shop. First panel—city says "no" to your sign. Second panel—buy an old van on the cheap that doesn't run. Third panel—have it towed to your location. Fourth panel—paint your business name on the side and claim it's a service vehicle for your business. Voila! You have a sign so folks can find you. They just kept reminding people about my sign issues, and it kept my shop name center of attention without a dime from me. All good.

An article the local paper had done early on listed my shop as one of the businesses that received loan money from the city to start my business. The gist of the article was that some businesses were not a good risk for the city's money. Most other businesses mentioned were late on loan payments or left the city stranded with simply not repaying the loan. The genius writer seemed to think I, a humble, harmless tea shop who always made her loan payments on time, belonged on this "unworthy" list because we "dabbled in the occult."

How did we accomplish that feat, you ask? Well, apparently the lighthearted, fun tea leaf readings we'd held a couple of times was "dabbling in the occult." I'm not sure how that put the city in any measure of risk of not getting their money back, but there you have it. No matter, I thought. More sweet free publicity.

By far, most of the publicity I got was on the positive side. I got two wonderful articles published in major magazines: *Midwest Living* and *Business Week.*

Out of the blue one day I'd gotten a call from a freelance writer that was hired to write an article on tea in the Midwest. The focus was on tea room menus because they always have elaborate presentations of a variety of finger foods and desserts. We got our "Pretty Little Tea Sandwiches" and "Lavender

Lemonade" recipes printed in the article with beautiful photos of our heart-shaped tea sandwiches. Well, not *our* sandwiches, but ones like it that they had prepared in their kitchens.

I even got quoted a couple of times throughout the article, and that was fun to see. The best thing about it was that being a Midwest publication, I knew it would reach an audience that was outside the immediate local area, but within a reasonable distance to visit the shop.

I tried so many other methods to get new customers through my doors. It seemed I'd exhausted every single type of traditional marketing, so I started to get really creative. I was open to any new idea, effort, or scheme that I thought would bring in new tea drinkers.

With a degree in education, teaching others about tea came naturally to me. Every customer that walked in the door learned something about tea that they did not know before. When I decided to offer tea tasting classes that gave me a chance to go into greater depth on history, production, processing, varieties, health benefits, and of course, I could demonstrate the proper way to make a perfect cup of tea.

That's when I decided to design the first tea tasting journal. The idea was borne out of my tea tasting classes. If someone took the series of three, they would taste twenty-four teas in all, and that was a lot of tea to keep track of. And I knew there were lots of serious tea drinkers out of local reach who might love a way to keep a diary of their tea impressions.

How to accomplish this was the first hurdle. I didn't think I'd get a publisher to publish such a thing, so I examined every angle of self-publishing I could find. Most of the self-publishing, publish-your-own-book online sources were so costly that I knew that wouldn't work either.

I looked into local print shops. I found that it wasn't that much to get a ring-bound item printed, like a small book of department policies some business might want printed for employees. So, I thought, ring-bound is OK, especially for a journal you want to lay flat for writing.

I asked if it had to be eight and a half by eleven, and they said it could only be that full page or a half page. Great! The half page was the size of most trade books, so that would work.

Next, I found that the cover and backing could be printed on the heaviest card stock, giving them some strength, and I could also add a plastic protective cover over the front and back. And, since this was a journal to be written in, I could get it printed on heavier paper than the usual book so that the writing would not bleed through to the other side. Perfect!

The very first formatted tea journal in print. Ta da.

It still ended up costing enough, with over two hundred pages in all, that I had to charge $19.95 for the journal. I didn't think that was a bad price point, and most people didn't bat a lash. But, of course, there's always one complainer. Someone somewhere in the internet ethers actually called me to ream me on the phone, demanding to know why this journal cost so much! Sigh. There's always one.

Besides just being a formatted tea journal, however, the first twenty or so pages included what I call my "tea primer." It is a compact and concise packet of information containing all the basics one might need to know if they were just starting out to investigate the fascinating world of tea. So, the journal could be used by novice and connoisseur alike. Thinking especially of the experienced tea geek, I included pages of official tea tasting terms that are used on the tea estates. Words like vegetal, earthy, astringent, metallic, and brassy.

I sold a number of journals to people taking the tea tasting classes, of course, and have had orders from across the country from those serious tea snobs. Many were as gifts for a serious tea drinking friend, which I felt was very thoughtful. I would chuckle when they asked me to inscribe it to their friend. A strange new experience for a new writer.

There have been a few other journals that have popped into existence since then, but it was a real feather in my cap to be the first one ever in print.

I thought having some credentials would add some weight and credibility to my teaching, so I signed up for a course in becoming a Certified Tea Master. I was able to Skype with the instructor, which saved me some travel and accommodations costs, but the program was still quite expensive. It was structured so that we met online once a week for several weeks and tasted a number of teas each time. There was a packet of information that came with the teas, but I found that there was not much, other than a brief description of the Gong Fu tea ceremony, that I didn't already know.

By the time we got to the end, I was feeling more than a little cheated. After all, the course deemed itself one in tea mastery, but it was mostly full of things I'd already learned on my own. The final "test" was to identify a mystery tea. I knew from looking at the leaf what it probably was, and one taste confirmed that it was a tea called White Monkey Paw. It was actually one that I carry and is one of my personal favorites. So, I "passed" the course with flying colors, but added little to my knowledge of tea. I did have a shiny $1200 brass pin that says I'm a Certified Tea Master, though.

I decided that I wanted to share my tea knowledge with a wider audience. I looked into any group that would have me speak. I have presented at senior assisted-living centers, talking about how tea can help keep you younger. I spoke at a local metropark to a group of volunteers the park was thanking for their service. I've spoken to groups while they enjoyed their own version of afternoon tea, such as libraries, charity groups, church groups, hospitals, and women's centers. All of this could potentially bring me new customers.

With the smaller groups, I was able to also do a mini tea tasting. I would take three teas to sample and that greatly enhanced my lecture. Right away, the group would get to experience the difference between the teas and also taste a properly prepared, good-quality tea. There are many people that have never had anything but tea bag tea, and when they experience their first taste of high-quality loose-leaf tea, it's an eye opener.

One of the most fun things I got to do was go on that Saturday morning news show I used to advertise with. It's one thing to talk in front of groups of thirty to a hundred people, but it's another thing to speak in front of a camera on the most watched TV show in the area. Talk about nerves! I was always shaking in my boots, but somehow managed to come across like I knew my stuff, which I did, of course. I got to show the whole community things like what quality tea leaves look like and how to prepare a proper cup of tea. Those opportunities were worth all the tea in China to me. (OK, I had to work that phrase in just once, didn't I?)

The pinnacle of my speaking engagements was when I had the opportunity to be one of the speakers at my doctor's yearly integrative medicine conference. He arranged speakers who talked on many different aspects of natural, alternative practices for health.

I'd approached my doctor about being able to set up a table at the conference. I knew they usually cost a thousand or two (easily paid for by pharmaceutical companies), but he knew I could not afford such costs. I convinced him that more people needed to know about the health benefits of tea, and I could do that by setting up an informational table outside the conference. He agreed, and thankfully offered that as long as I was giving away something for free, such as tea samples, I could have the table for free!

It was a lot of work to figure out how to prepare tea on the spot for a couple hundred people all day long. So, I took a couple of very quick heating hot-water urns, bagged up hundreds of teas, usually in three flavor choices, got a stack of paper cups, and was able to offer a cup of tea on the spot to anyone who wanted to taste!

After that first year, he was impressed enough with my knowledge of tea and health that he asked me to be a speaker! He knew I was very well-informed in tea, but since it was a medical conference, it was also a requirement that I had a medical degree of some sort. Thankfully, I have a degree in medical technology, and that worked to give me credibility with the audience of medical practitioners.

That was great advertising for my shop and my product. Free, in the sense that there was no outlay of cash required, but I can't begin to count the hours of preparation I put into each of the three lectures I'd give over the years. Still, I enjoyed it. It gave me a chance to use my science education, tie it in with my tea business, and get the word out to more potential customers. A win-win-win, for sure.

There were many print advertising schemes over the years that proved to be a waste of money. The backs of grocery coupons are hardly ever noticed. The frequency you need for print ads to be noticed is far beyond the budget of most small businesses. I'd learn what not to do next time, but was always searching for something fresh and new that might actually work to bring customers through the door or to my website.

In the search for new and fresh, there is always a certain measure of risk. Generally you put the money out with just a phantom promise of return on your investment. Never any guarantees. Sometimes you hit on success, at least a measure of it that made the venture worthwhile. And, sometimes life hands you very tough, very costly lessons.

One of mine was a potential advertising venture that sounded good, and I would be getting in on the ground floor of something new and exciting. The company was a new search engine called LeapFish. The campaign involved paying a certain ad fee to be guaranteed to come up in the first page whenever people searched for your keywords.

The internet had exploded from Yahoo into Google and on to other search engines like Bing! LeapFish sounded cool and trendy. It was a gamble. If it didn't take off and no one used it, it wouldn't be of much use. If it did, it could be huge. The cost was near $3000 as I recall, and I debated over it for a long time. And finally decided to take the plunge.

And that's what it turned out to be—a plunge. Down into the recesses of some lost netherworld. After all their hype, it never took off. After they had my money, they were almost impossible to contact and within a year had mostly disappeared.

A few years later, when apparently there were lots of people who had been burned by this disreputable gang, I got an email on a possible class action suit. I followed up and sent my information in, but nothing must have come of it as I never heard a peep about any compensation for losses.

That was a tough one. I was a bit wiser after that, and made my mind up to never again be tempted and taken in by another questionable scheme like that.

Marketing is an engaging and complex art, and much of it was sheer fun for me. It required my digging deep and finding the absolute limits of my artistry. Sometimes, it was a pressured situation, which took a bit of the fun out. Always there was that underlying worry: *Is this going to bring me new customers? Is it effective? Strong enough? Clever enough? Will it work?*

But it was always linked to my artist, giving me an intensely satisfying outlet for my creativity. That's another reason why we're here, I think. To be creative in the expression of ourselves. It's the antidote to a boring, tedious life. It is in our creativity that we express the fullness of our existence. Good news is, it's unlimited and endless.

Chapter 8

The Artistry of Tea and Retail

My most joyful moments in life have been when I was using my creativity and exercising the right side of my brain. Never am I more satisfied than when designing something new. The shop gave me massive opportunities to do just that. Marketing requires artistry to be sure, but here I'm also talking about creating the entire infrastructure of the shop. From the very beginning, just refining the whole idea was like taking a blank canvas and ending up with a beautiful painting.

There were all these creative decisions to make. What did I want the shop to look like? What would be its character? How would I decorate? What kind of fixtures would I use, and how would it all fit together? What would be my name? What kind of logo did I want? Art class was perhaps my favorite in school, and this was like living in art class.

I knew I favored the French country look. So, I decided that would be the shop's character. Everything was painted white and hunter green. Old, rustic tables and hutches worked, and were less expensive than most retail fixtures I'd seen in catalogs or online. Since the original shop had an herbal theme as well, I stenciled herbs everywhere. On the backs of the arched wooden chairs for the tea room. On the sides of hutches and bookcases. It really did take on a rustic charm.

Herbal wreaths and prints filled in the wall spaces between small decorative shelving units where we displayed merchandise.

Since the fictional herbalist monk Cadfael was our namesake in the beginning, I created a Cadfael corner. I'd found an old primitive wooden wheelbarrow and rustic mixing bowls, those very old gardening scissors that just pinch two large blades together, and lots of hanging dried herb bundles. It looked like you were stepping back into Cadfael's garden shed.

In that space I placed all the Cadfael merchandise. There were the books, on which the PBS series was based, that were written by Ellis Peters, the pen name of the English author Edith Mary Pargeter, OBE, BEM. I also carried videos (Yes, that was before the advent of DVDs.) from the PBS series. I filled out the corner with other books on herbs and herbal blends for potpourri and aromatherapy.

I framed an old herbal pamphlet that had a monk on the cover holding those same old garden scissors that were perched on the table as part of the decor. To fill out another empty wall space, I printed up the story of the character Cadfael, for those who were not familiar with the series. I printed another page with information about the author, as I knew most people were unfamiliar with her as well. To give these two pieces a monkish character, I used textured mat board cut in an arched shape and mounted the stories inside. So, it was like looking through two windows in some old monastery.

I was so touched when one of my customers who'd patronized the shop since the very beginning and was an avid Cadfael fan, came on the last day and asked if there was any way I'd sell her those two prints. Of course I did. It was just so wonderful that someone would so fondly remember the shop for a long time to come.

To complement the shop with other herb-related items, I included bath and body care and candles infused with natural herbal fragrances, and a line of herbal teas, tinctures, oils, creams, and sprays that were targeted toward natural solutions for medical conditions. So, there were herbal teas, capsules, and tinctures that could help you relax and sleep or perk you up. Ease your stomach and promote good digestion. Get you through a cold. Keep bugs away. Promote good kidney and liver function. And, of course, help your weight-loss efforts.

But the bulk of the shop had become the teas and tea ware. When I sent for my first samples of loose-leaf tea, I was taken aback by how many there were now available. Hundreds, in just this one catalog. As I'd mentioned before, I hadn't had good loose-leaf tea in years, and when I tasted these treasures, I was totally smitten. So, while I had maybe a dozen healthful herbal teas, I had over a hundred regular teas. There were even simply flavorful herbals, namely Rooibos, that I'd never heard of, which got added to the collection. Turns out that Rooibos is loaded with antioxidants too, so it is as healthful as it is tasty.

There was so much to learn about tea. There were so many varieties available. Most people in the US at that time were only familiar with black tea, as in English Breakfast and had probably heard of green tea but most likely had never tasted one. And maybe they'd heard of oolong, but most didn't know that they'd already been drinking it whenever they dined at a Chinese restaurant. So, I jumped onto the learning curve and made it my goal to bring all this goodness and variety in tea to as many people as I could.

One of the best resources for a retailer is trade shows. I soon found out that there is one specifically for tea: The World Tea Expo. My husband and I went to it for years. It was a great source for vendors, and I got to meet people from all around the world. They have educational sessions, and a few of them actually did fill in some tea information for me. But, some of them were not very informative, and in some, even though presented by well-known names in the tea biz, information was actually inaccurate. I suppose they really had no control over that, but when you see these folks back repeatedly, it's a bit disappointing.

It was a great resource though, especially for tea. Most of the vendors were tea merchants, and I found several new tea sources that way. It was a divine experience for a tea enthusiast. All the vendors had samples, so there were hundreds of teas to taste. At breaks in between sessions, tea was served in the large waiting area. It was a great way to meet some other people in the tea biz, and also to meet some of the big names in tea you see floating around on the internet. So, it was a fun and worthwhile experience until we'd been so many times that there wasn't enough new to satisfy my curiosities or justify the costs.

I learned everything I could so that I could talk about tea to any audience that would listen. I especially liked it in small groups like church ladies' teas or retirement homes. I usually did tea tastings along with the talk, and so got to expose a whole new audience to really good-tasting tea. That was a goal of mine, since so many people had only experienced tea bag tea, which is of the lowest quality, overbrews too quickly, and simply doesn't compare in taste to loose-leaf tea.

There were so many other things to be decided on besides the tea collection. The majority of merchandise consisted of various kinds of tea ware. There was so much more fun tea prep paraphernalia available now than just teapots and the traditional tea balls. It seemed like every time I got a new catalog or found a new tea vendor, there was a new tea gadget.

Starting with the teapot, which of course came in all the traditional shapes made out of porcelain, was usually bone china with floral designs or the solid colored classic squat shape as in the traditional brown betty, made of heavy clay which keeps tea warmer than other pots. Sadly, some of the bone china factories have gone out of business, as a taste for more contemporary pots reduces the number of people collecting and using bone china.

Bone china tea sets seem to have gone out of fashion,
replaced in popularity by limitless colorful and
quirky contemporary designs.

Then there are many contemporary variations with more
modern botanical, geometric, wildlife, or abstract designs.
They come in everything from the classic teapot shape to
every design imaginable. I've carried teapots that are square,
triangular, pots with a hole in the middle, pots that look like
butterflies, bumble bees, flowers, strawberries, lemons, apples,
teddy bears, cats, dogs, rabbits, squirrels, acorns, monkeys,
dragons, ducks, owls, fish, frogs, birds, and even toasters. You
get the idea. Pretty much unlimited variety.

Asian teapots were traditionally either porcelain or clay,
and the cast iron pots are as classic as it gets. Other materials are now employed and you see teapots made from steel
and glass added to the contemporary assortment. Yixing teapots from China are made from a special purple clay and are
works of art. Some well-known Yixing artist's pots are valued
in the tens of thousands. They can be quite plain in design,
but often incorporate botanical or animal themes. The pinnacle in design are those that are elaborate depictions of dragons where the tea pours from the mouth.

For a very long time, there were only two options for tea
preparation: putting the tea directly into the pot, or using a
tea ball. Putting the tea in the pot ends up having bitter, over-
infused tea if you don't decant every drop in the first pour.

Tea balls confine the leaf so may not be extracting the most flavor, and they are a pain to use. That's why, as with many people, even though I had discovered the pleasures of loose-leaf tea in my twenties, I got frustrated with tea balls and went back to the convenience of tea bags. The mistake in that choice is great loss of quality, flavor, and variety.

Infuser baskets are the best for ease of use and work for just one cup or mug, or a whole pot of tea.

By the time I'd sent for the first tea vendor catalog, I realized there was a whole new tea culture out there. There were now many clever new ways to prepare tea, all designed to make the process easier. First of all, there were open tea bags you could fill with loose-leaf tea. Just staple the bag shut and use a spoon to retrieve it from the cup or pot, and you still have the convenience of something disposable. Some clever vendor even came up with a clip on chain to make dunking these self-filled tea bags as easy as the ones with the string stapled on.

My personal favorite infusion method is the infuser basket. Basically it is a deep wire mesh or metal basket with lots of tiny holes. It is usually about three inches deep with wings of some sort so that it sits on top of a mug, cup, or the opening of a teapot. It will often come with a drip plate to set the infuser on in between cups. Loose-leaf teas have some staying power and most can be reinfused two to four times from the same leaf.

There were new versions of the tea ball but with many variations on the theme. It is popular now to make them out of some material that will stand up, giving the user something to hold on to with more substance than the traditional chain. One of the main problems with the traditional tea ball was that the chain had a penchant for falling in your cup or pot. The chain usually had a hook on it so that it could be hooked around the handle of a mug or teapot so that it didn't fall in. But, sometimes it still managed to unhook and slip in, and then had to be fished out. The newer versions have solved the problem, and are easier to open, load, and clean out since many of them open at the top instead of being hinged in the middle. One clever design had a plunger that when you pushed the plunger on the end, it caused the ball to open up. Some are still made of metal, but the newer silicone ones that came in lots of fun shapes, colors, and designs were a customer favorite.

There were several ingenious new contraptions for making tea that were not exactly teapots and not just another infuser gadget but something quite unique. There was one particularly clever device that was a flask of sorts to hold the water and tea leaves. The bottom of the flask had holes in it that were closed off while the tea was infusing. Then, when time was up, you put the flask on top of your mug and that depressed the bottom plate to open up the holes. Perfectly prepared tea then dripped into your mug. When you lifted the device, again, the holes automatically closed off. No dripping! Tea leaves could stay right in the flask until you added more water for a second brew. Ingenious.

One contemporary teapot of sorts was a glass pot that sat in a metal frame. It had a metal lid that had a knob at the top attached to a post that was then attached to an infuser basket that sat under the lid. When the hinged post was pulled up and turned on its side, the basket nested completely under the lid. When you lifted the post and let it drop through the hole, it lowered the basket down into the hot water. So, the beauty was that when infusion time was up, you could lift the basket and pour yourself a cup of tea and what was left in the pot would not overbrew since the leaves were no longer sitting in the tea water.

The best contemporary method, which I liked so much we made all tea in the tearoom with it, was the French press. It was another device where the leaves stay right in the pot, so no dripping basket to contend with. That was convenient for our tea service, but I had many customers who were disappointed that they didn't get a traditional teapot when they sat for tea in the tearoom. We stuck to our guns on that one, insisting that we were not a Victorian tearoom, but a contemporary one. We exposed lots of people to this great method of tea preparation and consequently sold more tea presses than probably any other tea shop in the country.

The only problem with the press was that all the tea had to be decanted or what remained in the pot would still overbrew and become bitter, even though the leaves were pressed to the bottom under the mesh screen. This is not a problem when making coffee in a French press, but tea is a much more finicky beverage. We solved that for the most part by having two different sizes of presses, so that most of the tea would decant in the first pour, depending on the number of people.

One company solved the problem of tea's proclivity for bitterness if left in hot water too long with an improved design of the press. They actually devised twisting plates on top of the mesh filtering screen, so that when it was plunged down after infusion, the plates could be turned to close off the filter, thus separating the leaves from the water. Perfect tea every time, and you didn't have to pour it all off any more.

So, with the vast variety of teapots and a never-ending parade of innovative loose-leaf tea gadgets, the merchandise filled the shop with lots to peruse for both novice and tea connoisseur alike. We were *the* destination spot for the latest, best tea prep gear and for great gifts for tea-drinking family and friends.

There was never-ending opportunity for creativity in arranging all these tea wares for display. I'd learned some basic principles of display from my stint at the bookstore, and it was always a fun day when the manager asked me to rework a display table for an upcoming holiday. It was pure joy for me to have a whole shop to arrange displays for from scratch.

The framework for the overall design of the retail area was five old farmhouse tables. The look of them fit perfectly with the French country theme. Then, I'd found these old tiered plant stands, which had perfect sized shelves for teapots. It got the merchandise up off the flat tables and at eye level and made for much more interesting displays. That was a key element in a good display that I'd learned from bookstore days. It took a lot of searching, but I eventually had one for each table, so it worked beautifully to create that one-of-a-kind presentation of merchandise.

Teapots and larger merchandise would sit on these slatted plant stands with no problem, but smaller items would fall through. So, I solved that problem with having acrylic pieces cut to size for each shelf, providing a flat, stable perch for whatever filled in the design of the display. And, a doily on each shelf added that touch of vintage we carried throughout the shop.

In other spaces where I needed just a bit of height and depth to a display, I'd use acrylic display stands to provide the needed tiering effect. I never seemed to have enough of those, and they were, for some odd reason, an expensive commodity. So, I got creative. I'd find a box with the size and depth I needed. I'd cover it with brown kraft paper and add some pretty ribbon around the edges to give it a more polished look. These worked really well, and had them in all shapes and sizes scattered across the shop.

Those five tables with the tiered plant stands formed the backbone structure for each of my four shops. With each move, I'd be in a real tizzy at first. All my merchandise scattered around in boxes and large garbage bags, and all the fixtures—

shelves, benches, hutches, racks, bookcases—piled around. It was daunting to the point of near panic.

So, first I'd clear the retail space. Everything got moved out, or at least over to the sides or corners, so I could get a feel for the cleared retail area. Then, I'd take those five tables and move them around the space until all of a sudden, in each subsequent move, they'd fall into perfect placing, perfect balance, and provide that skeletal structure for the shop. From there it was easy. I just filled in the spaces in between with what was left. Each shop had its own unique character and design, but the basic character of Elaine's Tea carried through to each new space.

There were so many fun ways to display merchandise. Every bit of floor space that wasn't part of an aisle that needed to be kept clear for walking through the shop was filled with some table, chair, bench, bookshelf, cart, bin or basket. And when we ran out of floor space, we went up. We hung wind chimes, birdhouses in the shape of teapots, and other garden art from the ceiling. It added dimension to the shop, and the small space was filled with loads of wares to peruse.

Arranging merchandise for
display was one of my favorite jobs.

If doing display work wasn't satisfying enough, I'd fill much of the rest of my time with creating all the graphic design needed for the shop. That started with the signs outside and moved inside to wherever any signage was needed for the shop. I made wooden signs with vinyl lettering for each of the tea sections: Black Tea, Green Tea, Oolong, White Tea, & Herbal Tisanes.

I can't count the number of times someone would ask what tisanes meant. It's just the French word for an herbal infusion. "Tea" really only comes from the drink prepared from the Camellia sinensis tea bush. But, over time, we've come to call almost any hot beverage prepared from plants other than coffee or cocoa *tea*. I preferred the correct term: *tisane*. Using that always gave me a chance to educate customers, another thing I loved to do.

I'd put small signage wherever needed to explain something about a product, list the price, or point out something new or a product that had been put on sale. Being cheap, err . . . I mean frugal, I'd simply print out a label on regular paper, cut it out to size, and "laminate" it with clear, wide shipping tape. It might not have been as professional as something from a print shop, but it cost me nothing but my time and ingenuity. And, I got the benefit of pure creative enjoyment to boot.

Sometimes, I'd find a stash of specialty paper that I'd used for some previous project and find that the shop graphics looked even better printed on that. Punch a hole in the top of it, put a ribbon through and tie it on a basket handle, and voila! A pretty display is created.

Early on, I'd purchased some acrylic easels that could be loaded with a sheet of paper saying anything you wanted. They were pricey too, but well worth it. Over the years, I can't tell you how much use I got out of those easels. They were quick and easy to change for wherever needed: in the shop, at speaking engagements, and events where I set up a booth with merchandise and information.

In the beginning, when I still had capital to draw upon, I used a local print shop to help design a trifold brochure with all the basic information about the shop: hours of operation, phone number, what we carried, tea and food menu, and other services and events. It cost a lot, and within a year or two, I could no longer carry that expense.

With a vast variety of graphic design abilities readily available on every computer, I found a template on mine that was trifold just like the one from the print shop, and began to design my own. The beauty of it was that I could print up in small batches as needed and make changes on a dime. With the print shop, I'd have to order 1000 at a time, and they'd go to waste when something significant changed, like my address after the first move. I really liked having the flexibility, and it made it easy to add a new tea to the menu, change my hours, or announce additions of new services.

Two of my brochure designs.
Once I started designing myself, changes were easy.

I designed my own business cards, flyers to announce an event, and postcards that told of our next move. I loved helping educate people about tea, and so all my little educational flyers were easy to print and distribute. The cornerstone was one on how to make a proper cup of tea. I eventually made it into a large postcard, color coded for each tea type and attractive enough to mount in your kitchen. Another important handout was on the health benefits of tea. The most frequent questions at every tea talk I gave were on health benefits. I made more detailed fliers that I could pass out at my tea lectures and classes with info on the types and varieties of tea, history of tea, tea leaf grading, the production of tea, and tea rituals. PS, all of this info is available on the website (wildorchidteas.com), if you're interested.

Tea Prep Guidelines — Elaine's wild orchid teas

419-885-1515
wildorchidteas.com

Tea Type	Tea Leaf/8ozCup	Water Temp	Infusion Time
BLACK Teas			
Traditional Black	1 rounded teaspoon	195-208° F	3-5 minutes
Darjeeling	1 rounded teaspoon	190-195° F	3 minutes
Pu-erh	Quarter sized portion	195-208° F	3-5 minutes
GREEN Teas			
Chinese Green	1 rounded teaspoon	175-185° F	1.5-2 minutes
Japanese Green	1 rounded teaspoon	175-185°	2-3 minutes
Matcha	1/2 teaspoon	170-180°	Stir 30 seconds–1 min.
WHITE Teas			
Chinese Silver Needle / White Tip	1 heaping teaspoon	185° F	2-3 minutes
Ceylon White Tip	1 heaping teaspoon	185° F	3-5 minutes
Traditional or Flavored Whites	1 heaping teaspoon	185° F	3-4 minutes
HERBAL Teas			
Floral / Leaf Herbal Blends	1-2 teaspoons	195-208° F	3-5 minutes
Fruited Tisanes	1-2 teaspoons	195-208° F	3 minutes
Medicinal Herbals	2-3 heaping teaspoons	208-212° F	10-15 minutes
OOLONG Teas			
Lightly Oxidized Jade Oolong	1 rounded teaspoon	180-190° F	1.5-2 minutes
Medium– Dark Amber Oolong	1 rounded teaspoon	190-195° F	2-3 minutes
Bai Hao (white tip) Oolong	1 heaping teaspoon	185° F	3 minutes
SPECIAL Teas			
Rooibos	1 rounded teaspoon	195-208° F	5-10 minutes
Yerba Mate	1-2 rounded teaspoons	Moisten cold, 150-185° F	3 minutes
Flowering Tea	1 pod / 4-6 cup pot	175-185° F	Until fully Blossomed

With each creation I got better and better at graphic arts. I got to know how to create a certain look or feel. I found fonts that were unusual but conveyed the right mood. I became very good at finding free clip art to add color and enhance visual interest.

Toward the end, my main mode of communication with customers was through a monthly newsletter. It was challenging but always got my creative juices going, and I could have it put together in a day or two if time got tight. Each month I'd announce new products, upcoming events, and special sales. I'd always include a blurb on the latest news in tea & health. And of course, it was a great way to make sure my regular customer base followed me to my next location after each of my moves.

It's funny, but no matter how hard you try, some people just aren't paying attention. Before my last move, I knew for a long time that we'd be moving, so I started letting people know months in advance. And, for at least six months after moving, mentioned our "newest" location in every newsletter. About a year later, a woman came in who had been a regular customer, but I had not seen her in quite a while.

She exclaimed, "So this is where you are! I'm so glad to have finally found you!" I told her that she should sign up for the newsletter, so she would always know what's going on with the shop. Her reply: "Oh, I'm on your newsletter list. I just don't read my emails anymore!" Disheartening. Not much you can do if people won't read.

Decorating the shop for each holiday season was a good way to freshen up displays, add a festive atmosphere to the shop, and come up with new gift ideas to sell. Springtime with Easter was a good time to feature floral teas. Autumn, Halloween, and Thanksgiving were filled with Pumpkin and Spice. Valentine's Day was a great time for us to make custom baskets with teas like Lover's Rose and heart-shaped compressed teas.

The Christmas season was the longest and most fun. It was also the time when small retail brings in about one-quarter of their revenues for the year. So, coming up with creative tea gift baskets and tea samplers was a must.

I'd found a small box of bindi tins that I thought would make a perfect tea sampler pack. Bindi tins are little round tins about an inch or two across with a clear glass lid. They are used by Hindu women to store the little dots (bindi) that they place on their foreheads just above and between the eyebrows at the point of the third eye chakra. These little tins are also used to store tiny watchmakers' parts and work exceptionally well because of the see-through lids. Because of that, they also were perfect for a tea sampler.

Sampler packs were popular year round for gift giving.

I ordered the size that would hold just enough tea leaf for three samples of each tea type. I'd number each tin on the bottom and printed out a chart with the name of each tea and placed it on the inside of the pack lid, similar to what you'd find in a box of mixed chocolates. The outer pack was made out of the same metal that the tins were made of, so it made for a unique and sturdy sampler pack. I made an attractive label for the outer cardboard box with an old world map faded in the background. It was perfect for those tea treasures that came from all around the world. I'd finish them off with different ribbons and, voila! I had an exclusive tea sampler. Others have copied it since, which I guess is a testament to the success of my idea. I'd sell out almost every Christmas.

One of the most innovative things I did was a creative twist on a rewards punch card, which I had put in place for a free cup of tea after seven cups and punches. I'd run across a Coffee Coin online and thought it was the coolest thing. It was a ceramic coin a little over an inch in diameter with the coffee coin logo on the front and a sticker on the back with boxes to be stamped with each purchase since it couldn't be punched.

I called the company and asked them if they would be willing to make a coin for tea shops. They had to make some minor changes in the coin front, but the back stamp sticker was the same. They said yes, and said they would make a Tea Coin for me!

As well as the points coin, they also had coins that could be of any denomination, where the coins could be used to replace a paper gift certificate. So, I also ordered coins in $5.00, $10.00, and $25.00 amounts. I figured that would allow customers to buy gift coins in any amount they desired.

The tea coins were a novelty and big hit with customers.

It worked! It was like giving so much more than a paper gift certificate, or even a gift card, which is so popular today. I had little muslin pouches I'd put the coins in, so it was like getting a little bag of money. Customers loved them.

I used those for many years, until I'd had enough breakage

that I started running out of some coins. I'd also found that an employee had given some to a friend that had not been paid for, so that kind of soured me on the whole idea. I decided to discontinue them and go back to a paper punch card and numbered gift certificates where I could keep better track of sales. Sadly, those are the kinds of measures you have to take to prevent loss.

I gave ample notice to customers through shop signage and our monthly newsletter that the coins had been discontinued but could still be redeemed. I did accept them until I closed, and again tried to let customers know that by the closing date all gift certificates and coins had to be redeemed. But wouldn't you know, someone contacted me months after closing and wanted to use a couple of coins he'd found in a drawer, years after they had been purchased. There was no way to do that in an online situation, and it would have been nice if the customer had understood. After all, he'd had years to redeem them. But, of course, he didn't. I think he'd also contacted someone from the state government, but when I explained that the shop was closed, there was nothing to be done. It's sad how irresponsible some people have become.

The coins were one of the more ingenious things I'd done for the shop, and turned out to be a marketing boon. I sold more gift coins than I'd ever sold paper gift certificates. There was just something so appealing and tangible about them that made people want to buy them. I think one or two loyal customers even kept a few as mementos. How cool is that?

Holding special events in the shop was a great way to get people into the shop and expose them to a deeper understanding of tea and its many benefits. I began with tea tastings, where participants got to taste eight different teas, properly prepared. I'd been offering classes on anything related to tea, including my four-part tea tasting course. I started to come up with other classes, not necessarily related to tea, just for fun. That sometimes brought in regulars who were looking for a bit of entertainment, something different to do. And often they would bring a friend, which in turn, got that new body into the shop.

My tea tasting classes were by far the most popular, and became a mainstay marketing tactic. It created those valued "regulars" who now knew good tea, came back often, and were adventurous enough to try something new from time to time.

The tea tastings were actually divided up into a series of four classes over four weeks, or sometimes the last two were combined into one. The first was always on black tea, which seemed the basis for the western world of tea drinkers. Lipton or Red Rose tea bags, or English Breakfast, the most common tea offered in restaurants, was the extent of the tea that many people had ever experienced, and that was all black tea.

Tea Tasting classes were always fun and a great way to introduce customers to the world of tea.

My class exposed them to so much more. That first taste of quality loose-leaf tea, properly prepared, brought many surprised smiles. First and foremost, I always taught them how to prepare tea. Most tea, besides being of low quality which greatly affects the flavor, is made too strong or infused too long. Water temperature is also important to the true tea snob who insists on enjoying the best flavor out of each cup they drink.

They would come to understand the main growing regions and what flavor notes each tea from each region should have. Assams from India are malty, Indian Darjeelings have a classic muscatel note, Keemuns from China are grapey and can even have hints of dark chocolate, and Sri Lankan Ceylons are light and smooth with almost no astringency. English Breakfast, and all similar mixed teas, are a blend of black teas from these different regions. It isn't until you get to the singular region teas that you get a taste of those original flavor notes.

Understanding how terroir affects the resulting taste of tea, and how each region had its own unique flavor notes, laid the foundation for understanding the world of tea. We tasted eight teas in each class, giving a good overview of each type of tea.

Moving on to green teas, which are predominantly produced in China and Japan—we would sample enough tea that participants would be able to tell the difference between a Chinese and Japanese tea by the end of class. Tasting teas side by side gives the best opportunity to discern the differences in flavor, texture, and character. Greens are my favorites, so we spent extra time on proper preparation as they are also the trickiest to attain that perfect cup. Green teas should be very light and delicate and can be easily ruined with any more than a two-minute infusion. I always felt triumphant when some would declare at the beginning of class how they never liked green tea, and would leave with a bag or two to add to their growing tea repertoire.

Oolongs are a fun class of tea. Most widely known as Chinese restaurant tea, it was also made popular by Oprah. She had a show featuring this tea for weight loss, so of course, every woman in America suddenly wanted Oolong tea. It was Oolong tea that was first noted in medical studies to speed metabolism and thus aid in weight loss, although now green tea and others have shown to do the same.

I loved it when the talk shows would bring me so much new business. But I was always dismayed by the scams that seem to follow retail sales. The particular tea Oprah featured was a brand called Wu-long. So, people came in, asking for that specific tea. It had to be Wu-long brand.

Now, the thing you need to know is, wu-long is just oolong tea. It's simply a different dialect of the same word, but exactly the same tea. It is a class of tea, not one special kind that only this company sold. I had the most difficult time convincing customers that any oolong would do the same thing claimed by this company on Oprah's show and I was a little disappointed in Oprah's staff for not researching this more thoroughly.

The same thing happened when Dr. Oz talked about Pu-erh and weight loss on one of his shows. Pu-erh is a different type of black tea, where the tea is fermented on top of the oxidation, giving it even more health benefits than regular tea. Everyone was clamoring for Pu-erh after that, and of course, we carried several. I was always careful to explain to customers that, while this tea did indeed have many exceptional benefits, it was no miracle weight loss cure.

But, the American population is always seeking the next weight loss magic pill, and I knew other tea vendors would take advantage of this. So, I decided to check out Teavana at our local mall to see how they were handling this new weight-loss claim. I posed as a regular customer who'd seen the Dr. Oz show and wanted some Pu-erh tea.

"Oh, yes!" the clerk exclaimed. "We have a delicious strawberry Pu-erh." Seems they had a delicious strawberry everything, with little attention to the tea itself. I asked to see it so I could judge the quality and validity. She brought out a large tin, opened it, wafted it toward me and invited me to smell. It smelled of strawberry all right. It had so many bits and pieces of fruit and flowers in it, the whole menagerie was pink.

Now, pu-erh tea is dark brown. I looked closely and said, "Where's the pu-erh? I don't see any pu-erh tea in this!" She was miffed, but assured me that there was pu-erh in the mix. She poked and flicked, flicked and fluffed, and finally found a pu-erh leaf. "See! There's one!" I bit my tongue hard, so as not to laugh right in her face. "Thanks," I said. "I'll have to think about it."

That's probably one, if not the main reason that I didn't make as much money as I could have. I just couldn't cheat or lie to people.

But, I digress.

Back to oolongs, which are a fascinating class of tea. They provide such intriguing flavor notes as hazelnut or oats or corn. They can have delicate floral notes, such as violet, and even fruity notes like apricot. We would prepare and taste several classic or more common oolongs, but I always included a couple very rare, high-end samples. One of my favorites was Wild Orchid Oolong with its classic long twisted leaf and delicate orchid notes, all from the tea itself, no flowers added. There are fake Orchid oolongs out there that are simply ordinary oolong with Orchid petals to scent the tea. Lovely, I'm sure, but not the real deal.

Milk Oolong was my very favorite. It actually has a buttery, creamy flavor in the cup with no milk or cream added. It is a real freak of nature. It turns out that it is only produced when the temperature drops severely the night before harvest, which is what changes the leaf to yield that creamy taste. Someone finally noticed this and now, when Mother Nature cooperated, they could reproduce this amazing tea. As you might imagine, it is rare and expensive, as it should be for providing such delight. Watch out for "milk oolong" teas that have an oily film on the cup when prepared. These are fakes that have been flavored after the fact.

Saving the best for last, the final class was on white tea. When I first got into the tea business, white teas were so rare in the western world that there were only two or three available from any of my vendors who carried hundreds of other teas. What makes white tea so rare and generally much more expensive is partially due to the fact that, of the whole three to four foot tall tea bush, only the top two leaves and the bud can be used to make white tea.

Many high-quality teas only use two leaves and the bud to make all their tea, such as quality Assams, Darjeelings, and Ceylons. But in whites, it *must* be just the top leaf and bud. For a Silver Needle or White Tip tea, it is only the unfurled bud at the tip of the stem. The processing is also different, where white teas should be air dried, which takes longer to produce than other types of tea. Now, due to the demand for this delicate treasure throughout the world, some are lightly steamed to speed up the process.

White teas are perhaps my all-time favorite. It's the one I always say I'll take when asked, "If you could only have one, which tea would you take to a desert island?" "Adam's Peak," an exquisite Ceylon White Tip tea, is what I always reply. I love it's delicate flavor, even lighter than green teas, and it's a very relaxing tea. The unfurled bud is the highest in L-theanine, a component, which literally relaxes the brain, and some white teas are all bud, making them the highest in healthy antioxidants.

All quality tea can be reinfused several times, but white teas can be up to five to seven times. It gets pretty weak by then, but you've managed to get out every last bit of those antioxidants if you do reinfuse. The Chinese Buddhist monks have an interesting saying about this: "You should drink (reinfuse) your white tea until it is completely devoid of flavor. When you do so, you will reach Nirvana." I personally think they were talking about much more than a peaceful state of mind. Since the Chinese have had tea the longest, know it best, and have observed its health benefits for millennia, I believe they were speaking more to a "Nirvana of perfect health" notion.

After taking the entire tea tasting series, participants would "graduate" so to speak, and get a certificate deeming them an Official Tea Snob. People loved this! It added a fun note and recognized their work and accomplishment. These Tea Snobs became my very best customers. I loved it when they came back in with their knowledge of tea, knowing what they liked and often open to trying something new. And I was touched when they would tell me years later that they still had their Tea Snob certificate hanging in a special place.

Completion of the entire Tea Tasting Series gained participants
Official Tea Snob status.

One advanced class was on tasting a number of high-end samples I'd gotten in. As these would be more expensive teas, I wanted to make sure they would sell. So, I took a group of my experienced tea tasters, had them all sample these teas and tell me which they thought were worth carrying. And which they would pay the higher price for. It was a win-win situation for both of us. They got to taste teas they'd otherwise never be exposed to, and I had real input on which would be worth carrying.

Another time, I gave them the opportunity to create their own unique tea blend. They were first to wander through all the tea shelves and pick three or four teas to "play" with. Then, I'd dole out an ounce of each of the teas they picked. I'd shown them how I found new blends by testing different combinations and proportions of flavors. They dug into it with gusto! They each had a French press and access to the hot water urn to prepare each new hopeful blend. In the end, when they'd found their perfect new tea creation, they got to name it and make a whole tin of it for them to take home. I have to say, that was probably the most fun of all the classes in sixteen years.

At one point, I decided I needed to change things up a bit by adding some variety of events to the tea tasting classes. The first variation was pairing tea with chocolates. I'd never thought of pairing tea with foods, but it was popular with wine, so why not tea? I'd actually taken a session on it at the tea convention in Vegas, so that gave me the basic structure for the class. It was always my most popular event, filling all seats every time it was offered. How can you go wrong with chocolate, right?

Almost equal to the tea and chocolate pairings were the tea leaf reading events. I thought that sounded like a very fun tea-related event for customers. I searched and finally found a woman, Retha Martin, whose specialty was reading tea leaves.

We'd have tea and scones, as with all the other events, but for readings, we put the leaves directly into the teapot—a real no-no for properly prepared tea. But participants would pour out a cup when the time was right so that some tea leaves would end up in their cup. They'd drink the tea, and when just a small sip was left, Retha would tell them how to turn the cup just so to prepare for the reading.

One customer who happened to be an expert on kimono, approached me about having an event where she would demonstrate the proper way to don a kimono. That one was well attended and lots of fun when several of the participants got to model. It was highly informative, too. I had no idea kimono were so elaborate and complicated to wear properly. One guest even came fully dressed in her kimono. And, yes, we sipped tea and munched on scones, as always.

Kerry Porter, a.k.a., the Kimono Lady,
demonstrates how to properly don a kimono.
Some participants even got to try them on.

Along a similar line, I knew a woman through my Tai Chi class who was studying to become a master of the Japanese Tea Ceremony. One of my most memorable events was the shortened version of the ceremony she agreed to do at the shop one evening. She came dressed in full kimono, and it was fascinating to watch her painstakingly careful preparation of the matcha green tea. Every movement had to be perfect. It made for such a sacred atmosphere, and you could almost hear a pin drop throughout the evening.

Most events brought me new, regular customers, so they were

worth the long, exhausting days. And they added an element of fun. Plus, gave an always welcomed boost for the bottom line.

"What else can I do?" I was always asking myself. "How else can I attract more customers?"

Since I carried some bath and body care products, I came up with an unusual tea facial evening. This gave customers a chance to try the entire line of tea-infused face products we carried. It was a bit messy, involving washcloths and removing makeup, but it was fun. I held it in the evening, so participants would just go home afterward with their freshly cleaned, exfoliated, moisturized, and tea-enriched faces.

It was always my goal to get as many people as possible interested in tea, and I thought, *Why not get 'em started young?* So, I came up with events for children that would expose them to anything tea related. I worked with Brownie and Girl Scout troops to hold a tea with a lecture on manners, a dress-up tea party being the perfect setting for this. They had to dress properly, and we had hats and gloves they could don while at the party. They learned the basics of good table manners and could practice them on the spot. They seemed to enjoy it, and I'd get a chuckle when one girl would remind another not to put her elbows on the table or to remember to take her gloves off while eating. The mothers loved it, and the troop leaders were happy to find a fun way for the girls to earn another merit badge.

I expanded further with classes that were just fun and an excuse to join others in taking tea and scones. Numerology was one class, where I taught how to find the significant numbers in your life, and what they meant. Chinese Archetypes was another out of the ordinary class. At least it is related to the birthplace of tea. There was a rather lengthy list of questions each participant would answer, then score and tally, which would give them which Chinese archetype was dominant for them: air, earth, wood, fire, or metal. It was interesting and fun, giving clues to personality traits much like astrology does.

Ayurvedic Doshas was another event similar to the archetypes, where after answering questions, you would find out which dosha was predominant in your life: Vata, Pitta, or Kapha. It could give clues to basic personality traits and was especially useful in understanding a proper diet for balancing your doshas and living a healthier life.

Vatas are generally thin and high-energy individuals. Vata imbalance may lead to nervous, compulsive behavior. Kaphas are generally stout and heavier in body, calm and steady in personality, and may often have red hair. Kaphas are great to have around in the event of something traumatic with their steadiness able to better handle the situation. But, when out of balance, Kapha types can be overweight and sluggish and sleep too much.

Pittas are somewhat balanced in the middle. Sharp in intellect and quick witted when in balance, but can lean to nervousness if tending toward too much vata, and toward sluggishness if having too much kapha. No one type is better than the other, with each having exceptional traits when in balance, and we all have all three of these types within us, just one that is our predominant trait, according to the ancient wisdom of Ayurveda.

It may not seem to have much to do with tea, but there were actually dosha tea blends, which were all sampled while nibbling scones and filling out the questionnaires. Each participant would note which tea they were most attracted to, and it was fun to see if it matched their test results. Most of the time, oddly enough, it did! And they got to take home a bag of their appropriate dosha tea.

With short attention spans and people getting bored easily, it was a constant challenge to keep trying to find new, fun things that would bring people into the shop. It was something I always enjoyed, though. A great distraction from the stresses of small-business life. It kept me busy and sharp, which is perfect for a pitta.

Chapter 9

Sri Lanka, the Island of Tea

China, as one might expect, is the largest producer of tea, and is the largest of all tea-producing countries. It is the place where tea was discovered nearly five thousand years ago. It evolved from its humble beginnings there into the lovely drink enjoyed around the world today.

There are many fables attached to the discovery of tea, but probably the most accurate one credits it to an early Chinese Emperor, Shen Nong. In 2737 BC, this tale tells that Shen Nong, who was also an herbalist, was traveling through the woods with his entourage, looking for herbs for use in healing. It came to be dusk, and they decided to set up camp for the evening. While boiling his drinking water to make sure it was safe, it is said that a strong wind arose, blowing some leaves from a nearby bush into the pot of hot water. His servants were sure they would be punished for allowing his water to be tainted, but he was an herbalist, always looking for new plants that might be put to good use. As the story goes, he was so captivated by the aroma that arose from the pot, he insisted on being served the new concoction. He tasted it. He loved it. And from then on, he requested his water be prepared with these leaves daily. Tea was born.

China had tea all to herself for the first three thousand years or so, and it wasn't until around the year 600, when Buddhist monks were visiting from Japan when they were sent home with gifts of tea bushes. Tea spread slowly to other parts of the world via the famous Silk Road. And then, with the advent of shipping, especially the era of the clipper ships, tea trade expanded its reach far beyond. And certainly much quicker than by camel.

India, another large country with perfect growing conditions for tea, is second on the list of producers. After that, some might be surprised to find that Kenya is the third-largest producer of tea in tonnes. But the fourth-largest producer of tea, while around a fifth the size of Kenya, and absolutely tiny in land mass compared to China or India, we find to be Sri Lanka.

Sri Lanka, a country unto its own, is actually a large teardrop shaped island off the southern coast of India. While tea is grown in many places around the world, no other place identifies so wholly with tea. It is the island's primary commodity, and its highly prized tea is exported around the world. For such a small country, it produces an awful lot of tea.

It's a very important tea-growing region. An exotic land, especially to someone whose only venture outside the US had been Canada. So, when an opportunity to take a tour of Sri Lanka and its tea estates, guided by one of my vendors I'd met at the Tea Expo had presented, I knew I must find a way to make it happen.

My husband was skeptical at first. It would be the most expensive trip we'd ever taken. Sri Lanka didn't hold so much intrigue for him as it did for me. But when I dug up all the details, figured out how we could afford it, he got on board. We both were excited at the prospect of traveling to such an exotic place.

I had traveled mostly across the US and had never been farther out of the country than the Blue Mountains in Canada. So for me, it was beyond my wildest imagination. I'd never dreamed I'd get to go somewhere so far across the globe with culture so wildly different from the USA. I always describe it as "the trip of a lifetime."

I'm usually a pretty nervous traveler. I don't like to fly. All right, I'm downright afraid of flying. *How the heck am I going to manage twenty-two hours in the air?* I worried. I thought about getting some meds from my doctor, but in the end, I was so excited for the trip that a bit of alcohol, as soon as a stewardess was to be found, got me through.

I'd met the tea vendor and host of the trip, Lalith Guy Paranavitana, but only once, a year or so before. Lalith is his Sri Lankan name, but he uses Guy as his American first name, and owns the Empire Tea Services in Columbus, Indiana. So, when we got to Chicago, where we were to meet up with the group, I didn't see anyone who looked familiar. To be completely honest, I had no memory of what he looked like. We had no choice but to board the plane and hopefully make connections somewhere along the way.

When we got to London, neither of us had been in such a monstrous airport as Heathrow and were completely overwhelmed in trying to find our way to the next gate at Sri Lankan Airlines. Fortunately, Phil was wearing the Air Force ball cap his son had given him, and a nice Englishman noticed it. He wanted to chat with Phil about the Air Force, and, also fortunately, he noticed how disoriented we were. He pointed us in the right direction to the shuttle we needed to take.

I thought that when we got to the gate for the Sri Lankan leg of the trip, we might see someone who looked vaguely familiar and could get connected with our group, and if not, then we'd just have to find them when we got all the way to Sri Lanka.

While on the shuttle, I was sitting in a seat that faced the back of the bus. There was an Indian/Sri Lankan looking man standing at the very back, talking to a small group of Anglo looking people. I thought it'd be pretty serendipitous if that was actually him and told myself that it probably wasn't. But, he kept looking at me, and I kept looking at him.

Finally, it was he who took the brave move to come up to us and ask if we happened to be Phil and Elaine. It *was* Lalith! So, we got connected before we even got to the gates. What a relief! Now united with our group, we could relax and enjoy the rest of the trip.

When we got through to the gate to get our boarding passes, I found that Phil and I were seated in the same row but not together. And, it was in a middle row about eight across, for the longest leg of the flight: fourteen hours! I panicked and started to freak out at the counter. The lovely, Sari-draped woman behind the check-in desk did not get angry at me. With a compassion I have rarely experienced before, she reached across the counter, gently put her hand on mine, and just said, "Do not worry, it will be all right."

It was like some kind of Buddhist or Hindu magic, but I instantly calmed down. The stewardesses were all adorned in Saris and all had a lovely, gentle demeanor about them. One helped get people in our row moved around so that Phil and I could be together for the flight. I have to say that I've never experienced a more pleasant flight, where all the stewardesses could not have been more kind and accommodating.

Our group had been scattered throughout the plane, so we joined up with the group again when we arrived in Sri Lanka. That was after I hit a bathroom to peel off my layers of winter clothing suitable for January in Chicago but not so much for the eighty-degree tropical year-round climate of Sri Lanka. I was also wearing the thick, tight sleeve on my right arm to prevent lymphedema after my breast cancer surgeries. Lymphedema, if it develops, is a horrible recurring swelling, and so, I was glad to have something that could help prevent it, but it was uncomfortable and hot. It was another layer that I was glad to get rid of as soon as we disembarked.

We were struck by all the armed military guards still very visible. The many years of terrorism and attacks from the Tamils had just recently been brought to an end, but the government was taking no chances, and their presence made us feel safer. Lalith had wanted to offer this tea tour for many years, but would not risk taking travelers there while the civil war was still going on with random bombings in the streets. With things now settled, we were the lucky first group.

Lalith got us to the banking counter where we could exchange our money and we were off! We stepped out of the airport and into a tropical paradise.

We were met by our English-speaking tour guide, Ravi, and boarded onto our small tour bus, which would be home for the next fifteen days. We headed to the Galle Face Hotel, over-looking the Indian Ocean in Colombo. The grandeur of this beautiful old hotel is a picture that hasn't receded from memory. I was struck by the exceptional service we received there and at every place we stayed. They seemed always happy to host visitors and were obviously very proud of their beautiful country.

The delightful hotel greeter, welcoming us with "Ayubowan," which means "Long Life," and Ravi, our tour guide.

Once settled in our rooms, the group decided to hit the streets of Colombo to experience the culture. That was our first ride in a tuk-tuk, so named because that's the sound the engine makes: tuk tuk tuk tuk tuk. It's a small three-wheeled vehicle with one seat for the driver up front and a comfortable two-seater in the back. After negotiating a price (which was expected) for the ride to the local shopping mall, four of us crammed into one of the tuk-tuks. We were stuffed on top of each other and laughing so hard, you'd have thought we were a bunch of teenagers.

Our driver got a mischievous glint in his eye, with this load of naïve Americans, and proceeded to give us the ride of our lives. Traffic was always heavy in Colombo and driving is different there. It seems like you can drive wherever there's an opening, roughly on your side of the road, but with lots of crossing over and diving back into your lane at the last second with only inches to spare before coming head on with a driver from the other direction. Our hearts jumped every time! But, it turns out, Sri Lanka has fewer auto accidents than most other countries, so somehow, they make this crazy system work.

Shopping was much different as well. The place we went to was actually a small two-story mall, but it was huge for Sri Lanka. Most shopping is just random strips of small cubby-hole shops, more like almost open-air markets but with roofs and side walls. Thankfully, we were able to pick up some souvenirs that night, as there was little shopping to be had for the remainder of the trip, which took us into the mountains.

Breakfast the next morning was a huge buffet with both British and Sri Lankan foods. In fact, every meal we had, at every place we stayed was that same type of large buffet. They don't seem to have restaurants with individual menu service like we are used to. It was fun to get to taste the very strongly curried Sri Lankan fare, but it was a bit too intense for me, and even though I usually like spicy foods, the bland British fare sat better with my stomach.

The first day, we were taken to the Colombo tea auctions, which few people outside the industry get to witness. It was a huge tiered auditorium, where representatives and buyers from each business came to bid on whatever tea lots they'd tasted and decided to try to procure. Each tea had been graded and samples shipped to all interested buyers. This is where all the big tea companies, like Lipton, get their Ceylon tea. It all happened very fast, but the buyers seemed to know exactly which teas they wanted and how high they were willing to go. It was exciting to watch, even if we couldn't understand many words.

Later in the afternoon, we were treated to an official tea tasting by a senior tea taster at one of the large corporate tea entities. I'd seen photos of all the teas lined up in their tasting cups ready for sipping with the wet leaf perched on the lid behind, available for sniffing the intense aroma of each tea. But this day, all those cups were lined up right in front of us and we got to do the tasting ourselves.

Tasting all those lovely teas,
only to be spit out into the rolling spittoon.

We were instructed in the official process. One thing we quickly found out is that tasters don't swallow the tea! They may taste several hundred samples in a day. There is an official tea-tasting spoon, with a bowl deep enough, like a large soup spoon, to dip in and get a large enough sample. Then the tea is slurped—yes slurped!—so that it becomes aerosolized into many small droplets to blast the taste buds. Try it sometime. You really do get a better sense of the taste that way.

The tea is then swished around and fully tasted, much like wine tasters do. The funniest part of the whole process is the large rolling spittoon that drains into a container underneath. It is moved along as the taster goes down the line, so that the tea can be spit out into the bowl of the spittoon. An experienced taster only takes a few seconds to taste and determine the quality of each tea sample. The grade and taste notes are jotted down and then on to the next. Thirty or forty teas are graded in just a few minutes.

It was a fun experience for our tea group and interesting to watch real pros do it so quickly. We asked one of the tasters how long it took him to learn the skill. He thought about it a second and said, "Well, I've been doing this for about ten years now. I taste tea every day, seven days a week, and I think I'm just getting good at it." Wow!

We headed back to the magnificent Galle Face Hotel for another night and set out to see our first tea estate the following day.

The first tea estate we visited was the famous Vithanakanda Estate in Ratnapura. It's a low-elevation estate, producing high-quality teas that are world renown. Usually the higher the altitude, the more delicate and highly prized the tea. But Vithanakanda is a notable exception.

The tea grading system is the same as used in India. The largest pieces of leaf and the best flavor of tea gets the highest tea grade: SFTGFOP, meaning Special Fine or Fancy Tippy Golden Flowery Orange Pekoe. The more broken the pieces of leaf, the lower the grade. The larger the pieces and the higher percentage of tips (i.e., unfurled bud in the mix), the higher the grade. This list shows the classic grading system:

- Special Fine/Fancy Tippy Golden Flowery Orange Pekoe (SFTGFOP)

- Fine/Fancy Tippy Golden Flowery Orange Pekoe (FTGFOP)

- Tippy Golden Flowery Orange Pekoe (TGFOP)

- Golden Flowery Orange Pekoe (GFOP)

- Flowery Orange Pekoe (FOP)

- Orange Pekoe (OP)

- Pekoe (P)

- Souchong (S)

- Broken Grades

- Fannings

- Dust

If it is exceptional, it's given Grade 1 after the letters. At Vithanakanda we tasted some of their finest SFTGFOP Grade 1 tea and got large samples to take home. Pure heaven for all of us tea lovers in the group!

One of the most remarkable things to me was the intense aroma of fresh tea as we drove into the estate and got near the factory. I'll never forget it. And the taste of tea processed that very day is different from any I've ever experienced. By the time we get tea in the US, it's past that ultra freshness we got to luxuriate in whenever we got near a tea factory.

The estate manager showed us through the factory. That's where I really began to understand the whole process: from the field to cup, so to speak.

Long poles help pluckers to spot the best tippy leaves.
They go through a second sorting to make sure only the best
leaves go to the factory.

First, the tea is plucked. By hand. That's what makes for the
best quality. We found out that it is, not surprisingly, mostly
done by women. Women seem to get stuck with the most tedious
and laborious tasks. Sigh. So, every day except for their religious
holidays (not sure if they had anything resembling a weekend),
they were out in the fields with their tea baskets secured to their
backs, often with a wide strap that went across their foreheads. I
kept thinking that they must have really strong necks!

The pluckers themselves came up with an interesting yet extremely simple tool that helped facilitate quickly spotting what and where to pluck. It consisted of a long stick, the size of a broom handle. It would be laid across the row in front of them, and thus help them keep track of the section they wanted to concentrate on. I wondered if also the stick laid into the bush at a height that might have helped to spot the two leaves and bud sticking up above it. At any rate, it seemed like an invaluable tool to some of the ladies.

They had a quota that they needed to meet every day. So, when they came to the collecting areas, their baskets were weighed before being dumped onto a large tarp. While they carefully plucked the proverbial "two leaves and a bud" in the field, there was a second sorting done when the tea was dumped out and any leaves that weren't of superior quality were discarded.

The tarps were gathered up and taken to the factory, where they were hooked onto a conveyor belt to lift them up to the withering bins on the second floor. These were large bins with wire mesh on the bottom, so that air could be gently blown through to speed the withering. Tea leaf is a thick evergreen, like a holly leaf. So, it took twelve to fourteen hours for the tea to be appropriately withered and ready for the next stage of processing.

After just enough moisture is drawn off the leaf and withering is complete, the tea is taken to the rollers. These large machines consisted of two plates about six to eight feet in diameter that faced each other about an inch or two apart. On the inside were raised spiral lines of metal that when these two plates rotated against each other, the withered tea leaves in between were pushed against the raised metal and crushed just enough to open their cells to facilitate the oxidation process. It made the leaves look like more of a mealy paste at that point.

Then the tea was taken to the oxidation tables. There, the crushed leaves were mounded up about two feet deep on large concrete pads or tables, and there they sat until they reached full oxidation required for black tea. That process took from thirteen to sixteen more hours.

It was fascinating to watch how this was monitored. The lot number & number of hours passed was written by finger into the top of the flattened tea pile. When the tea got to thirteen hours, the superintendent of the estate would come by and take a small sample to inspect. He would feel, smell, and also taste the tea leaves. His experience told him when the tea was ready, and if not, it would sit another hour. So, he'd wipe the leaves flat again and rewrite the next hour in the leaves.

When oxidation was complete, the tea leaves then needed to be dried. Moisture had to be driven off to no more than about 4 percent, as I recall. That way, tea will stay good when properly stored in a bag or tin, and not mold or mildew. This was done by firing in large woks or steaming. Steaming puzzled me, but apparently the intense heat of the steam evaporated the moisture of the steam itself and moisture in the leaf too. I guess like steam ironing where the clothes dry quickly, even though there is moisture in the steam. Sometimes large ovens were used to help facilitate this step, too.

By the way, since tea does still have that residual small percentage of moisture, it should never be stored in the refrigerator. Taking tea in and out of the cold will cause condensation of that moisture on the inside of the canister, which can redeposit on the leaf and can cause it to spoil. If the moisture condenses outside the tin, the tea would become dryer and lose flavor. Room temperature is fine for all tea except matcha powder. Matcha is actually preserved best by keeping it in the refrigerator, or better yet, the freezer. It can be kept at room temp as well if it is something you consume regularly and will use up in a reasonable amount of time.

After that came sorting. As I previously explained, the larger the pieces of leaf remaining, the higher the grade and quality of the tea. So, we saw things like vibrating conveyor belts with different sizes of mesh underneath, to allow the various sizes of leaf to fall through into separate bins. Those bins with the largest leaves also had the largest percentage of tips in them. The tips, being an unfurled bud, did not crush or fall into pieces, but usually remained mostly intact, and thus would separate out only into the last bin for larger leaves.

Once the tea was separated into appropriate grades of leaf by size, samples would be taken to tasting rooms so that each lot could be officially assigned a grade by the expert tea tasters. That final grade was based primarily on taste and not the look or size of the leaf. Once graded, each lot could be bagged up for shipment. The outside of the bag would be stamped with the lot number and the grade of tea. These thick, heavy, multi-layered paper bags were twenty kilos in size, so they were about two feet wide by four feet tall and maybe a foot thick. That's one huge bag of tea!

Estates stored the tea until sold off in auction to those huge tea retailers like Lipton, Twinings, Tetley, and Red Rose. Commodity auctions work well for the tea trade. The producer gets his product sold for the highest dollar it can command in the market, and rules are that payments must be made within thirty days, as I recall. That way, it works for both buyer and seller. The product moves quickly, and the manufacturer isn't taxed with collecting payment later.

We have lots of wonderful photos of the ladies who plucked the tea. They wore colorful outfits and were thrilled to have their photos taken, although a few looked quite shy. When we got to meet them up close, we could see how stained their fingers were from plucking tea all day.

One cute impish tea-plucking lady popped up behind a half wall overlooking the lovely rows and rows of tea bush. Grinning ear to ear, she posed, and we obliged by taking her picture. They told us she did that all the time. She just loved to get her picture taken by visitors. They chased her away as a nuisance, but I found her delightfully funny.

One tea-plucking lady who loved having
her photo taken and one who was really shy,
but agreed to take a photo with us.

The estates were always trying to find ways to make their
work easier. They designed finger cots so that they wouldn't
get this staining. But, the ladies didn't like them and so
wouldn't use them. They were always trying to find better
harnesses for the tea baskets that would shift the weight to
the shoulders instead of their heads and necks. But again, the
ladies seemed habituated to what they had always done and
would rarely accept the changes.

We got to go into some of the fields and pluck leaves ourselves. Let me tell you, those rows and rows of groomed tea
bushes look beautiful in photos, but what you don't see is how
lumpy and uneven the soil is beneath them. It was not easy to
walk on, and I could imagine that twisting an ankle might be
a common work hazard.

We were taken on a tour through the medical center, using
that term rather loosely. It covered all the basics of medical necessity, but looked nothing like the average American health facility
in cleanliness, décor, and amenities. Because estates are usually
very far away from towns, all workers lived on the estates, even
the superintendent. So, all their needs had to be met by the estate.
Ladies had babies there in the medical center.

They were given small houses to live in and a plot of land
on which they grew their own vegetables and tended their

own animals if they had any. Their children were schooled on the estate. The superintendent had his own cottage, which was much more of a house than any of the workers would ever see. Of course, the super's wife and family would maybe live in the nearest town with some social amenities, and he would shuffle between two homes to see his family occasionally.

What I saw for the first time was a markedly different existence than what we have in a first world country. Sri Lanka is considered a developing country. In the remote countryside, we would see houses with no windows and in poor repair. But, with temps at eighty degrees year round, all you really needed was a roof overhead for the monsoon season. It must be different by now, but when we were there, a large percentage, something like 70 percent of the population, did not have electricity.

When we got into the cities, the picture was quite different, and we started to see many people sporting cell phones. In the cities, professional, working people have a lifestyle similar to ours. Even better, in some ways. Having servants is common for most professionals and is commonplace in their culture. Professionals don't cook, clean, or maintain their gardens. Their salary affords them the ability to hire those tasks to be done for them. Sometimes I think that part of the crazy in the US is that we have to do too much work to maintain a reasonable lifestyle. Many highly educated professionals here are not paid enough to hire housekeepers and cooks and gardeners. But in Sri Lanka, even a teacher would enjoy this luxury.

At any rate, what we saw at the estates was that the people were well cared for and treated fairly, even if the work was hard. The estates even offered and paid 100 percent of college education for any child of an estate worker who desired to go. One estate we visited had just graduated the first child of a worker who had received his MD. They were so proud of that. Mothers there are like mothers everywhere, and we heard stories of them desiring less-difficult labor for their children than plucking tea in the fields. Totally understandable.

As an aside, the fact that upcoming generations were becoming more educated, it made me realize that at some point in time, hand-plucking of tea would become a thing of the past. Some places, like the US, where hand plucking would never be done by Americans in the first place, have already developed machinery that mows off the top six inches of the plant. The loss in quality is enormous and completely unacceptable to any true tea connoisseur. It makes me wonder if someday, it will not even be possible to obtain hand-plucked tea. Or, if it will be so expensive that most will not be able to afford it. Makes me truly appreciate every cup of high-quality hand-plucked tea I sip.

The second estate we visited was Nuwara Eliya, which had been formerly managed by our host, Lalith Paranavitana. Nuwara Eliya is among the highest elevations where tea is produced in Sri Lanka, and generally, teas from higher elevations have a more delicate, highly prized character. That Adam's Peak Ceylon White Tip tea that I'd take with me if I ever got stranded on a deserted island, that tea comes from Nuwara Eliya.

We stayed at some of the most wonderful hotels along the way. Most were four- and five-star rated and the Grand Hotel in Kandy was luxurious. It was the first time I'd ever seen a lobby that was totally open air. No walls other than the one behind the check-in desk, just completely open to the environment on the other three sides, and having a canopy overhead to protect guests and sitting areas from rain. Sitting and sipping drinks in these beautiful surroundings with the background of nature all around was an incomparable treat.

The next estate was the Pedro Estate, which sells under another name you might have heard of called "Lover's Leap." It was established in the early 1880s, and since the first tea estate in Sri Lanka started in 1867, Pedro is one of the oldest. It is also located in the Nuwara Eliya region, so their teas are high growns as well. While there, we got to meet with scientists at the Tea Research Institute. We were all so looking forward to talking to these researchers to get their insights into the technology, chemistry, and cultivation of tea.

Besides the valuable information they shared with us about tea, we experienced firsthand one of tea's amazing properties. We were all getting tired having trekked to many places by day nine of our trip. On top of that, we had just come from one of those large buffet lunches.

At first, everyone was groggy and almost falling asleep. But we had our pens, papers, and questions at the ready and we were preparing to fight the grogginess to garner as much information as we could from these knowledgeable scientists. There was so much to learn here.

As is customary, we were served pots of tea before they began to speak. Within just a few minutes and a few sips of tea, we were no longer slumping in our chairs. We were alert and gave those experts brain pickings like they'd probably never had. I think they actually enjoyed being asked so many questions and sharing their knowledge with such an eager group. I was so elated to get to talk to these experts and learn the most current information and research on tea.

From Pedro we headed for the Uva region, where we were to visit the fourth tea estate: Somerset. Established in 1880, again this was a very old, well-established estate. Here we got a more detailed look at tea production. We spent more time out in the factory and fields, and enjoyed tasting the "tea dhools" fresh off the dryer. We got more great photos of the ladies plucking tea, sorting, withering, grading, drying, and packing up for shipment. I now had a clear picture of how tea got from field to table.

This was the estate where we would stay overnight in the superintendent's cottage. What an experience it was! While it was supposed to be just Phil and me, another couple from the group stayed there with us, switching from their original assignment because they came from a town in England called Somerset. That was not a problem with us, except that the estate was not prepared to host two couples. At the last minute, they scurried around and prepared a second room as best they could. As luck would have it, we got the second room.

That turned out to be one of the interesting highlights of our trip. While the first room was comfortable and lovely and well decorated, our room consisted of two single cots with a sheet tucked over the thin mattress, and one for on top and a lumpy pillow. There was a dresser across from them in the large, mostly empty room, and the only other piece of furniture was a small table between the two cots. No light for reading, and just a bare bulb strung from a cord in the center of the room.

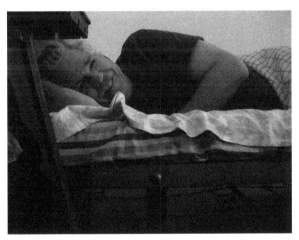

Our "not-so-luxurious" digs at the superintendent's cottage.

Well, there we were, so we had to make the best of it. After dinner and some conversation over drinks, we retired for the evening. We were to get up very early the following day so that we could experience the fresh tea coming off the driers in the morning. When we settled in our room, we looked at each other from our respective cots, chuckled at the sparse surroundings, and tried to go to sleep.

About fifteen minutes later, I felt something crawling in my bed! I jumped up, expressing my horror to Phil, and he scrambled for the light switch across the room on the wall. It was some sort of bug, not exactly sure what, but I wasn't about to lay down with it again. We made sure it was gone. OK, we killed it. But I was sure there were probably more critters lurking about, and I wasn't sure how I was going to get to sleep.

From my experiences in New York City once, where cockroaches were common, I learned that they would scurry when the lights got turned on if you went to the restroom in the middle of the night. So, we kept that bare bulb on all night long to keep the bugs away, and I honestly don't know how we actually got any sleep.

Morning came, and with it, one of Sri Lanka's traditional luxuries: bed tea. Bed tea is where you get served your morning tea in bed, still sporting your jammies. What an enigma that was! Enjoying luxurious bed tea in this stark room from our lumpy cots. Phil and I chuckled whenever we thought of that unexpected, enigmatic adventure.

After lunch, before we left, we gave our host a gift to thank him for our accommodations, such as they were, and the in-depth education into tea production. We had decided it should be something that was symbolic of where we were from. So, what we came up with to represent Toledo, the Glass Capital of the World, was a beautiful glass paperweight from the Toledo Museum of Art, also one of the most noted museums in the US. I didn't know if the superintendent would have much use for it, but thought, perhaps, his wife might appreciate the artistic gesture.

The rest of our accommodations were more than adequate and most of them were in grand style and comfort. The last, Bentota Beach Hotel, was my favorite. It had the most splendid lobby, with the entire ceiling decorated with a checkerboard of beautiful batik squares about three feet by three feet each. There must have been a hundred of them! In the dining room, there was a huge metal sculpted bird, a good fifteen feet tall and at least that long. The hotel is perched right on the Indian Ocean with stunning views and a beautiful, groomed beach. I didn't want to leave. If I should ever make it back to Sri Lanka, I'd plan to spend a week there.

The exotic front desk and one of the
many batik panels that lined the ceiling of our hotel.

After leaving Vithanakanda, as we headed for the other estates scattered in the central, mountainous part of the country, we took leisurely days in between, where we saw many historical points of interest. The rides were along narrow, often one-lane roads. In some places, when two vehicles met, whoever was closest to the last turnoff had to back up and pull over to let the other vehicle pass. That might be a half mile back, but those were the rules. Perhaps that's why I felt so confident about our drivers. Anyone who could back up a winding one-lane mountainous road had to be damn good at it. There were beautiful waterfalls and spectacular views with sheer drop-offs at the edge of the road. At every turn, there seemed to be something that held my interest, especially the rows and rows of tea bushes. I felt an unexplainable calm on these drives through the mountains, and just like with the wild tuk-tuk ride through the streets of Colombo, it was actually fun!

When we got up into the higher elevations, we were weaving in and out around each peak. The mists I'd read about, hovering over these high elevations, are what make the perfect terroir, producing the most exquisite teas. It was so beautiful and each turn brought another stunning view. One day, when we were surrounded with this otherworldly mist, we saw the beginning of a rainbow. It was cut off by one of the peaks. But when we rounded the peak and came out on the other side, which took more than a few minutes, we thought it would be gone but were delighted to see the other half of the rainbow as vivid as the first. It seemed to all of us that it was some sort of good omen bestowed on our trip.

En route to the central region, we stopped at an elephant sanctuary at Pinnawala. We got to see baby elephants being bottle fed and the whole herd getting their daily jaunt in the river. There must have been fifty to sixty elephants living there. Many of the elephants had disabilities of some sort. One had even lost one of its feet. How it could support its massive weight on only three feet while walking was amazing, but somehow it seemed to manage just fine. The sanctuary was for the ones who can't live in the wild anymore and need human intervention. When they have babies, although normal, they of course get to stay with their families. So, there are some normal elephants who will live out their lives in this protected environment.

At one point, we were standing along the edge of the river near some steps that went down to the banks. One of the caretakers/handlers saw us and motioned for us to come down to get a closer look. We quickly went down to the bottom few steps, and he carefully brought one of the elephants over to us. My absolute favorite photo of the whole trip is when I got to pet that beautiful creature. One of the handlers took the photo for us, with Phil and me grinning from ear to ear. It was an almost spiritual experience. I was amazed at how their hide was so very dry and rough. Being in the presence of their powerful yet beautifully gentle spirits will always be one of the peak moments of my life.

Much rougher skin than I expected,
but a gentle energy emanated from this beautiful creature.

We followed the herd down a long road toward a lake where they also got to bathe if they wanted. Another great photo I took is of Phil with his hand on one gorgeous male with his trunk in the air, showing off a massive smile. They look like best friends who haven't seen each other for a while. I could have stayed there for hours and hours, but it soon came time to move on. I was looking forward to the following day, where we were supposed to be able to ride an elephant if we wanted to.

Somewhere along the way, even though we had been warned to not drink the water, both Phil and I got violently ill for a day. It might have been from the water that was used in food prep, but somehow, we both got what I'm sure was Giardia, a typical parasite travelers encounter. Being the more susceptible of the two of us, I got it first.

Having worked in microbiology, where one of the substations was parasitology, I knew exactly what this tiny little creature looked like with its one cute eye and undulating flagella for a tail. Cute as it is, I now experienced firsthand what havoc this little guy wreaks on the fragile American digestive tract. After spending hours on the toilet with a bucket in hand, my visions of Giardia no longer included anything cute. Evil monsters are more like it.

I was better enough the following day with some medicine to help settle my stomach. It was funny when Phil found a nearby "pharmacy" to find something for me to take. When he asked for what he wanted, they said, "Of course. How many would you like?" Apparently, everything was sold by the "each," so he got how many he thought would get us through. Fortunately, he bought enough because the following day, he came down with it, too.

Another odd thing, the pharmacy was about the size of two lanes in a bowling alley. Long, narrow, with each side wall lined with remedies and a small check-out counter up front. It was an eye opener to the excesses of life in the US and how modestly some people get by. By the way, Sri Lanka provides healthcare for all its citizens. I was so worried when we were planning the trip, and called my insurance company to make sure they would cover it if I got sick when I was over there. Turns out I didn't need it. Sri Lanka covers everybody, even foreign travelers. This developing country sees health care as a human right. Imagine that.

The day I was sick, I missed a destination I would dearly love to have seen. It's an ancient rock fortress called Sigiriya. It required a long climb to the top to see some of the world's earliest known Frescoes etched into the rock around two thousand years ago. There was no way I could handle that, being inseparable from my new friends: toilet and bucket. But Phil managed to make it before he got sick, and at least I got to see his firsthand photos.

On the way back from Sigiriya, the group stopped at the spot where you could ride an elephant. Phil didn't take a ride, but I sure would have! There were a couple in the group who did get to take that memory home. I had to console myself with the fact that at least I got to pet one.

Other sites included several Hindu and Buddhist temples. About 70 percent of the country is Buddhist. Hindus make up around 12 percent, with 9 percent Muslims, and 8 percent are

Christian (6 percent of that Catholic). So that's why the people are so serene, by and large. That's why the sari'd woman at the counter at the airport was able to calm me so quickly. I loved this about the people, and while we were constantly on the move for fifteen days, I don't think I have ever been more relaxed in my life.

The incredible art, carvings, sculptures, paintings, and ornate metalwork were breathtaking. The staggering beauty of the Hindu temples was almost too much to take in. And we saw how seriously these people take their religion. All of the tuk-tuk drivers had decorated their front cabs with symbols of their religion: beads, metals, photos of saints. Even our bus driver had these around the dash of the bus and would stop at little shrines along the way to place offerings of coins out of respect to his faith.

Having some experience in carving from my sculpture days, I couldn't believe it when I found myself standing in front of one of the famous *Reclining Buddhas*. Its massive size and sacred countenance was awe inspiring. It must be about fifty feet long. The head, on its side, is as tall as an average man. The one we visited was the *Reclining Buddha* of Gal Vihara at Polonnaruwa, which is from the 12th century. The energy coming from that enormous modeled stone somehow emanated just what it was created to depict: the storied, peaceful moment of the Buddha's death when he transcended into Nirvana.

One of the world-famous *Reclining Buddhas*.

Equally impressive, in the same area, we also saw *Buddha in Meditation*, a colossal sitting figure. I could have stood there for hours and had trouble pulling myself away. The only reason I didn't stay longer was that, out of reverence for these statues, we had to take our shoes off about thirty feet from the statues. The ground was rough, crushed stone leading up to them, and my feet were starting to hurt! After gazing for as long as I could stand, I hobbled back to my shoes, both needing comfort for my feet and wanting to absorb more comfort for my soul from these beautiful sculptures.

Another famous relic was at the Temple of the Tooth. Under a large bell-shaped dome was claimed to be the tooth of THE Buddha himself. Again, that wasn't the only holy place claiming to house the tooth of Buddha. Who knows if it was really there? Or perhaps there was more than one tooth that had a shrine built around it.

I remember that there was a photo of a large majestic-looking elephant named Raja in the temple of the tooth. A little further along, not just a photo, but the taxidermied (Is that a word?) guy himself! Raja was the elephant who had led the procession for the yearly festival of the tooth for many years. The dome (or perhaps a smaller container inside) would be mounted on his back and carried through the streets for the celebration.

Raja, this majestic "tusker," was so revered that he was declared a national treasure. That was only the second time an elephant had received such an honor. He died in 1988, after fifty years of service, and his replacement didn't have such long, magnificent tusks as he did. We wondered why, and they explained that many elephants were being born with much shorter tusks, and some even without them at all. At least at that time, they were at a loss as to why.

As we were leaving one of the temples one day, four saffron-robed monks passed near us, heading toward the temple. I turned around to see them and was struck by how the color of their robes stood out from the mostly bland surroundings. That was a moment in time that begged to be preserved. I followed an instinct and grabbed my camera, aimed, and snapped. I have to say, it's a fantastic shot and my second most favorite photo from the entire trip.

One of those special moments in time.

On our way to Nuwara Eliya estate, we visited a spice garden somewhere near Dambulla and the large central city of Kandy, the former royal capital of Sri Lanka. That was fascinating to me for a number of reasons. In addition to tea, I sold herbs and spices at the shop. I've grown my own herbs for years, and love harvesting and cooking with my small crop each year. At this lush garden, though, we got to see some exotic spices not grown in any western garden.

There were groves of cinnamon trees where parts of the bark had been cut off and harvested. Cinnamon comes from the bark, in case you didn't know. We also saw cloves, vanilla beans, and nutmeg growing. I hadn't known that mace comes from the outer lacy layer of nutmeg, which is ground to make the spice mace. Nutmeg is the hard "nut" in the center. They have such strikingly different flavors; I'd never have guessed.

Cacao beans were another surprise. I had no idea how

large the pods were—about eight to ten inches on average. The cacao beans are actually inside these large, red outer pods and go through drying and grinding to get to the powdered cocoa we use for baking and making luscious hot chocolate. Who knew? Well, until then, I hadn't.

The artist in me was quite well nourished when we spent an afternoon at a spectacular batik factory and shop. We got to tour the entire facility and observe firsthand how these beautiful works of art are made. Like the tea, there is much hand labor involved. It was interesting to watch the ladies paint the wax on the cloth in intricate patterns. Wax must cover every place where color is not to be deposited. Then the fabric is dipped in the next dye color, after which the wax is melted off and wax applied again to the next area to be covered. The entire process is incredibly laborious.

I was actually amazed at what I thought was quite a low cost for such elaborate, time-consuming handwork. Those wares would have cost much more in the US. So, we didn't get out of the shop before buying a couple of wall hangings, a shirt for Phil, and a beautiful silk caftan for me. I wear it often and remember that beautiful shop and dedicated artists whenever I put it on.

I could have spent all day at the Batik factory.
Fascinating detailed work.

The final highlight of the trip was a Jeep safari into the wild sanctuary at Yala National Park. There we saw exotic birds, including peacocks, up close. We waited but couldn't get one to open his colorful tail feathers for us. There were water buffalo, crocodiles, monkeys, wild deer, sloth bears, and of course more elephants. Sloth bears were rarely sighted, but we were lucky to see one with her cub climbing a mountainside. The real prize was to spot a leopard. The populations are dwindling, so it isn't always a given that you get to see one.

We had a great driver, though, who kept his radio and cell phone going, to get any tips from the other drivers if they were in an area with a leopard. He had heard something promising, and we were off at a fast clip to the area where one other jeep was stopped. We came up beside them slowly, stayed very quiet, and watched. We started to slowly creep along the path and finally, we saw one napping in a tree. It was getting close to dusk when they usually start hunting, but he didn't seem to be in much hurry, or perhaps he just wasn't hungry. I got a pretty good photo of that one by zooming in, even though he was quite far away.

Our driver decided to move on slowly to a different area, keeping his experienced eyes peeled. After about ten minutes, suddenly he stopped. He turned around and pointed. Not very far away, maybe thirty or forty feet, he'd spotted one. The leopard saw us, and looked curious. He started to slowly creep toward us. There was a small outcropping of bushes about a dozen feet from the vehicle. He stopped, crouched near the bush, but out far enough that we could see him well and he could keep his intense focus on us. I remember thinking, *I wonder if he's sizing us up for dinner?*

He never moved closer, thank heavens, as he could easily have jumped into our open vehicle. I guess he decided we didn't look tasty! Phil, being the real photographer in the family, got the best shot of this guy, and only our jeep with us and the couple from Somerset got to see him in the flesh.

It was getting dark quickly by that time, and our driver cranked up his speed to get us out of the bush since headlights are not permitted. They keep this sanctuary as close to the real wild as possible. Well, except for a few jeeps roaming through now and then, but headlights are never permitted. He kept going as fast as he could without spilling us out onto the heavily rutted terrain. By the time we reached the entrance, it was completely dark. I was sure glad he knew the way.

Toward the end of our stay, Lalith had arranged a reception for us with the representatives we'd met from the estates we visited and their wives. It was a lovely event with dinner and socializing into the evening. As I spoke with some of the wives, I remember thinking, *This feels like America in the 1950s.* None of the wives had careers. They were draped in lavish jewelry and dress. Their role simply seemed to be to help entertain their husbands' work contacts, raise the children, and manage the home. The development in Sri Lanka was happening fast. While some 70 percent of the population, if I remember correctly, was still without electricity at that time, cell phones were becoming commonplace. They were demanding the expansion of utilities infrastructure so that each home could have a refrigerator—and a computer! Understandably, they wanted their fair share of what was out there to be had. And they wanted to be connected with the rest of the world via cell phones and computers.

I hope, in this rapidly developing country, they don't make the same mistakes we have. The tea companies' conglomerates own many of the large hotels and other businesses. There seemed to be a sort of monopoly going on. I don't know anything, really, about their government. But I sincerely hope they monitor their growth and have wise and fair leaders to guide that beautiful island nation to a good place. And, I sincerely hope, as this growth expands, these lovely people do not lose their kind and gentle nature.

Our last night was back in Colombo at the Mount Lavinia Hotel. Some of the scenes from the movie *Bridge on the River Kwai* were filmed there, depicting the colonial command post of the British Army. It had a definite British air of formality about it. The service and accommodations were lavish. There wasn't a door we could walk up to that wasn't opened for us by a crisply uniformed attendant. Right on the coast, overlooking the Indian Ocean, it's another place I'd love to go back to visit again.

On our last night, we found a tuk-tuk driver and paid him to just drive us around for a half an hour. He didn't take us into the city for a joyride. We just tooled around up and down the coast at dusk, watching the sun lower into the ocean, just as it was setting on our amazing Sri Lankan adventure.

I'm not sure I've ever been more relaxed as I was by the final day of that wonderful journey. I remember thinking, as we boarded the plane, *I don't want to go home.* I knew as soon as we stepped foot in America again, all the "hectic" of living here would set in again. We've got some waking up to do here. I learned a lot from the serene, gentle Sri Lankan people, and I will carry it with me forever.

Chapter 10

The Politics of Business; the Politics of Life

air warning: You may want to skip this chapter if you can't handle a load of truth and hard-core reality about the politics of small business in America today.

I used to live under a rock. Like many Americans. Before I had my own business, I knew little of the political side of things, the real workings of the economic world of business. I went to a regular job, put in my eight hours, forgot about it when I walked out the door at the end of the day and on weekends, and collected my paycheck every two weeks.

But politics has a way of seeping into everything. Even arenas where you think there would be none. Take Tai Chi, for example. I have practiced Taoist Tai Chi for many years, on and off. In the beginning, I was very interested in the organization, so I decided to serve on the board. I thought I would just offer my time and energies to help this wonderfully health-oriented organization grow. I thought, *This is a Taoist organization, surely everybody will be on the same path and come from a gentle, Taoist perspective.* I couldn't have been more wrong.

There were factions, I discovered. Some who wanted to call all the shots and rule over others. They had strayed from the national guidelines, and wanted to run it with a more western mentality. They had not kept up with the fine nuances of the form, so people weren't getting the best instruction to improve their form over time. And, while they stated they wanted to grow, some would not agree to move from a restrictive location that was costing far more than it should and was too remote to allow for much growth.

Lots of battles ensued. Eventually, with the help of my dear cousin AJ, who had also fallen in love with this healing art, and another truly dedicated instructor, Nancy, who wanted to get us back on the right path, we succeeded in accomplishing moves that led to the growth and realignment we wanted and the local organization desperately needed.

It took a toll. It tainted the pure Tao of my practice for a while. The battles were fierce at times, and that took away the serenity of the form for me. I eventually got away from the politics when I resigned from the board and realigned my practice purely for my own health and growth. In the end, the experience left me with a greater skill to fight for what I knew was right. It turned out to be invaluable when I entered the world of small business.

Delving into business gives you a front-row seat to how things really work in the world and a clear vision of the ugly politics embedded in our capitalist culture. You find out that slicing out your piece of the American pie may turn out to be more than you can chew. The American dream looks like more of a nightmare at times. And there is absolutely no more going home after a day's work and forgetting about things.

Work hard, do what you love, and the money will follow, so they say, and so I thought. No one could have worked harder than I did to keep this business afloat for sixteen years. It seemed like for every step forward, there was some stumbling block that prevented real growth and often forces that pushed me back a step or two.

I've analyzed and reanalyzed why I was never able to get much past break even to a reasonable profit. The results revealed a complicated puzzle. There was no one piece that even stood out as the main culprit explaining why I could only seem to just get by. But, several factors caught my eye, and in my opinion, if they don't get some serious attention from our government, small businesses of unique character will cease to exist in this country.

What became clear and made for a not-so-pretty picture of capitalism was the disheartening decline of customs and conventions that at one time made America the best at everything. What I saw over those sixteen years was that America had become hostage to Greed—with a capital G. And that's a one-way ticket to doom.

In the first three years, business grew on an upward curve, as might be expected. By year three in 2003, I'd nearly doubled what I did in the first year. I expected it to peak and level off at some point, but instead, the aftermath of 9/11 seemed to take a toll that permanently changed the psyche of the country. People were hit hard that something this horrible could happen on our own soil, and the lingering caution manifested itself in tightened purse strings.

Where sales should have at least stayed level, sales started dropping off year by year. It just didn't make sense. I was getting more well known in the retail landscape and had a growing register of new customers. I had a newsletter list (consisting of only those who volunteered their email address and were regular customers) of over two thousand people. And I had a bevy of very regular regulars who came in so often that I knew them by name. But, by the crash of 2008, I'd slid back down to the meager profits of my first year, and no matter what I did after that, I just couldn't get the growth back.

I think one puzzle piece of the problem was location. I don't mean which building I was in or street I was on and how much traffic flow there was. All four shop locations were on streets with the highest traffic flows in Toledo. I think the problem was Toledo itself.

Toledo is one of the cities that just didn't seem to recover fully from the trauma of 9/11 in 2001, and even more so, from the crash of 2008 and subsequent recession. Other cities have rebounded back to what they were before the crash, to some semblance of normal. Not so for Toledo. It seems that for every new business that opens, one or two established businesses close.

I can also tell you this: Toledo is one of the least friendly cities to small business. Now, I've never done business in another city, but I can see how businesses thrive in cities nearby—Ann Arbor, Columbus, and Cleveland. Toledo is large enough; it should have followed suit. And I've talked to enough business owners who operated in other cities to know that there's a striking difference in attitude.

But, no matter how hard this little engine tries, it just can't seem to get over the hill of stagnation. Lots of new businesses come, and few are able to stick around for more than a couple of years. Toledo has a beautiful riverfront that for some unknown reason, it just can't ever seem to develop into a lively and thriving community of businesses.

I remember back when I was just out of college, a famous poet with whom I was familiar, Jorge Luis Borges, came to Toledo for a poetry reading or some other event; I don't recall the particulars. He was interviewed by the newspaper the next day and asked about his impressions of the city. I will never forget what he said.

He said that he had traveled all around the world. He had seen many cities with beautiful riverfronts, which usually gave rise to development thriving with activity. But he said that he had never seen one with a riverfront so wasted and undeveloped as Toledo. These cutting words appeared in an article in the local newspaper the day after his event.

I was embarrassed. I was disheartened. And ever since, I have been one of the biggest cheerleaders for the city, following every effort to help it grow. I'll never figure out why, but my experience seems a sad parallel to the stagnation of our riverfront. I will never figure out why a city with such potential fails to realize it. And why they are so positively stifling to small business.

Another example so ardent I will never forget it, is when Ed Schultz, from his MSNBC news show, *The Ed Show*, came into town to film one of his segments. I don't remember the exact year, but I'd probably been in business five or so years. They usually didn't come to places like Toledo, but the hot-button issue of the moment was on labor, and Toledo has a strong presence in the world of unions.

He was driven from Toledo Airport, about ten minutes outside of Toledo's west side, through the west side and central Toledo, and then into downtown, where the location of his show was filmed. In that twenty-five-minute drive, he got to see a good slice of the city. As soon as he got on air, and before he even got into his show, he said he had to mention something that he couldn't help notice on his ride in from the airport.

He said something very close to this:

"Well, I gotta tell you, folks. I travel all around this country, and I've seen a lot of cities across this great land. But, as I rode across this city on my way in from the airport, I gotta tell ya, I've never seen anything like it. Buildings shuttered and out of business, vacancy after vacancy, and as many spaces for lease as filled with active business. This is a ghost town when it comes to thriving business."

That made my heart sink. It was embarrassing to have that so openly revealed on national news, even though it was true. It was disheartening to hear that brazen truth spoken out loud. I will never forget his shocked disappointment in the face of this city, so reminiscent of that of Borges so many years before.

Toledo has gotten its negative notoriety in a few other instances, too. Who can forget John Denver crooning about the sidewalks rolling up by ten? His visit to Toledo was so dull and boring, he describes it as having spent "a week there one day."

So, for whatever reason that no one can seem to figure out, Toledo sits in stagnation. Growth is a struggle here. Survival is a struggle. But that was where I was living, and I didn't want to relocate or travel every day to try to run a business, say, forty minutes away in Ann Arbor.

I was driven, in spite of all the handicaps, hardships, and setbacks, to save my business. I spent every waking moment, and I swear in my dreams too, on tweaking the business or solving whatever current problem had arisen. I'd try any new feasible-seeming idea to help bring in new customers. But the city, or just retail life in general, threw one curveball after another. Let's take regulations for starters.

I've already mentioned some of the health department regulations that ended up costing me money. I'll reiterate that I was more than willing to keep things safe for my customers, but the imposition of regs that don't make sense or shouldn't apply to you only shows how mindless and unthinking government agencies have become. In my opinion, it is the single most destructive element in business and our society today.

Imposing regulations like requiring a grease trap for ANY operation that serves food is a prime example. When I tried in vain to explain to the health department that I didn't put any grease down the sink, it fell on deaf ears. When I questioned the validity of imposing this unnecessary expense on my type of business that it should not have applied to, I was told that there were other businesses, like gas stations, that also had to have three compartment sinks with grease traps, and they only sold prepackaged food. So the fact that the rule was applied even more unfairly to someone else was supposed to make me shut up and accept it. Wow. *That's pretty absurd,* I thought.

In a city which is always struggling to grow, I would have thought they would welcome a delightful new business with open arms. One would think they would bend over backwards to help a new business get its doors open. Maybe even have some funds to help shoestring-budgeted new small businesses get a start. You know, like there's all kinds of money available to large corporations. But just getting an occupancy permit to open those doors was a nightmare of hoops to jump through. And there were constant power plays that seemed to exist for no rational purpose than power itself.

Apparently, you needed to get that occupancy permit if you had done any major electrical, plumbing, or structural changes to a suite. My first opening was held up by all of the extra nonsense inspectors had imposed on me. Each subsequent opening got better. In part because the second two shops were in Sylvania Township, not Toledo proper. They seemed a little more lenient and less nit-picky. By the fourth shop, I had it down pat and managed to skirt the whole process.

I'd gotten a licensed plumber to install my sinks. He was supposed to have his work inspected, but I don't think he ever did. I never saw any documentation on it, and I didn't really care. I just wanted to get open as quickly as possible. I knew the sinks were installed and functional and that's all I needed. Except that embedded in his charges were monies to cover inspection fees, and he pocketed that money. Why do so many people cheat?

The electrical was so minor—just putting in two extra outlets—I wasn't going to call an electrician for that. It would have cost an exorbitant amount, and my husband, who is pretty good at electrical work, did it himself. No inspection needed then. I wasn't going to open myself up to harassment over the poor electrical conditions that no doubt existed in this old building, and the city would insist that I as a renter, not the building owner, would have to upgrade the building.

We actually found out later, when my husband went to change an air filter in the ceiling, that the electrical up there had so many code violations it wasn't funny. At least what Phil had installed was up to code. So, obviously, because these costs, which should have been borne by the landlord, were always passed on to the tenant, many others before me had done their own electrical work as well. It is way cheaper to have your friend or brother or husband, who knows a little about electrical, install changes than to have to pay a licensed contractor.

Later when I was having so many problems with the landlord, and would have loved for him to get in trouble with the city, I reported the unsafe electrical in the ceiling. It took numerous and extreme efforts (phone calls, messages, letters, registered letters, and the threat of getting news media involved) on my part to get the inspectors to even come to the building. Clearly, they were dragging their feet in hopes I would drop the issue. Clearly, they were protecting the building owner. Since the electrical problems were put in by someone other than me, and they were discovered after I'd been there for a year, it would fall on him to bring them up to code.

Nothing ever happened while I was there. No electricians ever showed up, and I can pretty much guarantee that that building is still grossly out of code and unsafe to occupy. But, as the landlord rubs elbows with the city government officials, and probably donates to their campaigns, just as in national government, he gets away with leaving the building out of code, hoping the next unsuspecting tenant will get inspected and have to foot the bill to upgrade his building. Sheer shenanigans.

The only changes we made to the suite were to fill an opening in a wall and added a service counter. That's all. So, I figured that qualified as no major structural changes, and I opened my doors in record time with NO inspections. Maybe I was skirting the absolute letter of the law, but by this time, I knew what I was doing, knew what was safe, and knew better than to invite trouble in the front door.

Another example of regulation absurdity was my teapot-shaped sign in the front of my fourth shop location. I already had a $4000, top-of-the-line, individually lettered, backlit sign to hang on the front of the shop. I paid around $400 to have it mounted and wired to this new storefront. It looked nice but just wasn't getting much notice since it was difficult to see.

The shop was too far back from the street and there was a large old oak tree just off to the side of my storefront that blocked the visibility of it totally when coming from the west. It was blocked from the east by the neighboring business's large sign, which hung out perpendicular to the building. By the time customers could see it coming from the east, they would have passed the parking lot driveway.

Getting found and being easily seen by customers is paramount for any business, and especially challenging for a very small business. You don't have that large of a building to put a very large sign on. You can see big department store signs blocks before you hit the parking lot. But, with tiny businesses, often there is only one small spot in front for mounting signage. Too easy to miss.

And when customers miss your shop, sometimes they just drive on by, and you lose the business. I had countless customers tell me their frustration in finding me and, luckily, how many times they drove back and forth before they got to the right driveway. Those are the ones who persevered, but I'd never know how many just gave up and never came back.

So, I thought, I'll put another sign in the front yard of the shop, close to the road, that will get noticed as people drive by. You see these sandwich board type signs in front of many small shops. I knew the city didn't permit sandwich boards, although many businesses would put them out anyway, in desperation to get their businesses noticed until the city fined or harassed them enough. According to a barber shop down the street from me, "If you don't let me keep my sandwich board sign out by the street, you might as well shut me down because I'll be out of business in no time."

I decided to put in a properly mounted, in-ground sign. I already had the large teapot-shaped sign, as it was the sign I had over the door of my first shop. I had the old Cadfael's name taken off and new lettering put on both sides so that it could be seen from both directions of traffic passing the front of the shop. I'd simply reached my limit on the many complaints from customers that they couldn't see the sign above my doors in this shop, huge as it was, until they passed the shop.

In business, especially a very small business, you cannot afford to lose even one customer. Your continual challenge is in removing any deterrents to getting customers in your front door. So, when customers express a frustration like mine did with the signage issue, you try to fix it as soon as you can. And it is a necessity to do it as inexpensively as you can.

Since I had the teapot sign already, it was cute and would be an attractive addition to the neighborhood, and I knew how to properly mount it, my husband installed it in front of the shop. I was careful to make sure that it was back from the road far enough to not block the vision of traffic coming from either direction or exiting the parking lot. Customers noticed and it worked for me too, to be able to say, "Just look for the big white teapot!" Many thanked me as they could now easily find the shop.

The "illegal" teapot sign.
After lots of haggling, I won and it stayed.

The city *may* have let it slide, but a neighboring business—the one with the large sign that blocked mine—had complained about it. That was in retribution, since I had complained about an ugly hand-lettered, huge A-frame sign he had put out that was infringing on my shop frontage. So, they came to inspect the sign and blindly imposed some more regulations on me.

Technically, I had not gotten a new permit for the sign. I said I'd be happy to. But they also said it could not be left where it had been placed. It was outside the sidewalk, and according to sign code, it had to be inside the sidewalk. Problem was, on my side of the street, instead of the sidewalk being the typical three feet from the road, it was twelve feet. A sign placed inside that wouldn't have been seen any better than the one over my front door. More money wasted, and my customers still wouldn't be able to find me.

There existed, I found out, a variance procedure, which was designed to address such issues, where a variance could be granted to bypass the letter of the current regulation when there were special circumstances. Or at least that's what it looked like on the surface. Of course, there was a cost of $150 just to apply for a variance. Variance hearings were only held once a month, and from many other businesses and citizens who had applied for variances in the past, I'd been told the answer was always "NO."

I was also told by the city inspector, while wielding his abusive power over me, that the answer would absolutely be "NO" if I applied for a variance because I was outside the letter of the regulation. I asked, "Then why even have a variance procedure if you won't ever allow a slight variance from the regulation?" And of course, I got no reasonable answer, just a runaround. I did apply, but I'd told them that I couldn't afford $150 for a charade if the answer was just going to be no. In the end, the city wouldn't even hear my variance request and sent my money back.

I was left with constant harassment and threats of stiff and recurring fines if I didn't take the sign down. So, I waged my fight-back campaign. The local papers got wind of it and it got a lot of notice from two significant articles in *The Toledo Blade*, our main newspaper. There was also a short blurb on it in the "Hip Happenings" posted in the city paper.

I'd asked customers for support, and many sent me emails to forward to the city, asking them to leave me alone since they needed my sign to find the shop and it was attractive, properly mounted, and wasn't impeding drivers' vision in any way. One customer even sent a letter to the editor of *The Blade*.

After several meetings with the whole neighborhood of businesses, all expressing the need for yard signs, the city relented and said they would make an addendum to the code that left our neighborhood of businesses free to place signs, even A-frames, in the yard space in front of their businesses. Within new parameters, of course.

Ultimately, I don't think they ever wrote and placed the new parameters in the code and basically just dropped it and left us alone. So, this time was one of those small wins. What it took out of me in time and stress level was another story. But I tried to see the positive side of it all. I did get a lot of free publicity out of it, I got to keep my sign after all, and eventually the harassment stopped.

While I'm on the topic of city-related things, I'll share another bit of shady business and the reason, I believe, our city has such a difficult time making progress and keeping businesses afloat.

That same city councilman had meetings with our neighborhood of businesses because the city had received grant money from the state of Ohio for development of retail districts in old, stable neighborhoods. The idea was to pattern after districts in Columbus, Ohio, our state capital, which were very successful in revitalizing old neighborhoods and attracting good quality businesses to them. There are several of these neighborhoods like German Village and The Short North that everyone familiar with Columbus knows.

The concept is a great boon to businesses in these neighborhoods. In addition to being in league with other great businesses, it's a considerable benefit to be able to say to customers, "I'm in the Short North," and have them know immediately where you are located. I, and all the other businesses on my strip, were very excited about the concept and interested in seeing this plan developed.

It had been at least two years and still nothing had been done with this grant when I first moved into the neighborhood. I'd heard about it, but nothing ever seemed to materialize. I and a few others made some inquiries about it, so the city finally responded and about a year after I'd moved in, there was a meeting with the city councilman to discuss getting this project going. We were all excited at the prospect.

We were told at that first meeting that the original grant amount was for $150,000. But, in the years that nothing was happening with it, the councilman said he'd given half of it away to another councilperson for a project they were working on. That was curious, because I was under the impression that grant money had to be spent on what it was granted for. Still, we thought we should be able to do something useful with the remaining $75,000.

Ideas were tossed out about getting signs or flags to place along the mile so that people could get to know exactly where the district was. It was a mile-long strip on Sylvania Ave. The working name the city was using was The Sylvania Avenue Mile, but no one liked that and it was decided that we would need to come up with a new name first off. Everyone gave their contact information, and we left with hope and anticipation for the next working meeting.

It was at that first meeting that every neighboring business spoke up about the sign issues after I brought it up. With so many businesses explaining that if they couldn't keep their little road-side signs up, they might as well shutter their doors, the councilman relented and said he'd get the city off our backs. Power in numbers.

As for the follow-up meeting, it never came. Not in good time, anyway, and not arranged by the councilman. It was another year later, when I'd started talking to other businesses about us having a meeting with or without the city council's participation. One other shop owner said that she was thinking the same thing. She said she knew the councilman and would invite him to the meeting.

Good, I thought. *We'll get things going again.* I wanted to get this shopping district on the map and noticed by the city. It wasn't doing any of us any good to sit on this pile of grant money and do nothing with it.

But, by the time the next meeting was held, the story about the money had changed. It became some convoluted string of excuses for why not much money was left. We had decided to put up flags on the light poles to let people know where the district was. The city put up about a half a dozen abstract American flags on poles along the mile. The councilman said that it cost $2400 out of our budget to put the flags up. I'm sure they were just sitting in some city warehouse from a previous Fourth of July celebration and pulled out at no cost to be reused on our mile. The whole money issue was already fishy, but now it was starting to really stink.

What? How was that going to tell anyone anything about a new neighborhood district? Abstract American flags? No name, no information, no identity. At the next meeting I brought up the issue that we needed our name out there. We had decided on The West Oak Walk, or WOW District. I remember voting on new flags, which I thought were going to have our name on them, but somehow just different American flags replaced the original ones. Each time those few flags were put up, we were told that the cost was around $2400. Now, I'd looked into things like flags and signage enough to know that was a blatant lie. Fish were stinking again.

What, again with the American flag thing? So, I pressed the issue at the next meeting to get the name of the district out there so that people would know of its existence. For the third time, more flags were voted on, and finally a few went up with the name on them. No announcement by the city, no hoopla, so, basically, people still don't really know about the WOW District. I've never heard anyone mention it. If I told someone that I was in the West Oak Walk, or WOW District, they'd just say, "What's that?"

Another thing I tried to get put into place to help get the district noticed was park benches along the sidewalks in front of businesses. The benches could have the WOW District logo on them, and that would surely help get the district known. That mile got more foot traffic than most in Toledo, so benches seemed like a great idea. When they were brought up, the councilman agreed and said that the city could get them made with the logo on them, but that each business who wanted one would have to pay for them.

Seriously, WHAT? What the hell happened to the $150,000, or the $75,000, or even the $67,800 after those expensive, recycled American flags were "purchased"? That should have bought quite a few benches. They would be the property of the city, paid for by city grant money. Why should any business owner who is renting space have to buy a bench that would stay there after that business closed or moved on? None of this made any sense. It sure wasn't on the up and up.

The results—after years of ineptitude and graft, there was no real benefit to the businesses on that neighborhood mile. The councilman was just trying to find out a way to justify the dwindling of a pot of grant money, which was never spent on what it was designated for: the development of a neighbor-hood shopping district. Whenever he was questioned on these explanations that didn't make sense, he just came back with something more convoluted that dodged and didn't really answer the questions. He actually joked about it once and said that people were telling him that he was turning into a true politician, and he seemed quite proud of that.

I believe to this day that the money was given away to cronies of the councilman. I can't know for sure, but why else would you request grant money for city development, lie about the amount of money and fudge expenditures, and drag feet until overwhelming frustration set in, and the whole idea was dropped?

What ever happened to that original $150,000 grant money? And as I said before, as far as I understand, grant money cannot be given away or spent on any other cause than that for which it was granted. But, again, the state apparently does little or no follow up on grant money, just as they wouldn't follow up on the money given to banks for interest rate reductions that should have been passed along to the businesses.

Most Americans have a pretty good idea that graft and corruption abound in our federal government. But trust me, it's metastasized all the way through state governments, and on down to the local level. And, it's much worse than one might want to believe. The fact that the councilman was in charge of obtaining all of the city's grants, not just our $150,000, left me wondering just how much had his cronies profited, in turn obliging them to donate to any of his future political campaigns.

We've got some heavy-duty cleanup to do in our political sectors: federal, state, and local.

Small businesses have few means to protect themselves from corruption or losses that the public might bring about. In the beginning, I hired an attorney to set up my business as an LLC, a Limited Liability Company. That means, anyone who sues your company for some reason, cannot go after your personal property. So that limitation assures that your personal property and assets are protected, and one can only take from the business to settle any lawsuit against your business.

In order for that to work, you would need to be able to sign loan documents, leases, and any other legal agreement in the name of the LLC, with you as a member of the LLC. In my entire sixteen years in business, I don't think I was able (allowed) to sign any document in the name of the LLC. I had to sign in my name as a personal guarantee, which meant that anyone suing me could come after both the business and any of my personal assets. So, what point was it to pay an attorney to even set up the LLC? Truthfully, none.

I also paid him to read an over-thirty-page fine-print lease agreement for me to alert me to anything different from past leases or anything of concern. I remember him saying, "Sign it. It's all standard stuff." But none of it was standard to me. He charged me a couple hundred dollars for his time and didn't even have the courtesy to explain things to me like all my financial liabilities that were riddled throughout all that fine print.

Another time my attorney failed to protect me was when I wanted to renew my lease on the Monroe Street shop. That's the one where the building got sold out from underneath me and I had to move with little notice. I had been trying to renew the lease for months, and the realtor simply wouldn't return my calls. I even went to the realty company's physical offices to try to make contact with them.

All of this left me with a very uneasy feeling. So, I decided to start writing letters to them so that I had some documentation of my efforts to renew. Even when I was able to get the realtor on the phone one day, he gave me a flimsy excuse that the building owner was out of the country and promised he would get the lease signed as soon as the owner returned.

A few weeks later, I came to work to find the notice on the back door, telling me that I would have to vacate the premises soon. So, I thought, *Call an attorney.* Since my early years, I'd found another one who I thought would be more effective than my original one.

When I explained the situation to him, I was told that since the letters I'd sent were after the required notice period of intent to renew, even though I'd been trying to renew months before, that I had no choice but to vacate the building. As lying is rampant in our society, he knew that the realtor would just lie about when I first contacted him, especially since he'd been lying to me about the owner being out of town. He'd only been waiting to seal the deal on selling his building and didn't want the encumbrance of another several years' lease. Had I been able to sign a new lease, it wouldn't have prevented him from selling the building, but the new owner would have to essentially buy me out if he wanted me to move before my lease was up. As it was, my current lease was up in about a month.

So, I had no protection and my only alternative was to leave. That buyout would have gone a long way toward paying for my move, an always costly endeavor. And it would have given me some leverage in leaving the building in a more comfortable time frame. It was beyond disappointing that my lawyer did nothing to at least try to fight the issue or help me get some sort of buyout in the spirit of cooperation.

Lesson number "who knows which?"—*Attorneys have an overblown opinion of what their time is worth.* In all my years, I don't think I've ever gotten any real help or my money's worth from an attorney, and try to stay away from them as much as possible.

Retail is in serious trouble in this country. Big and small. Large department stores are barely holding on. Sears filed bankruptcy and has closed so many stores, it may as well be totally out of business. Penney's has had to close stores. Pier One Imports and Bed Bath & Beyond have closed. The way they do business has had to change, just to stay alive. Several large, well-established specialty stores have left our local mall. There's just not enough business, enough revenue to stay alive.

One thing that has dramatically changed the retail landscape is big-box discount stores, like Kohl's. Now, I love Kohl's and watch for my discount coupons like anyone else. But what they, and others, have created is a mentality that almost everything is on sale and at a hefty discount. Something is on sale all the time. People barely notice 10 percent or 15 percent anymore. You've got to hit 30 to 50 percent or more to get attention these days. And, on top of the sales discount already marked in the store, Kohl's gives an occasional 15 to 30 percent *on top!*

The items they carry are mostly of reasonable quality and comparable to most regular department stores. So, people aren't willing to pay more regular pricing with little or no discounts for merchandise of equal or not-much-better quality. Consequently, the regular department stores are also having to put merchandise on sale all the time in order to compete.

This is where capitalism has gone awry. Competition is usually a good thing, and has traditionally promoted the development of a better widget in order to get your widget noticed over your competitor's. Have we reached a pinnacle in quality, where it's just not possible to make your widget stand out? Is it because goods are so readily available from all over the world? A market that used to produce "better" is now producing price wars. The cheapest price is the new variable that wins the business, not necessarily the better-quality product.

The internet hasn't helped much either. Without the overhead of shop space and having to employ as many workers, internet businesses can sell the same product as a brick-and-mortar store at a lower price and still make a comparable (or better?) profit margin. Expedited shipping and effortless cruising of thousands of products from your easy chair has made it quick and painless to shop the internet instead of physically trudging to the store.

And if all of this hits even the big stores, you can imagine what it has done to truly small retail businesses. Well, unless you carry the mentality that small doesn't count. I remember trying to explain to a customer how the crash in 2008 had impacted my business dramatically. He looked incredulous, and he mumbled something like, "How could it? You're so small!" As if because of the smallness, the economy couldn't touch us. Truth is, it impacts small businesses to a far more devastating degree.

Larger businesses have a buffer that gives them some protection. Larger budgets, so more money to play with, to cover losses, to make changes. Greater profit margins, so some losses and dips in income can more easily be absorbed. Those buffers make it possible for them to ride out a storm.

Not so with the very small mom-and-pops. The budget is tight—small at best and sometimes almost nonexistent. There simply is no buffer with which to ride out a storm. What I had to do when the near depression hit in 2008 was to take out of my own pocket. Thankfully, I had tucked away a generous wedding gift from my great aunt, and thought, *Now is the time to use it.* So, I put that into the kitty to cover expenses that slim revenues just couldn't. Thanks, Aunt Anna!

Large businesses have another serious advantage over mom-and-pops and that is buying power. Large, chain retail stores can buy in huge quantities, thus getting the lowest wholesale pricing available. When you're small, firstly, there is simply no room to store large quantities of product, even if one could purchase more to get better pricing; and secondly, the budget simply doesn't allow such large expenditures.

For example, let's take an average teapot. I still have minimums to meet for wholesale ordering, like I might have to buy a minimum of three of each style of teapot to get wholesale pricing at all. So, I would pay $10 per teapot for one I could sell for $20. A medium-sized store or small chain would be able to buy say, twenty of those teapots, and might get a wholesale price of $7 each. So, when they sell, they get $13 per pot, where I only get $10.

And, when it comes to the large and megachains, like Kohl's, Meijer's, Walmart, and Costco, they are buying direct from the manufacturer, and in very large quantities. I've never been privy to actual numbers, but they get their wholesale costs down so low that there's no way anyone smaller could ever compete with them.

And, another thing, by the time you'd sell a very large quantity of something, it might not be good, if perishable, or might go out of style or desirability. I tried to carry popular tea items, like clotted cream, but it always went out of date before I could sell the quantity I had to order.

In the beginning years, I sold tons of English fine and bone china. I'd stock up especially at Christmas, sure I'd sell most of what I'd ordered. I watched my sales so closely, I adjusted whenever I needed to, and over the years, English china has fallen seriously out of fashion. Toward the end, I would only order it by special order, and carried almost none of it in the shop. I think I had the same two or three teapots that sat on the shelves throughout the last five years, never selling. They finally went to another tea shop who bought most of my leftover wares after I closed the shop.

Other inequities lie in the fact that when you are small, you pay the most for everything, not just merchandise. I paid a much higher utility rate than any large factory or retail store in town. My cable for internet services cost more. My credit card fees were the highest. A large company might only pay 1 percent or less (One such company recently told me that they pay 0 percent!) for each credit card sale, but my rate is over 2.5 percent and sometimes over 3 percent.

Most of these inequities are impossible to get around. Believe me, I tried. I'd spend stubborn hours dealing with credit card companies, trying to find a way to get my rates down. I'd try to find ways to do things usually only large companies could do. I was always scheming. So much so, for sixteen years, that three years after closing, I still have trouble trying to get my mind to chill and not overanalyze everything.

When I came up with the first *Tea Taster's Journal* ever, I figured out a way I could get it printed. It wasn't really a book, because it only had about twenty pages of tea information in the beginning of it. The rest of the pages were simply empty formatted journal pages for recording your impressions of teas you tasted over time. So, I figured out I could do a spiral bound book at a regular office store printer, basically publishing the book myself.

I had no idea how it would sell, so I couldn't risk buying too many copies all at once. I bought a batch of a hundred for starters. It sold slowly, but eventually I had to reorder another batch. Subsequent batches weren't any larger than the first, again, because of budget and storage space. So, a hundred copies cost me significantly more than what I'd have paid had I been able to order a thousand at the start.

Advertising was another arena riddled with inequity. Ads are expensive, but the more you can buy, like everything else, the less they cost. So, while I'd like to pay a much lower cost for my ad spots, I simply couldn't afford the quantity I needed to buy to get that lower price. The double whammy in advertising was that ads don't work well unless they are used in very large quantities. People need to be bombarded these days before ads have much impact. None of that really mattered. Reality is, you must live within your budget. If I could only afford four ads a month instead of forty, that's what I had to live with.

Rents are another big hit for the very small enterprise. And the price for the space is the price for the space. There's little wiggle room, unless you are so sure of your business longevity and success that you can sign leases for more years at a time. So, a Subway that can fit into the same-size suite as I did, pays the same rent as I (or maybe even less if they could commit to longer leases), but the revenues from a day at Subway are significantly larger than those from a small tea shop, or unique gift shop, or used bookstore, or an independent clothing boutique.

As far as the building owners are concerned, it's simply not their problem. And it really isn't. It ends up falling squarely on the shoulders of the unique, small-business owners, trying to figure out how to make it work in a business climate solidly stacked against their success.

When you add the internet into this whole mix, with the low overhead advantage for internet businesses, it's a wonder any small business can make it anywhere. That statistic I'm sure most have heard, which says something like nine out of ten small businesses fail in the first three years is a gross misnomer. Those true innovators, grassroots entrepreneurs who put their blood, sweat, tears, hearts, and souls into their businesses are *not* failures. The inequitably stacked system is where the true failure lies.

Given the same parameters, restrictions, and inequities, just as many large and megabusinesses would fail, too. It's just that they get all the advantages that help them to get to sustainability and huge profits. Lower product costs, lower utilities, lower advertising rates, lower credit card costs, lower costs all around, and many times, extra help from city, state, and federal government programs. And, let's not forget huge tax breaks. Give those same advantages to small businesses, and how many more might be able to succeed?

When you look at some of the grosser inequities in other businesses, such as the oil industry, it gets even more maddening. I read an article a few years ago that mentioned that for big oil, the profit margin on every barrel of oil was 1:32. Mine, on every teapot was 1:2. But, who, on top of that kind of profit margin, gets all kinds of government subsidies? Big oil. There are no subsidies for small businesses. The mentality is simply that you don't count. You're on your own to figure out how to cut a deck that is solidly stacked against you. And if you can't cut it, we'll put you down as one of those nine out of ten that couldn't make it.

It's disheartening, to say the least, and at times I probably reached a level of fury over the hard-core, unfair realities of running a small business. After a while, I learned that my anger made for no changes, and only drained my energies. And I needed all the energy I could muster to make it through my days. I got more and more clever at finding ways to balance out the inequities and kept my focus on never quitting, no matter how hard it got.

Not all people are as hardheaded as me, and many people choose to just get out. Even that's a difficult thing to do, especially when you have all that heart and soul wrapped up in it. At times, I almost felt it was truly going to kill me or that I'd end up so debilitated physically and mentally that I'd have a heart attack or stroke. Perhaps all that healthy tea I consume prevented that from happening, despite all the heart disease in my family. Who knows? But I do know this: it should not be this difficult. It should not take this much from one's soul and very being to keep a small business running. It's absurdly unfair.

I truly feel that if we don't get a handle on this, there will come a sad day where we have nothing but big box stores and the internet. No character, no charm, no innovation, no originality. No face-to-face interpersonal connection, nobody knowing your name. I have often thought and said that if this country does not begin to value these small business gems that add much charm and character to the landscape of our cities and towns, we will end up in a very dull, gray world without them.

This is where it becomes a very political issue. Capitalism run rampant and riddled with corruption as ours has become, simply doesn't work in the long run. It has slanted the field in favor of the large and powerful. And with added subsidies, when their profits are already substantial, they are enabled to reach shameless levels of greed and wealth beyond all reason.

Things are out of whack. There used to be standards and formulas. When everyone lived within those parameters, things worked better. General rule of thumb in retail was that wholesale pricing was based on a reasonable markup from production costs. Retail costs were based on a reasonable markup from wholesale costs; generally, retail was set at twice the wholesale. But in this era of extreme greed, it's become *charge whatever you think you can get away with*. That's got pricing of goods way out of whack.

Another practice that's skewed pricing into insane territory is the conditioning of the American consumer into thinking that they need to get an "on-sale" price *all the time*. It might have worked at first, for a little while. But, you just can't turn a profit by offering goods "on sale" all the time. So, in order to make that work, original prices have had to be adjusted up.

Look at the numbers. An item that is worth $50, and you sell it for $50, you get $25 to replenish your stock with another item, and you need the $25 profit off that item to make your ends meet. Out of the $25 profit, you can pay your overhead, and you have a little left over to pay yourself. At least that's roughly how it should work.

But then you start to offer items on sale, say for 30 percent off because customers are conditioned to not buy unless things are on sale. Soon, you will find that $10 profit instead of the normal $25 profit may not even allow you to pay the bills, and there certainly won't be any money left over for yourself.

So, what you have to do, once you get into this insidious game, is raise the original price to a falsely high retail price. So, you raise the "retail" price to $72 and tell the customer you're selling it at 30 percent off! The consumer, who in this country has also been conditioned to not think, is happy because it looks like they are getting almost $22 off of a $72 item. You are left with a little over $50. I.e., you have your original $25 to replenish the item in your store and $25 to cover your overhead and your paycheck.

What that's done to our market is, for one thing, people don't have a handle on the real value of things anymore. The lines are so fuzzy, I don't think real values even exist anymore, at least in the minds of most consumers. Retail has become such a game, and consumers are too confused by it to bother to figure it all out. And whoever can play the dirtiest, wins. Imagine what happens to the profits when the seller now lists that $50 item at $100! That puts an **extra $25** of pure profit in the pocket of the seller, and you are paying much more than the item is really worth. I've seen items marked that much higher than their intrinsic value, and you probably have, too. You just might not have noticed. But we are so swayed by that huge percentage-off SALE that many people overlook the original price. Unless you've bothered to do the math, you might have been tricked by that dirty scam. Sadly, I'm sure you have been, a time or two.

My point is, we seem to have completely lost a sense of worth and value in this country. There used to be a sense of what something was worth. A loaf of bread was worth some amount based on what it actually cost to produce it, not "whatever we think we can get for it." In a rational society, there should be rational standards, which the value of most products are based on. Otherwise, you get a market in rampant chaos like we now live with. It's crazy, unstable, and lends itself to manipulation and abuse of the consumer.

I get that worth and value are ultimately variables in the eye of the beholder. You might think a vase listed at $20 isn't worth that, but to me, if I love the design or it fits perfectly a use I have, I might think it's a steal at $20. But, in recent years, I've seen things priced way out of line. Prices way beyond what inflation would have increased. Consequently,

I notice younger generations, ones who were not exposed to true value, don't have a clue on ultimate worth, and are easily taken with outrageous pricing, just because an item is highly desired.

Desire alone does not justify a high price. The outrageously overpriced iPhone, rapidly increasing with each new product generation is one current example. And, this manipulation doesn't just affect product pricing. Service values are by nature more difficult to evaluate. Often being based on desire as much as need, they consequently lend themselves to even greater abuse. The appalling cost of American health care is a prime example of a society's economy run amok and abuse of the most heinous kind.

My point is, we are running down a path of explosive economic destruction. There is no level playing field, not for the consumer, nor for the small-business owner. If some changes aren't made to rein in the rampant abuses in our economy, we risk losing many good things. One of which is those charming, unique small businesses that add such delightful character and charm to our retail landscape. I, for one, don't want to lose them. And, I hope there are enough intelligent minds and caring hearts left in our country to avoid that ultimate disaster.

Stepping down off my soapbox now.

Chapter 11

Vision Accomplished: Lessons & Rewards

My life is divided into two major parts: before tea and after tea.

We all grow throughout our lives. Some more than others, but we are all different at thirty than we were at twenty. We're wiser at sixty than we thought we were at thirty. But sometimes, something happens in our life that makes for huge leaps in growth and change. That's what happened after I entered my journey into tea.

Before that, from very early on, I was not very adventuresome or brave, having lived a pretty sheltered existence in a small close-knit farm community. I was terribly timid even in high school. I remember once when I went with my parents to take my sister to college her first year, we went to the University Union Bookstore. They had BGSU sweatshirts that I was drooling over. I asked my dad if I could get it and he said I could if I went up and paid for it. I couldn't do it. There was just something so intimidating about that huge place with all those books and new students ready to fill their brains with knowledge. I begged, but he stood his ground. He knew this would either push me past my fear or teach me a tough lesson with the consequence of going without the sweatshirt. From that incident on, I knew I had a lot to learn and overcome.

Much later, when I was fully established in my med tech career and wanting to satisfy my more artistic side, I again had to work on building bravery. I started looking into classes at the university and found the classes were taught at the Toledo Museum of Art. Intimidating. But, I wanted to explore 3-D art, to which I had an intense attraction. The consequences of not expressing this side of me outweighed my intimidation so much so that I simply signed up for a sculpture class, having not done anything more difficult than a simple coil-built clay pot in high school.

What I found, when I went to my first class, was an odd mixture of sheer terror and delicious excitement. The terror peaked when the professor announced the first assignment: a self-portrait head (as opposed to a bust, which includes the shoulders). At first I panicked. My stomach had that horrible sinking feeling, like you get when you're in way over your head. But, since I was only auditing the class as an adult, it's not like I had to worry about a grade. I had no idea if I could do it, but I thought, *I've got nothing to lose, and if I can pull this off, just think how much that will build my confidence.*

I couldn't get my hands in the clay fast enough. And you know what? My finished self-portrait head actually looked like me! Well, an idealized version at least, since I employed artistic license to take off a little excess weight around the cheeks and chin. Better than life! But the main thing is that it really looked like me.

I was hooked. And when I'd gone through all the sculpture and pottery classes I could at the museum and then at BGSU, I needed to find another structured art environment. A friend told me about a woman named Joe Ann Cousino who was an artist who taught sculpture classes out of her home. It sounded perfect. I got her phone number and called.

Again, some fierce desire got me into her class. When she first questioned me about my art experience, she thought it sounded like I had already had so many art classes I wouldn't be a good fit for her group. My determination seemed to have a life of its own, and I explained that I wasn't an accomplished artist by any means, and needed just her type of guidance to be able to keep working in clay. She relented and said she'd give me a try.

The funniest thing about it was that I was more intimidated about getting into her house than anything else. She had told me to come around the side of the garage to the back of the house and just come in the back door and go down the stairs into the basement where her studio was. I showed up for that first class, which was in the evening. Her side yard light wasn't working that night, so it was like going into some dark abyss and then down into some unknown void. I seriously almost turned around and went home. But something stopped me, or rather propelled me to keep going, knees knocking. Perhaps it was the lesson from my father that carried me on. I knew this was a golden opportunity for me, and did not want to suffer the consequences of losing out on this class.

Getting married at forty-three was a highly life-altering passage, after living alone for twenty plus years. I perhaps should have noticed how important tea would become in my life when my husband (boyfriend at the time) had me over for dinner on our third date. At the end of the meal, he pulled out his grandmother's Hall Aladdin's lamp teapot and made a pot of loose-leaf tea to have with dessert. Wow. We first connect over art and now over tea. I think I knew then that we were soul mates and that this guy was a keeper.

Of the many teapots I've collected over the years,
this one is the most precious.

He was an important part of my tea journey as well. I couldn't have opened any one of the four incarnations of my shop without all his selfless help. And having a partner who never once suggested the shop was a mistake, even though we worried constantly about not being able to pay off the debt, was key to my survival. His encouraging daily notes he left on the breakfast table are treasures to me, especially now that he's passed. My champion and best friend is no longer in this realm, but his hundreds of daily notes remind me that I had his constant support for over twenty-five years and all through my tea journey.

Jumping at a job in lab management with no management experience and nothing other than that compelling hunger to learn and grow, demanding to be fed, was another leap of faith that prepared me for my tea journey. So, when the harsh smackdown of losing my job suddenly befell on that Friday afternoon, I was ready to go for something much bigger and more soul satisfying.

While these early experiences all took me to new places, nothing was so dramatic as my leap into the world of tea. It was vast and so different from anything I'd done before. I had so very much to learn. I ran up against corruption and evil. I would need to be repeatedly brave and face many challenges, or I'd fail. That simply wasn't an option.

All of that changed me. After tea, I was no longer timid. I found a fulfillment many never do. After tea, I could stand up to bullies. Chat comfortably with strangers, thanks for the push from my art teacher, Jody. I had much practice in solving problems quickly and frugally, thanks to the fires of necessity. Consequently, no matter what happens now, I have a deep feeling that I will be able to solve and survive. Panic has no hold on me anymore. The full manifestation of my creative side had been unleashed, and it's become second nature to bring any idea into reality. I relish any way to apply my creative juices to even the most mundane daily projects. It has brought me great satisfaction.

One of the things all small-business owners want to achieve is the full realization of their vision, or (the American) dream, if you will. There were a couple of moments when I was able to step back and say to myself, "I made it!" Those were the times where I felt that I had actually gotten hold of the dream and was living it.

The first time was right before the grand opening. I'd worked so long and so hard on bringing this ethereal dream into reality, and when the last teapot was in place, the last batch of tea bagged and on the shelf, every doily perfectly straight, I knew. The excitement of the day carried me over the sheer exhaustion I was carrying from the big push the night before. I stopped and whispered softly to myself in that quiet moment just before I turned over the "OPEN" sign for the first time, "I did it."

Another milestone, which gave me a solidity that carried me through the rest of my tenure as shopkeeper was when I had successfully moved my shop to its second location. I was bound and determined not to become one of the nine out of ten from that nagging statistic on small businesses that fail within their first three years. I'd defeated the "landlady from hell" and the evil tenant next door, who tried pushing me out of my space before I was ready to go. I found a new spot, planned all the details, and pulled off that move in record time. And I was now in my fourth year. That gave me a confidence I'd never before experienced. And I said to myself, "Wow! I guess you *can* do anything you set your mind to, and I did it!"

Perhaps the most fun moment came on one of my rare vacations while running the shop. My favorite place to go was Kelleys Island in Lake Erie, and my husband and I vacationed there many times over the years. It's only about an hour's drive from my home to the ferry dock at Marblehead, followed by a relaxing half-hour ferry boat ride. And I absolutely LOVE ferry boats because every time I've had to take a ferry to get to a place, it turns out to be quite special. By the time I got off the ferry, only an hour and a half from home, I felt like I was in another world. Perfect getaway.

My husband and I spent the great majority of our trips there at one particular B&B, The Morning Glory Inn. We got to know the wonderful innkeeper, Penny. I'd occasionally take tea orders from her and her friends to replenish their tea stashes with "the good stuff" I carried, especially in comparison to anything available on the island or even back at the mainland groceries.

So, on one of my trips there, we'd checked in at Morning Glory and had gone downtown to grab lunch and visit some of our favorite shops. When we got to Kelleys Cove, a favorite shop of mine, I found another Kelleys Island piece of apparel I just had to have. I swear, I have the biggest collection of Kelleys Island wear of anyone on the planet. When I went up to the check out, knowing that the owner and Penny were friends, I mentioned to her that I was staying with her friend Penny at Morning Glory. She lit up and said, "Oh, you own the tea shop! I'd heard TheTeaLady was on the island!" *Wow!* I thought, *Now I know I've really made it!*

Throughout the constantly trying years, until I'd reached that point when I knew it was time to close, I kept wondering if I would get out of this alive and intact. I worried that I might not get out clean (i.e., without owing on the loan still), which would seriously handicap our retirement years with the burden of a big mistake.

But, as sometimes happens, it all came together in the end. I was able to make enough in the final sales to pay off my loan and walk away clean and clear, with a little left over even. I hadn't made a lot of money in sixteen years. Hell's bells, I made on the average under a dollar an hour when I did the calculation! But I could at least walk away from this with my head held high. No bankruptcy, no debt, free and clear. Richer in more ways than any amount of money could buy. Wiser for the myriad life experiences I'd tackled and conquered. And my soul having found a peace I'd longed for my whole life before.

When I closed up shop that last day, locked the door, that final sigh of relief hit me. It was touched with melancholy this time, but still, I was full and satisfied and felt entirely accomplished. "Wow. I did it."

I actually thought it would be more difficult that last day. I thought I'd be sobbing in my teacup all day. But many of my regular customers showed up to say good-bye. Some came to say how much they'd miss the shop. I was extremely touched. Some to thank me for giving them such a lovely place to visit. I was very honored. All were needing assurances that they would still be able to get my tea, and I promised that it would be available for a good long time to come.

I was sad, absolutely. With that deep melancholy that floats over those major life passages you'd rather not experience, but you know you can't prevent: the ending of good things. Like the very last day of school with friends you've seen every day for twelve years. Like moving out of the first house that you could call your own, even if you were going to a bigger and better one. Like saying good-bye to a dear friend who is moving across the country for a new job. Bittersweet. Bitter because of the loss. Sweet because of how lovely it was, that thing you had.

If there's one most important thing I'd learned in those sixteen years, it's acceptance. Resistance is the ugly culprit that always makes things more intense and difficult. But on this very last day, I was in total acceptance that it was time to close up shop. I would get to preside over this lovely world I'd created one last time, and it was a joyful day.

I'm not sure there's a place for this kind of business anymore in America. The Ma & Pa kind of small business. If I had a family with a couple of children and a mom or mother-in-law for some free help, maybe. But then that means this type of business can't survive without free (i.e., slave) labor. Expenses are too high. Everyone has a hand in your pocket, and they take too large a portion before you even make your first nickel.

And, you have to work harder and smarter than anyone else to survive. It's so incredibly hard. Much harder than I thought it would be. I worked so many hours with little to no financial recompense. I worked for years without vacation time. I worked through planned vacations, because employees quit at the last moment because they wanted time off and to hell with their interview promises to me. I worked through many, many migraines. I worked when my back was out or my fibromyalgia was so bad I needed a combination of two opioid pain pills to get through the day.

If these very small businesses had the same kind of breaks that big businesses get from the government, the statistics would be reversed. Nine out of ten small businesses would easily succeed. Because one thing they have that simply isn't there in a large corporation is that burning desire and will to manifest a vision of one's unique contribution to the world. But, small businesses don't get those big business breaks.

There's no level playing field for small business. The deck is stacked way against you. You are somehow expected to pay the highest rates and fees for everything. Utilities, phone, credit card services, internet, and merchandise. Where large businesses get breaks on all of these things, small businesses get nothing. The message is constantly if you're small, you're not worth it. Somehow, you just don't count.

I beg to differ. Small businesses bring so much color and character to the landscape of our communities. I know I've said that before, but it bears repeating. The bulk of new ideas and creative ingenuity comes from small businesses. They may have grown into large chain franchises, but most, if not all, started out small, with that spark of an idea from someone with a burning desire to create and share that creation with their communities. Without that, it would indeed be a dull, gray world in which to live.

The creation of those new ideas is a bedrock of capitalism. It's supposed to spur innovation and the desire to come up with a better widget. And then, what should follow is a reward for bringing new ideas and products to the market. However, it doesn't often work that way anymore, especially for small businesses. Besides not getting the financial breaks given to big business, the internet has changed the whole landscape. Because of that whole internet sector operating with little to no overhead, the playing field hasn't simply become uneven, it's been completely shattered.

With all that constantly hanging over my head, and the knowledge that it would never change, it was such a relief when I was released from it upon closing my brick-and-mortar doors. A huge weight had been lifted from my shoulders. One that I'd been saddled with the entire sixteen years. I honestly think I was suffering from a certain measure of PTSD after dealing with the constant stress for so many years. And it took me about a year and a half before I started to feel even somewhat normal again.

So, would I recommend taking that leap into entrepreneurship to others? I would, but with great caution attached. I would offer some truth and reality for them to consider before taking the leap. It's not something one should go into blindly. And it's certainly not something one should depend on for their main financial means, at least for the first few years.

If you've got a dream, take the plunge and bring it into your reality. If you think you've got the stamina, courage, and tenacity, then I can't urge you strongly enough to "Go for it!" You will not find anything more rewarding, as long as you value more ethereal rewards than just a paycheck. You will be tested like never before, but your world will expand beyond measure. You will discover things about yourself that you might never have known. You will learn and grow in ways you could never have imagined. What are you waiting for?

There are many lessons I've learned through my sixteen- year experience. When I look at them all together in the list below, I'm amazed.

- Riches are not always in the form of money.

- You're stronger than you think.

- Passion is what carries you through the fires of hell, if necessary.

- One must never give up.

- Don't take recommendations from folks who know nothing about business and are suggesting using "a guy I know."

- Never rent one more square foot of space than you need.

- Some people are just lazy, selfish, or never satisfied. Don't worry, you'll never be able to please them all.

- Lots of people will tell you what you "should" do with *your* business.

- It's your money on the line, not theirs. It's your dream. Manifest *your* vision.

- If it isn't written in law that a business, landlord, contractor, bank, or whoever cannot do something, someone will definitely do it.

- City inspectors impose the letter of the code on small-business owners, but let the building own-ers get away with not keeping their buildings up to code. Especially if they donate to their political campaigns.

- Small businesses run nothing like large corporations. Compared to them, you have no power, no leverage over anyone.

- You CAN stand up to bullies, and when you do, they tuck tail and run.

- People lie. Even in interviews. Especially in interviews.

- When you're right, stand up for yourself. It feels good, and you won't have to take so much crap from people.

- Attorneys have an overblown opinion of what their time is worth; avoid them if and whenever possible.

- You can stand up to evil and, win or lose, remain standing with your integrity intact in the end.

- And ... sometimes, you actually win!

In truth, it's all in how you define "win." I've never been one who believes that whoever has the most money wins. I was instilled with a set of values where I hold learning, growth, and experience as much more rewarding in the long run. I can't even begin to enumerate all I've learned and the richness of experience I am left with from those years in business. To see what began as a simple dream progress to defined vision, and finally manifest into physical reality has been the greatest satisfaction of my life. To know that I added something beautiful and healthy and wholesome to the Toledo business community for sixteen years gives me a sense of pride far beyond what any regular job would have done. In spite of not making a lot of money with my venture, I'd have to call that a sure win.

Brené Brown says that "Connection is why we are here. We are hardwired to connect with others; it's what gives purpose and meaning to our lives, and without it there is suffering." Of all the rewards I gained in my tea shop years, I'd have to say that it is the lovely, delightful, and even amazing connections with others that was my greatest reward.

What those connections brought to my life is astounding when I look back on all of it. Many of those connections have become friends. One customer-friend helped me navigate one of the loan changes I had to make by sharing her financial expertise with me. Some supported me throughout my cancer journey. My former cop/customer/friend Smitty helped me evaluate my brother's gun collection and get it sold after my brother's passing. Several holistic nursing friends helped me throughout my husband's illness and subsequent passing. They did healing touch on both him and me and gave me aromatherapy to deal with the intense stress that ordeal brought.

Some showed up to help me with some of my moves—packing, transporting, and setting up each new shop. My friend, Sheila, who I'd actually fired at one point, came back and stuck with me the entire last three years until I closed the shop, in spite of all the horrible building problems and even dangers from the negligent landlord. Some who'd been patronizing the shop since the very beginning, showed up on the last day for one more cup of tea and a scone.

All this connection brought me to a much larger life than I would have had if I'd stayed in corporate America. Like they say, even something that seems very bad can turn out to bring something good into your life. That nasty corporate downsizing did just that, and I'm so happy that I lost my job that day, and that it happened just the way it had. Had it not been as intense as it was, I might never have had the guts and determination to leave the corporate world for good and take the plunge into opening my own business. So, as one of my favorite sayings goes, "Life is good."

All these connections are because of tea. Because in searching for that perfect commodity to sell, one that had goodness and health connected with it, I found tea. And these connections reach far beyond the friends gained through regular customers. I connect regularly with tea friends from Maine to Washington state. I've met tea vendors from India, Sri Lanka, China, Japan, Taiwan, and more.

Had I not fastened my life to tea, I'd never have met people from around the world. I'd never have traveled to Sri Lanka. I'd never have petted an elephant. I'd never have seen one of *the* famous *Reclining Buddha* statues. I'd never have ridden in a tuk-tuk or slept at a superintendent's cottage on a tea estate.

I've tasted tea that sells for hundreds of dollars a pound. I've seen tea growing in the fields and plucked it from the bush. I've seen it processed into the form we can purchase and prepare, and I'll never forget the intoxicating aroma of fresh tea as our tour bus neared every one of the tea estates.

I produced the first tea journal so others could record their own "Journeys into Tea." I became comfortable lecturing to large audiences of people. I stood up for myself and learned how to fight for what's right and protect what's mine. I got to use and hone my graphic-arts skills. I found an abundance of ways to satisfy all my creative impulses.

There were many difficult times. Especially dealing with the politics of my city, state, and federal governments. Satisfying incredibly demanding customers. Suffering the antics of unscrupulous, feckless landlords. Working through migraines, fibromyalgia flares, colds, broken bones, and cancer treatments. None of that was much fun.

But for all of that struggle, there was an equal amount of pure fun and from time to time, sheer joy. Using my creative artistic skills was on the joyous end of the spectrum. Teaching about tea through the tea tasting classes and the many lectures, from nursing homes to medical conferences, satisfied my unfulfilled teaching degree. Turning someone on to the world of tea, helping a customer find that perfect unique gift for a friend or family member, watching little girls (and sometimes boys) dress up and practice their best manners during a tea party was all thoroughly gratifying.

I heard Bruce Springsteen once say, "It's your insecurities that move you forward." Well, I had more than enough insecurities when I started. So it's perhaps those, along with an intense desire to find and fulfill my passion that have propelled me into a much grander sphere of existence than I lived in before tea.

Had I not taken the plunge into entrepreneurship, I'd have never met so many wonderful people. I'd probably still not know how to successfully stand up to bullies. I'd not be as adept at and might never have found the joy in talking with strangers. I'd still be living in a much smaller world. And I'd not have ever answered the question, "Can I manifest my version of the American dream and successfully run my own business?"

It's all answered now, and I get to carry the satisfaction and accomplishment with me for the rest of my life. I have all of that as a foundation for living more fulfilled for the rest of my life. *Life is good.*

My grandmother's teacup.

I still love tea. I will always love tea. I hope to die while sipping gently from my favorite cup of tea. I've done enough research and correlated enough data to be confident in my conclusion that there is nothing, absolutely no other food or beverage one can consume that is healthier than tea. I am grateful to have been able to expose so many others to the rich and healthy benefits of tea.

And I am so happy to have devoted the largest sector of my working life to that jewel of nature known as TEA.

About the Author

ELAINE TERMAN holds degrees in both education and medical technology, but these days is known as "TheTeaLady" because of her extensive knowledge of tea. After a corporate downsizing ended her nearly twenty-year career in laboratory science, she decided to follow her entrepreneurial dream and opened Elaine's Tea Shoppe in 2001. Starting out as a self-taught entrepreneur, her business evolved into a successful enterprise for sixteen years.

She is a Certified Tea Master and published the first and only journal for tea tasting, *Tea Taster's Journal, A Primer for Those New to the Journey into Tea* in 2007. Her teas, tea sandwiches, recipes, and tea prep guidelines have all been featured in national magazines. Although she considers herself mostly retired, Elaine's Wild Orchid Teas are still available through her website at www.wildorchidteas.com.

Milton Keynes UK
Ingram Content Group UK Ltd.
UKHW052246280524
443311UK00008B/171